SAGE was founded in 1965 by Sara Miller McCune to support the dissemination of usable knowledge by publishing innovative and high-quality research and teaching content. Today, we publish over 900 journals, including those of more than 400 learned societies, more than 800 new books per year, and a growing range of library products including archives, data, case studies, reports, and video. SAGE remains majority-owned by our founder, and after Sara's lifetime will become owned by a charitable trust that secures our continued independence.

Los Angeles | London | New Delhi | Singapore | Washington DC | Melbourne

ECOLOGY, CULTURE and HUMAN DEVELOPMENT

ECOLOGY, CULTURE and HUMAN DEVELOPMENT

Lessons for Adivasi Education

Ramesh C. Mishra
John W. Berry

Los Angeles | London | New Delhi
Singapore | Washington DC | Melbourne

Copyright © Ramesh C. Mishra and John W. Berry, 2018

All rights reserved. No part of this book may be reproduced or utilized in any form or by any means, electronic or mechanical, including photocopying, recording or by any information storage or retrieval system, without permission in writing from the publisher.

First published in 2018 by

SAGE Publications India Pvt Ltd
B1/I-1 Mohan Cooperative Industrial Area
Mathura Road, New Delhi 110 044, India
www.sagepub.in

SAGE Publications Inc
2455 Teller Road
Thousand Oaks, California 91320, USA

SAGE Publications Ltd
1 Oliver's Yard, 55 City Road
London EC1Y 1SP, United Kingdom

SAGE Publications Asia-Pacific Pte Ltd
3 Church Street
#10-04 Samsung Hub
Singapore 049483

Published by Vivek Mehra for SAGE Publications India Pvt Ltd, typeset in 10/12 pt Times New Roman by Diligent Typesetter India Pvt Ltd, Delhi, and printed at Chaman Enterprises, New Delhi.

Library of Congress Cataloging-in-Publication Data Available

ISBN: 978-93-866-0259-6 (HB)

SAGE Team: Abhijit Baroi, Vandana Gupta, Shaonli Deb and Rajinder Kaur

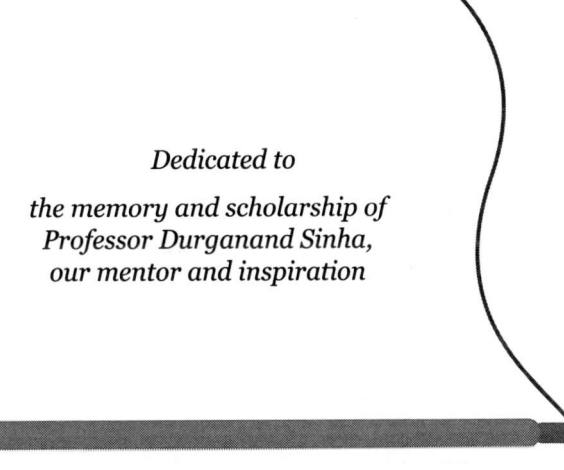

Dedicated to

*the memory and scholarship of
Professor Durganand Sinha,
our mentor and inspiration*

Thank you for choosing a SAGE product!
If you have any comment, observation or feedback,
I would like to personally hear from you.

Please write to me at **contactceo@sagepub.in**

Vivek Mehra, Managing Director and CEO, SAGE India.

Bulk Sales

SAGE India offers special discounts
for purchase of books in bulk.
We also make available special imprints
and excerpts from our books on demand.

For orders and enquiries, write to us at

Marketing Department
SAGE Publications India Pvt Ltd
B1/I-1, Mohan Cooperative Industrial Area
Mathura Road, Post Bag 7
New Delhi 110044, India

E-mail us at **marketing@sagepub.in**

Get to know more about SAGE

Be invited to SAGE events, get on our mailing list.
Write today to **marketing@sagepub.in**

This book is also available as an e-book.

Contents

List of Tables ix
List of Figures xi
Acknowledgements xiii

1 Cognition in Cultural Context 1
2 Human Development in Ecological and Cultural Contexts 18
3 Influences on Development of Human Behaviour 47
4 The Cultural Groups 76
5 Capturing Cultural and Cognitive Dimensions 106
6 Cognitive Styles in International Context 123
7 Cognitive Style and Educational Achievement of Adivasi Children 135
8 Revisiting the Culture–Cognition Relationship 171
9 Adivasi Education in Cultural Context 186

References 199
Index 213
About the Authors 217

List of Tables

5.1	Questionnaires, Tasks and Measures Used in Work with the Adivasi Children	119
6.1	Participants in the International Study	124
6.2	Differentiation: EFT (Max. Score = 6)	124
6.3	Differentiation: HWT (Max. Score = 16)	126
6.4	Contextualization: Syllogistic Reasoning (per cent correct)	128
6.5	Contextualization: Syllogistic Reasoning (Mean per cent of persons making requests for additional information)	129
6.6	Contextualization: Unfamiliar Words	131
6.7	Contextualization: LOT—Mean Search Time (in seconds)	133
7.1	Ecocultural Groups and Participants: Number, Gender, Age, Acculturation	137
7.2	Mean Scores of Groups on Cultural Dimensions	141
7.3	Mean Score of Groups on the SPEFT	144
7.4	ANOVA Outcomes on the SPEFT	145
7.5	Mean Score of Groups on the HWT	146
7.6	ANOVA Outcomes on the HWT	147
7.7	Mean Score of Groups on the SRT	148
7.8	ANOVA Outcomes on the SRT	149
7.9	Mean Score of Groups on the UWT	150
7.10	ANOVA Outcomes on the UWT	151
7.11	Mean Time Score of Groups on the LOT Under Appropriate (LOTA) and Inappropriate (LOTI) Object Place Conditions	152
7.12	ANOVA Outcomes on the LOT	153
7.13	Mean Discrepancy Score of Groups on the LOT	154
7.14	ANOVA Outcomes for Discrepancy Scores on the LOT	155
7.15	Mean Score of Groups on the Language Achievement Measure (Lach)	156

7.16	ANOVA Outcomes on the Language Achievement Measure (Lach): Total Score	157
7.17	Mean Score of Groups on the Mathematical Achievement Measure (Mach)	157
7.18	ANOVA Outcomes on the Mathematical Achievement Measure (Mach): Total Score	158
7.19	Mean Score of Groups on the Science Achievement Measure (Sach)	159
7.20	ANOVA Outcomes on the Science Achievement Measure (Sach)	160
7.21	Inter-correlation among Cultural Dimension Variables for Different Subsistence Economy Groups	161
7.22	Inter-correlations among the Cognitive Style Measures	163
7.23	Factor Analysis of the Cognitive Style Variables (pooled data)	164
7.24	Correlations of Contextual Variables with Cognitive Style Measures	165
7.25	Correlations of Contextual Variables with Educational Achievement Measures	166
7.26	Correlations between Cognitive Style and Educational Achievement Measures	167
7.27	Summary of MRA Outcomes	168

List of Figures

2.1	The Ecocultural Framework	30
2.2	Acculturation Strategies of Groups	40
3.1	Hypothesized Relationship between Two Cultural Dimensions of Societal Size and Social Conformity and Subsistence Strategies	66
3.2	Four Cognitive Processes	69
3.3	Hypothesized Relationship between Two Cognitive Styles of Differentiation and Contextualization and Subsistence Strategies	70
6.1	Mean Scores of Groups on the EFT	125
6.2	Mean Scores of Groups on the HWT	126
6.3	Mean Per cent of Correct Responses on the SRT	128
6.4	Mean Percentage of Participants Requesting Additional Information	130
6.5	Mean (guess and correct meaning) Scores of Groups on the UWT	131
6.6	Mean Search Time Score of Groups on the LOT	133
7.1	Map of the Major Sites of Work	139
7.2	Mean Scores of Groups on Societal Size and Social Conformity Dimensions	141
7.3	Mean Per cent Score of Groups on Social and Individual Connectedness	142
7.4	Mean Scores of Groups on the SPEFT	144
7.5	Mean Scores of Groups on the HWT (word repetition)	146
7.6	Mean Scores of Groups on the HWT (nonsense word repetition)	147
7.7	Mean Scores of Groups on the SRT (reasoning measure)	149
7.8	Mean Scores of Groups on the SRT (request measure)	150

xii Ecology, Culture and Human Development

7.9   Mean Score of Groups on the UWT (meaning measure)   151
7.10 Mean Score of Groups on the UWT (request measure)   152
7.11 Mean Score of Groups on the LOT (appropriate place)   153
7.12 Mean Score of Groups on the LOT (inappropriate place) 154
7.13 Mean Discrepancy Score of Groups on the LOT   155

Acknowledgements

A cross-cultural study like the one reported here requires involvement and support of several people. We would like to thank all those people who have given us their support with which this work has become possible.

We are extremely thankful to our research colleagues, Dr J. Peter Denny, Dr Jo-Anne Bennett, Dr Zheng Xue and Dr Nigel Turner, who made significant contributions to the evolution and refinement of our research ideas. They rendered great help in the collection of data with Canadian, Chinese and Ghanaian groups for the international study and also made the cultural life of these groups known to us through their ethnographic writings. On several occasions, we have returned to them for discussion of data analyses and their cultural interpretations. We appreciate their involvement and generous help in this project.

Fieldwork with Adivasi groups in India became possible through active involvement of Dr Azariah Hans (Ranchi) and Dr T. Jha (Gumla). They happily shared the responsibilities of fieldwork and proved to be wonderful academic friends and hosts. We thank both of them for their help and support. Mr Ishwar Dutt Dubey and his family made us feel home whenever the research team was there for fieldwork. We are grateful to Dubey family for their warm welcome and generous hospitality. Mr Yugant Kumar took great pains in collecting data from Adivasi children by travelling to many remote places and accepting many discomforts of the field. We deeply appreciate his involvement in the work and thank him for his invaluable help.

The work of John Berry on this book was done within the framework of the Basic Research Program at the National Research University Higher School of Economics (HSE) and supported within the framework of a subsidy granted to the HSE by the Government of the Russian Federation for the implementation of the Global Competitiveness Program.

We acknowledge the Educational Research and Innovations Committee of the National Council of Educational Research and Training (New Delhi, India) for a generous financial support to the Adivasi component of the project. We also thank Dr Lauren Crane, Department of Psychology,

Wittenberg University, Springfield, USA, for inviting Ramesh Mishra to spend part of his sabbatical year at Wittenberg as a Scholar-in-Residence, and inviting John Berry as an academic visitor. This arrangement allowed us to work together for some time to complete this book.

Our special thanks are due to all those parents and children who participated in the study and provided useful data, which allowed us to understand cultural features, psychological resources and cognitive strengths of the Adivasi society.

Ramesh C. Mishra
John W. Berry

1
Cognition in Cultural Context

Introduction

This book seeks to examine the development of some features of the cognitive performance and cognitive styles of peoples who live in varying ecological and cultural contexts. It pursues the basic goal of cross-cultural psychology, which is to seek out and interpret linkages between features of an individual's culture and the behaviours that they develop and engage in (Berry, Poortinga, Breugelsman, Chasiotis, & Sam, 2011). It builds upon the basic findings of the field of cross-cultural psychology that the culture in which people develop shapes many features of their behaviour. The book is also based on the perspective of ecological anthropology that argues that many features of cultures are long-term adaptations to the ecosystems in which they developed and now operate (see Kottak, 1999; Moran, 2006; Sutton & Anderson, 2010; Townsend, 2009). A third important claim of the fields of cross-cultural psychology and anthropology is that psychological processes and a number of features of culture are universal. That is, they are shared by all human beings, even though the actual behaviours and customs that are developed and expressed are variable across cultures and ecological settings as a result of this shaping.

Taken together, these perspectives allow us to examine the behaviour of individuals and their customary practices in relation to their ecological and cultural habitats and the recent changes taking place in them due to contact with other cultures (acculturation) and due to urban, industrial and educational experiences of individuals. These common features of human life allow us to make comparisons of behaviours and customs across cultures, based on the underlying similarities.

In essence, the book aims to show that by carrying out comparative research (based on the underlying psychological and cultural universals) we may discover systematic relationships between varying ecological, cultural and acculturation contexts and variations in the cognitive life of individuals who have developed within them. We also seek to use these findings to make suggestions to improve the educational processes and outcomes for children in these varying contexts.

The scope of the book is large, having an international focus on cultural groups in a number of societies (Canada, China, Ghana and India) that live under differing ecological and cultural conditions. The main focus, however, is on the Adivasi children living in the state of Jharkhand in India. The international scope provides a frame within which to understand the findings obtained with Adivasi children within their own ecological and cultural context. It also provides evidence for the existence of universal features of ecological settings, of cultural practices and of psychological processes. And it provides a basis for the search for systematic relationships between ecocultural contexts, cultural adaptations and cognitive development.

Culture and Cognition: Some General Issues

The search for the relationship between culture and cognition is not something new. 'How does culture shape our perception and thinking?' This is a very old question. And 'How do culture and mind make each other up?' is one more general current form of the same question. The question has been asked in other ways also. Are there cognitive processes that are universal, that are common to all humankind? And at what level does culture play a role in cognition? Throughout our careers, these questions have been of concern to both of us. We have had several opportunities to contribute our own conceptions and empirical research to the field of 'culture and cognition', and also to review research findings of cross-cultural studies carried out by colleagues in different parts of the world.

About five decades ago, Berry started to concentrate his research on ecological and cultural influences on perceptual and cognitive functioning (Berry, 1966). A book on culture and cognition (Berry & Dasen, 1974) summarized much of the work carried out in this field until that time, including the theoretical, methodological and empirical issues related to cross-cultural studies of cognition. These attempts were followed by wide-ranging work in many societies, particularly among hunting-gathering and agricultural societies (Berry, 1976; Berry, Van de Koppel, Senechal, Annis, Bahnchet, Cavalli-Sforza, & Witkin, 1986; Mishra, Sinha, & Berry, 1996) and surveys of research in sections of textbooks of cross-cultural psychology (Berry, Poortinga, Breugelmans, Chasiotis, & Sam, 2011; Berry, Poortinga, Segall, & Dasen, 2002; Segall, Dasen, Berry, & Poortinga, 1999), which exemplify Berry's sustained interest in this field.

Mishra has reviewed research on culture and cognition in two handbooks of cross-cultural psychology (Mishra, 1997, 2001) in addition to contributing his own research in this area (Mishra, 1996a, 1996b, 2008). Together, we have examined the role of ecological and cultural factors in the development of cognitive styles in the Adivasi children in India (Mishra & Berry, 2008; Mishra, Sinha, & Berry, 1996). We do not intend to repeat here all this material in any detail. On the other hand, we do intend to raise a few major issues from this earlier work that are directly relevant to the study reported in here.

In the following pages, we will summarize some of these concerns. These issues have been raised much earlier by Berry and Dasen (1974), and more recently by Dasen and Mishra (2010). Studies pertaining to the role of ecology in cognitive functioning have been reviewed and discussed by Mishra (2011a) and Berry (2017a). Our text closely follows these recent sources.

The first major question is whether there are cultural differences in basic cognitive processes, or whether these processes are universal. In spite of decades of research on the topic, the controversy regarding 'cultural universality' versus 'cultural specificity' of cognitive processes (and most other psychological processes as well) still continues. Advocates of 'great divide' theories (see review by Segall et al., 1999, p. 132) have usually pointed to large differences between different cultural groups around the world. One of these is the claim that there is an opposition between 'Western' and 'non-Western' thinking, using various labels such as 'civilized' versus 'primitive', literate versus illiterate, abstract versus concrete and so on. For example, about a century ago Lévy-Bruhl (1910) had characterized thought in 'primitive' societies as 'pre-logical'. In his view, 'primitives perceive nothing in the same way as we do' (1910, p. 10). Having been attacked by anthropologists like Boas and Malinowski, who advocated the 'psychic unity of mankind' (i.e., universality), Lévy-Bruhl (1949) reconsidered his statement somewhat later and wrote, 'I should have said: primitives perceive nothing exactly in the same way as we do' (p. 245).

Wundt (1916), however, argued for the existence of similar cognitive processes among groups of mankind, with differences between populations being due, not to the underlying psychology, but to the 'general cultural conditions' in which the different groups lived. His main conclusion was 'the intellectual endowment of primitive man is in itself approximately equal to that of civilized man. Primitive man merely exercises his ability in a more restricted field; his horizon is essentially narrower because of his contentment under these limitations' (p. 113).

Much of this work on great divides has been done in relation to the concept of 'intelligence', in which intelligence is considered to be 'one thing', that is, to be qualitatively the same (universal) in all human beings, just varying in 'amount'. In this work, researchers have applied standardized psychometric tests to derive an index of intelligence, called 'intelligence quotient' (IQ). Differences noted in the IQ of individuals or groups are interpreted as showing different levels (or amount) of intelligence. An early example is Porteus (1917, 1937), who took his 'maze test' to many societies around the globe, assessed people's performance and placed different societies hierarchically in terms of their intelligence with evolutionary innuendos. More recent examples are Jensen (1969), Eysenck (1971, 1988), Herrnstein and Murray (1994) and Rushton (1995). We certainly do not share these views about there being a hierarchy in intelligence across cultures. We have also often shown our disagreement with such interpretations of cognitive performance of different cultural groups (for a rebuttal, see Berry et al., 2011; Mishra, 1997; Segall et al., 1999, p. 137).

Another recurrent theme is in studies that attribute cognitive differences to 'racial' or genetic factors. This view considers that such differences were due to biological factors, specifically to 'race' (e.g., Shuey, 1958). These genetic interpretations have found a resonance in some contemporary writers, such as Rushton (2000) who argues that genetic factors (distributed differently according to 'races') are strongly related to cognitive life, especially to intelligence. In his view, higher levels of intelligence were selected for in 'Caucasoid' and 'Mongoloid' (in contrast to 'Negroid') peoples. These former groups 'evolved in Eurasia, and were subjected to pressures for improved intelligence to deal with problems of survival in the cold northern latitudes' (Rushton, 2000, p. 228). This great geographical divide is simply too far-reaching across very diverse cultural populations to be creditable.

Another great divide view of intelligence is in the work of Lynn (2006), who examined over 500 studies that reported IQ mean scores for countries. These scores were not examined for either their cultural validity or their equivalence. His main findings were that the average world IQ is around 90, and that there is a gradient across countries, with mean scores declining from north to south. This variation is explained in evolutionary terms: intelligence is related with the need for survival in cold climates. The argument is that as human beings migrated from Africa they encountered a cognitively demanding environment where survival (e.g., keeping warm, hunting rather than gathering) required greater intelligence than in the warmer homelands. As noted previously, this simplistic use of environmental determinism was largely dismissed in the last century, but appears again as an 'explanation' for population differences in IQ scores.

While over the years the vocabulary has changed towards a less ethnocentric (and possibly a more positive) version, several theories have emerged and flourished during the 20th century. The most recent one is the opposition between individualism and collectivism developed by Hofstede (1991) (see Kagitçibasi, 1997; Kim, Triandis, Kagitçibasi, Choi, & Yoon, 1994; Triandis, 1995). A large amount of this research on these contrasting psychological orientations has led to the view that the world can be divided into two broad categories—one characterized by individualistic attitudes, values and behaviours and another by collectivistic attitudes, values and behaviours. A strong proponent of this contemporary version of a basic cognitive dichotomy is Nisbett (2003) who advocates a clear opposition between Western and Asian thought: 'Two utterly different approaches to the world have maintained themselves for thousands of years.' Nisbett (2003, p. xviii) denies that 'everyone has the same basic cognitive processes ... or that all rely on the same tools for perception, memory, causal analysis, categorization and inference.' This view will be discussed further in Chapter 3, in relation to the concept of cognitive style.

While all these views accept that there are important differences in cognition, they interpret these differences in opposite ways. Some views assert that there are qualitative differences in cognition, but they do not deal with the question of whether one way is better or worse than the other; in other words, whether or not these views have ethnocentric or racist connotations. Even Lévy-Bruhl did not see prelogical thought as 'a-logical' or 'anti-logical', and not even as a stage prior to logical thought (despite the prefix pre-), but simply as a totally different worldview. In some ways, it is an extreme form of cultural relativism.

The second approach demonstrates what Berry et al. (2002, p. 324) have called an 'absolutist' orientation. In this approach, cognitive processes are assumed to be universal and measurable with standardized instruments without taking cultural and contextual variables into account; quantitative differences are, therefore, usually attributed to biological factors. The typical claim is that some cognitive performances are better and some worse according to some absolute criterion. What we know from much cross-cultural research on cognition, our own and that of others, including what will be presented in this book, leads us to disagree with both of these extreme approaches and to advocate an alternative position: psychological processes are universal, shared features of the human organism, but their development and display are shaped by life experiences (ecological, cultural and acculturation). This position is essentially a third alternative between absolutism (culture does not play any role in the development of human behaviour) and relativism (culture is all-important in the development of behaviour, even shaping the underlying processes).

Contrary to approaches claiming qualitative differences in cognition are claims to the universality of cognitive processes. This claim is inherent in the approach of intelligence, in which cognition is considered as a 'unitary process' measured by standardized (although usually translated and Western adapted) tests, such as the WISC (Wechsler Intelligence Scale for Children). Georgas, Weiss, van de Vijver and Saklofske (2003) make such a claim on the basis of a comparative analysis of normative data obtained from a large-scale research programme carried out in 16 countries. They argue that one should first check the structural equivalence of measures across the samples with factor analysis and other statistical techniques. Once this is established, any remaining country variations can be studied against the background of this commonality. Georgas et al. (2003) provide convincing data for '... a remarkable similarity in factor structure across these countries. The factor equivalence suggests cognitive universality in the performance of WISC-III across these cultures' (p. 289).

A major problem with their conclusion about 'universality' based on the Georgas et al. study is that all their samples are drawn from highly literate, industrialized and fairly affluent countries. The question is: Can we find a similar pattern of performance in other parts of the world? The authors (Georgas et al., 2003) attribute the (fairly small) country differences to 'educational factors'. This explanation appears rather unsatisfactory because the samples were not selected purposely according to some theoretical scheme. Also, their procedures cannot deal with possibly different definitions of intelligence (Berry 1987), since it imposes one particular sampling of skills to define and assess IQ.

The points raised above make it obvious that we have some reservations with this approach to IQ which leans towards absolutism and tends to disregard cultural differences, or at least considers them as less interesting than the demonstration of core universal processes. This is what Poortinga, van de Vijver, Joe and van de Koppel (1987) have called 'peeling the onion called culture', which, in the extreme, amounts to 'throwing the baby out with the bath water'. From our point of view, it is important and interesting to document both universality and cultural differences. Neither of these can be assumed ahead of time, but have to be empirically demonstrated. This is why we need systematically organized comparative cross-cultural research to deal with this issue.

As long as studies are confined to one single society, whether Euro-American or any other one society, and not include samples from the 'majority world' (Kagitçibasi, 2007), or to studies in the 'indigenous psychology' tradition (see Allwood & Berry, 2006; Berry & Bennett, 1992; Berry, Irvine, & Hunt, 1988; Heelas & Lock, 1981; Kim & Berry, 1993; Kim, Yang, & Hwang, 2006), we logically cannot find out what is common to two or more societies. In order to claim the universality of cognitive processes, we need to carry out culturally sensitive studies, such as those advocated by cross-cultural and indigenous psychologists, or by ethnography or anthropology, but using a culture comparative design.

This is what we have set out to achieve in this book. With respect to empirical results concerning cross-cultural research on cognition, we partly agree with one summary conclusion presented by Cole, Gay, Glick, and Sharp (1971, p. 233): 'Cultural differences in cognition reside more in the situations to which particular cognitive processes are applied than in the existence of a process in one cultural group and its absence in another.' The point of attraction for us in this conclusion is the idea that basic cognitive processes are indeed universal, that is, they are potentially available, at least as an underlying way of dealing with life's circumstances, to all human beings. However, the way they are used or combined, and the contents and contexts to which they are applied, vary widely across cultures. We consider 'basic' cognitive processes to include analysis, recognition, labelling, classification, remembering, problem solving, making inferences and logical reasoning. Many of these researches by Cole and his colleagues in Liberia, Mexico and elsewhere, and by other researchers (see Berry et al., 2011; Mishra, 1997) in different parts of the world, point to the fact that the basic processes exist, but depending on a number of situational factors they are developed and expressed in very different forms when they are applied to different contexts.

To illustrate this point we may take the process of classification. It refers to the way any complex set of information is simplified to make it more manageable. This is a basic process without which even language itself would be impossible. For example, when we think of a 'chair' as a piece of 'furniture' to sit on, we can include a vast number of different objects under that same word. But in some societies, chairs do not exist. People sit on stools, benches, cots, or mats. What exists everywhere is the basic process of classification, that is, using a prototype or best example for different objects related to a particular category. On the other hand, classification can take different forms. One form of classification, which is particularly valued in the Western world and fostered by formal schooling, is taxonomic or semantic classification, that is, classifying objects into subordinate categories, such as 'chairs, stools, cots and tables are all furniture'. This choice is opposed to functional grouping; for example, instead of putting the knife with the scissor (because they are cutting tools), or the cassava with the yam (because they are root vegetables), the knife is grouped with the cassava, because it is used to cut the tubers.

In much developmental psychology, taxonomic classification is considered as more 'advanced' than functional classification, because it is found in older (and more schooled) children. However, there are now several studies to show that in many contexts, functional grouping is the preferred mode (e.g., Mishra et al., 1996; Troadec, 1999) including for adults (Mishra et al., 1996; Wassmann & Dasen, 1994). Ciborowski (1980) reports an anecdote from the studies by Cole and his colleagues in Liberia. On a sorting task, the majority of adult Kpelle systematically produced functional groupings. When one of the researchers probed for reasons for the groupings, his informants said that this was the clever way to do it. 'Acting on a hunch, Glick asked a subject to do the classification task as a stupid Kpelle person might do it. The result was dramatic. Under the new instructions, the subject produced a perfect taxonomic grouping' (Ciborowski, 1980, p. 283).

We do not know whether this story is a fact or fiction, but the implication is clear: the Kpelle informants had at their disposal several ways of solving the task. Choosing one or the other may be dependent on circumstances, on how the informant interprets the instructions and gives meaning to the task, or on previous experience with similar situations, the familiarity with the testing materials and so on. In other words, it is not the 'presence' or 'absence' of the cognitive process that is at stake, but whether it is applied to problem situations and how.

In studies of cognitive development driven by Piaget's theory, Dasen (1984; see also Dasen & Heron, 1981) came to a similar conclusion. By using training techniques (Dasen, Lavallée, & Retschitzki, 1979; Dasen, Ngini, & Lavallée, 1979), it was found that after the age of 12, children who apparently could not solve Piagetian tasks at the concrete operational level, could do so after a very short training sequence. This finding suggested that children had the underlying process and competence for this type of reasoning, but did not use it spontaneously in the testing situation (i.e., at the performance level). The conclusion is that concrete operational reasoning is 'universal' at the competence level, with cultural differences manifested in the way this competence is actualized in particular settings. This is not to deny the fact that there are cultural differences in the rhythms of development (i.e., the age at which particular stages occur) under the influence of the value attributed to each conceptual area in each society. For example, there is a more rapid development of spatial concepts in hunting and gathering societies, and of quantitative concepts in sedentary, agricultural societies (Dasen, 1975).

Another illustrative example is syllogistic reasoning, which we also use and discuss in this monograph. Luria and Vygotsky carried out an early cross-cultural study in Central Asia (Uzbekistan and Kirghizistan) in the 1930s, which came to public attention much later (Luria, 1976). The researchers presented illiterate adults with problems of the following type:

> In the North, where there is snow all year, the bears are white;
> Novaya Zemlya is in the far North;
> What colour are the bears there?

When presented with this problem, the illiterate peasants typically said, 'How should I know what colour the bear was? I haven't been in the North. You should ask people who travel. We always speak only of what we see; we don't talk about what we haven't seen.'

When the same adults were given literacy training for a year, they had no problem answering the syllogism in the expected manner. Luria (1976) concluded that literacy produced new reasoning processes, namely, hypothetico-deductive or 'theoretic' logical reasoning.

Scribner (1977) compared the reasoning of illiterate and literate adults in Liberia in a study in which she also presented syllogisms that corresponded to the informants' daily life along with those which were unfamiliar to adults due to being beyond the range of their normal experiences. The results indicated that for the familiar syllogisms, the participants had no problem using the normative reasoning. For syllogisms with unfamiliar or hypothetical content, on the other hand, they either refused to answer, or changed the premises to suit their personal experience and knowledge. This is what Scribner called the 'empiric' mode of thought. Summarizing the overall results, she concluded that verbal logical problems are a special genre, a style of discourse that is frequently used in school, which explains why the 'theoretic' mode is common among schooled informants. The willingness to engage in this style does not reflect a different form of thought, but the habit of applying a common form of logical reasoning to a new context.

Schliemann and Acioly (1989) carried out an interesting study in Brazil with lottery bookies whose levels of schooling ranged from 0 to 11 years. The bookies were asked to solve permutation problems that contained familiar and unfamiliar contents (e.g., 'Find out all the possible ways to arrange the letters A, B, C and D', or 'the letters in the word *casa*'). All informants were found to be equally efficient in solving permutation of numbers problems at the workplace, but the unschooled group refused to attempt solving the unfamiliar problems. For example, Felix, a bookie with no schooling, gave the following answer to the problem with the word *casa*:

> F: This one is worse because I don't know how to read.
>
> E: But you don't have to read. (Repeats problem)…
>
> F: This one is too complicated because to read is more difficult than to deal with numbers. …
>
> E: What if you do it like this: The c stands for number 1, the a for 2, s for 3, a for 2? Couldn't you do it?
>
> F: No, because one thing is different from the other. (Schliemann & Acioly, 1989, p. 206)

This informant under consideration does not lack the cognitive process to solve permutation problems with numbers in the context of his job when he sells lottery tickets, but refuses to transfer this skill to the context of letters, which he considers foreign to him because he cannot read and write. The process exists, but the situation in which it is applied has to be familiar and meaningful. This is a typical example of the 'empiric' mode of problem solving for which the participants with limited schooling showed a preference.

A preference for the 'theoretic' mode of thought may be brought about by schooling because most activities in school are decontextualized; or possibly they are due to literacy, because writing and reading imply a double abstraction from reality (Goody & Watt, 1963). But research indicates that it is the Western type schooling, and not literacy, which encourages theoretic mode of cognitive functioning (Berry & Bennett, 1991; Scribner & Cole, 1981; see also Mishra & Dasen, 2004).

For Nisbett (2003) who has advocated a 'great divide' between Western and Eastern thinking, the 'theoretic' mode of thought is a Western inheritance from the early Greek philosophy. He reports that, independently of educational level, East Asians (in this case, Koreans) '...are more likely to set logic aside in favour of typicality and plausibility of conclusions. They are also more likely to set logic aside in favour of the desirability of conclusions' (p. 171). Nisbett's interpretation is similar to that of Scribner in so far as it is not a difference in the *capacity* for logical thinking: 'There is no question of this difference being due to the Korean participants being less capable of performing logical operations than the American participants. Koreans and Americans made an equal number of errors on the purely abstract syllogisms' (p. 170).

An obvious question here is: If it is not a difference in the capacity or cognitive processes, then what kind of difference is it? We believe that it is a difference in the cognitive style that people use when they try to solve a problem. We observe a cognitive style when different individuals (or different groups) react differently to a cognitive problem (task, test, experiment, etc.) in some systematic way even though they have the same underlying cognitive capacity or competence (Dasen & Mishra, 2010). They 'choose' to react in this particular way for a variety of reasons, such as their age, gender, previous experience, and socialization. This is not necessarily a conscious 'choice'; it is in fact more likely to be unconscious, linked to habits, customs, or preferred values, or generally speaking to 'culture'. An important aspect of cognitive styles is that there is no judgemental aspect to this choice. It is not inherently 'better' or 'more advanced' to react to a task or situation in one way or another.

We believe that we can usefully reinterpret many of the cross-cultural findings in terms of cognitive styles. The 'empiric versus theoretic mode', 'taxonomic versus functional classification', 'competence versus performance reactions' to Piagetian tasks, all can be interpreted as stylistic differences in dealing with the tasks. We also think that the Asian versus Western modes of thought, despite Nisbett's (2003) affirmation discussed earlier that 'the research shows that there are indeed dramatic differences in the *nature* of Asian and European *thought processes*' (p. xviii, our emphasis), is an example of the use of different cognitive styles. In fact, Nisbett's colleagues are more moderate in this respect. We believe that the following quote can easily be interpreted in terms of cognitive styles:

> Although both systems of thought are in principle cognitively available to all normal adult humans, cultural experiences may encourage reliance of one system at the expense of another, giving rise to systematic cultural

differences. These differences in cognitive orientations are believed to be rooted in different social worlds.... (Norenzayan, Choi, & Peng, 2007, pp. 577–578)

We will discuss these stylistic differences in cognitive functioning in some detail in Chapter 3. In the same chapter, we will review some selected studies in which one particular cognitive style—the field dependent/independent cognitive style—has been examined in a cross-cultural perspective. This research suggests that it is possible to predict the cognitive style of individuals and groups from the knowledge of their ecological and cultural characteristics. These findings have practical implications for dealing with the problems of education, health, social change and development of individuals and groups (Mishra et al., 1996), but especially of those who belong to the Adivasi communities, and whose life is changing due to the acculturative influences of education, urban contact and industrial experience. Thus, the study of the conditions in which people develop different cognitive styles appears to be a more attractive issue of psychological inquiry than other issues that seem to fulfil mainly academic concerns.

The Adivasi Peoples of India

We have indicated earlier that, while the book is international in scope, the main focus is on the Adivasi Peoples of India. Here, we portray their current general situation, particularly with respect to schooling and education programmes. Later, we will portray their cultural and ecological characteristics.

The development of the Adivasi Peoples (sometimes called 'Scheduled Tribes' or 'Tribals') has been a major concern of the Government of India since the time of Independence in 1947. Scheduled castes have also been of concern; however, these groups constitute an element of the main stream of Hindu society, while the Adivasi represent an outcaste group. To pursue the integration of Adivasi individuals with those of the larger mainstream Indian society, a variety of developmental programmes have been started by the central and state governments. Among others, education through formal schooling has been proposed as the most important programme for their overall development.

Education has been considered by many to be the most powerful route and vehicle for improving the position of Adivasi people within Indian society (Singh, 1996). However, in most cases this programme has failed

Cognition in Cultural Context 13

to bring about the desired improvements (Jabbi & Rajyalakshmi, 1997, Mishra, 2007; Singh, 1995; Singh & Jabbi, 1995). This is possibly because the Adivasi Peoples have not generally been attracted to these educational programmes (Joshi, 2009; Mishra & Joshi, 2015).

The reasons for the apathy of the Adivasi Peoples toward child education (particularly among the more traditional groups, such as the Birhor and Birjia) are not well known. The pressures of the family making a living in a subsistence economy and other demanding physical activities have been suggested as being responsible for the low participation of Adivasi children in these educational programmes (Mishra, 2007, 2008; Mishra & Joshi, 2015).

However, the incongruence between the cognitive and other abilities of children who have been nurtured in their particular ecological and cultural settings, and those that are valued and transmitted in schools, seems to be a more important reason (Mishra, 2005; Mishra & Sinha, 1998; Sinha & Mishra, 1997). In addition, the use of standard tests of intelligence has often been proposed as 'evidence' for the low IQ among Adivasi children (Singh, 1996). Most cross-cultural psychologists do not accept that standardized tests can provide any insight into the 'intelligence' of children raised in cultures that are different from the one in which the test was developed (e.g., Berry, 1972; Irvine & Berry, 1988, 2011).

We do not accept the claim that there are any cognitive or intellectual deficiencies on the part of such children. On the contrary, we feel that psychological instruments used in the assessment of their cognitive abilities have not been sensitive to their needs, aspirations and abilities (Mishra, 2005; Sinha & Mishra, 1997). Instead, they are considered to be competent in numerous other ways that have been nurtured in their particular ecocultural settings (sometimes referred to as their 'indigenous cognitions; see Berry, Irvine, & Hunt, 1993). By not understanding and assessing their actual cognitive abilities, the performance of Adivasi children in schools has often put them in the category of 'low achievers' (Singh, 1996). As a result of all these factors, the dropout rate among them, even at the primary school stage, is very large (Mishra, 2007; Mishra & Joshi, 2015).

Objectives of the Book

In this book, we attempt to assess and analyse the cognitive styles of children and adults in the context of their ecological and cultural adaptations, and their experience of acculturation. Our purpose is to reveal the existence of some basic ecological and cultural dimensions across cultures, and to show that variations on these ecocultural dimensions may account for much of the variation in cognitive processes and cognitive styles of individuals living in these diverse settings. We argue that an understanding of these dimensions and the relationships among them is important in developing any effective programme for the education of different cultural groups.

The work reported in this book attempts to expand our previous conceptualization and empirical assessment of the culture–cognition relationship (Mishra et al., 1996). We first report on the main concepts and findings from the work in a broad international study of these relationships in a number of societies (Canada, China, Ghana and India), and then with the Adivasi groups (Birhor and Oraon). Our intention is to situate the development of the cognitive style of the Indian Adivasi children in this broader international context.

We attempt to show that the way people carry out their cognitive activities varies substantially across cultures. As noted earlier, we assume (the *adaptation* assumption) that the way people carry out their subsistence activities (in their ecological contexts) is a major factor in the genesis of some core dimensions of sociocultural and cognitive variations. As noted earlier, we further assume (the *universalist* assumption) that people everywhere share the same basic cognitive processes, but they develop them (as abilities) and use them differently (as performances) according to the needs of their daily lives.

A major question facing the disciplines of psychology and education is the nature of the relationship between cognitive development and performance of people, and the ecological, cultural and acculturation contexts in which they have developed and now carry out their daily activities. As noted earlier, simplistic claims about the relative 'intelligence' of differing groups have served to make even the posing of any question about such relationships a difficult and sensitive concern, and researching it a hazardous enterprise. Nevertheless, the field of cross-cultural psychology has documented substantial relationships between cultural contexts and individual development in a wide range of psychological domains (see e.g., Berry et al., 1997, 2002, 2011; Segall et al., 1999), including cognition (Berry & Dasen, 1974; Mishra, 1997; Schliemann, Carraher & Ceci, 1997; Sternberg & Grigorenko, 2004).

In this book, we examine the relationship between culture and cognitive style in a way that 'neutralizes' the issue. This is accomplished in two ways. First, we view cognition as *adaptive* to the ecological and cultural contexts in which individuals develop, without any implication of superiority or inferiority of these cognitive outcomes. The only criterion is whether a cognitive activity enables persons to survive and thrive in their particular setting. Second, we focus on the *style* of processing cognitive information (the *how*), rather than the *amount* (the *how much*); in this way, we can avoid any suggestion of higher or lower levels of cognitive development. This dual approach allows us to understand and interpret cognitive performances across cultures simply as differences rather than as deficiencies (Dasen, Berry, & Witkin, 1979; Irvine & Berry, 1988; Mishra, 1998; Witkin & Berry, 1975).

The *universalist* theoretical framework allows for comparisons of cognitive performance (on the basis of common underlying psychological processes), but makes comparison worthwhile and interesting (using the surface variation as basic evidence). This approach is based on the well-established distinction in psychology between *process, competence* and *performance*. These distinctions will be elaborated in Chapter 2. Briefly, processes are the *ways* in which individuals carry out their basic psychological functions, such as cognition, perception, emotion and social interactions. Competence refers to the *extent* to which these underlying processes are developed as a result of experience during the course of development with the environment. Performance refers to the *display* of these competencies in the appropriate settings. In this book, we use the concept of cognitive style to refer to the pattern of performances on cognitive tasks that may be used to reveal the underlying abilities and processes.

General Outline

Our book examines the cognitive functioning of individuals across a range of societies that vary in their ecocultural adaptations; these will be described more fully in Chapter 2. First, these ecological variations consist of a range of societies that are rooted in hunting and gathering, through agriculture, to urban/industrial ecological contexts. Second, we propose that there are related variations in the cultural adaptations made to these contexts. Hunting-based societies typically have small communities and little hierarchy in their social relationships. In contrast, in agricultural societies, larger communities are common, which have more hierarchy and more pressures toward social conformity. Urban communities have even larger populations, but there is thought to be less hierarchy and fewer pressures to conform to social norms. Third, we expect that cultural adaptations of the group will result from contact with outside cultures; this contact initiates a process of acculturation. And fourth, we expect that there will be related variations in the cognitive life of peoples in these societies, and that these variations will be adaptations to the underlying ecological, cultural and acculturation features of their societies and communities.

Based on these ecological and cultural dimensions, we have included two sets of societies in our work. The main focus is on the Adivasi children in the state of Jharkhand. To provide a broad comparative context within which to understand the findings from the Adivasi children, we carried out the international part of the work, with a focus on adults in Canada, China, Ghana and India.

The Adivasi children are drawn from two groups: one is the hunting-based Birhor and the other is the Oraon. Among the Oraon, we selected three groups of individuals: those who engaged in two kinds of farming (dry agriculture and irrigation agriculture) and those who had settled in an urban area and who were wage-earning.

The international work includes two communities from Canada: the hunting-based Oji-Cree indigenous people from the community of Big Trout Lake and the surrounding area in Northern Ontario; and an urban sample of Euro-Canadians from the city of London, in Southern Ontario. In China, we worked with the Han people from a farming village in the Province of Guandong. The groups from Ghana included the hunting-based Vagala and the farming Wala people. In India, we worked with gatherers of the Birhor Adivasi culture in the state of Jharkhand and with farmers of Hindu culture in the state of Uttar Pradesh. These cultural groups and samples will be described in detail in Chapter 4.

The book has the following objectives:

1. To assess and analyse the ecological dimensions of societies based on a range of subsistence strategies ranging from hunting to gathering to agricultural to urban/industrial contexts;
2. To assess and analyse the cultural dimensions of 'societal size' and 'social conformity' and relate variations in these dimensions to the subsistence strategies of groups;
3. To examine the development of the two dimensions of cognitive style. The first dimension concerns the degree to which individuals make distinctions within a set of cognitive information. We call this 'differentiation' (intra-unit distinctiveness). The second dimension

concerns the degree to which individuals make connections between various sets of cognitive information. We call this 'contextualization' (extra-unit connectedness);
4. To relate performance on these two cognitive style dimensions to the ecological dimensions based on the group's habitat, subsistence strategies and acculturation experiences;
5. To understand the relationship of the two cultural dimensions of 'societal size' and 'social conformity' with the two cognitive style dimensions of 'differentiation' and 'contextualization';
6. To examine the cognitive features of children of the Adivasi groups in India in relation to the subsistence strategies of the groups;
7. To assess the cognitive style of adults in a number of societies around the world;
8. To compare the findings from the study of the Adivasi children to the findings from the study of international adult groups;
9. To consider the implications of these findings for the education of Adivasi peoples in India.

2

Human Development in Ecological and Cultural Contexts

Introduction

In this book, we attempt to show that the varying ways in which people carry out their daily lives in different ecological and cultural contexts give rise to the development of different behaviours. This ecological perspective is both a long-standing one (Forde, 1934; Kroeber, 1939) and a current one (Nettle, Gibson, & Starr, 2013) in our search for an understanding of cultural and psychological similarities and differences around the world. As noted in Chapter 1, we also situate our work within the twin fields of cross-cultural psychology (Berry et al., 2011) and acculturation psychology (Sam & Berry, 2016). In these approaches, we adopt two fundamental perspectives. The first is the *universalist* perspective, which posits that people everywhere share the same psychological processes, but that they develop and use them differently according to the needs of their daily lives. The second is the *adaptation* perspective, which proposes that the way people carry out their subsistence economic activities in their particular ecological context is a major factor in the development of their collective and personal behaviours. The behaviours of particular interest in this book are in the cognitive domain, particularly the cognitive styles and cognitive abilities that are developed by the Adivasi Peoples, and how these may impact their formal education.

The field of cross-cultural psychology has evolved over the past 50 years, from an interest mainly in the overt differences in behaviours that individuals develop in different cultures to one that also searches for underlying commonalities in human behaviour across cultures, while still seeking explanations for the sources of behavioural variations

Human Development in Ecological and Cultural Contexts 19

across cultures. This venture has involved the examination of individual behaviours as they are developed and are exhibited under different cultural conditions (Sam & Berry, 2017). Thus, this venture has required the use of the comparative method, in which numerous separate cultures are studied as collective phenomena, behaviours of individuals are studied as personal phenomena, and the two sets of observations are examined for any consistent relationships between them.

The sister field of acculturation psychology approaches the culture–behaviour relationship by examining such relationships in situations where the cultures are in contact with each other, rather than being separate or independent of each other (Berry, 2017b). So, in addition to the ecological and cultural influences on the development of human behaviour, we also need to examine the influences stemming from contact with other cultures. The main question is: If individual behaviours are shaped by the cultural experiences that people have, what happens when these individuals come to experience multiple cultures? Following contact between different cultures, the process of acculturation results in both cultural and psychological changes in all groups as they interact and influence each other both collectively and individually. The field of acculturation psychology has frequently addressed these issues in indigenous communities. This is because the original peoples in many parts of the world were massively impacted by colonization and enslavement. India and China both engaged is this form of domination in Southeast Asia over millennia. More recently, European countries did the same with respect to the peoples of the Western hemisphere, Africa, Asia and Oceania (Dudgeon, Darlaston-Jones, Nikora, Waitoki, Pe-Pua, Tran, & Rouhani, 2016; Kvernmo, 2006). Within this broad international context, the main focus in this book is on the effects of colonization (both by European and Hindu cultures) on the Adivasi Peoples of India (Tripathi & Mishra, 2016). The issues relating to the process of acculturation will be elaborated later in this chapter.

A major application of the conceptions and empirical findings of cross-cultural and acculturation psychology is in the domain of education. The core question is how these cultural and intercultural phenomena impact individuals during the course of their formal education. That is, what is the nature of the relationship between the behavioural development (particularly their cognitive development and performance) of people on the one hand, and the cultural and intercultural contexts in which they have developed and now carry out their daily activities (Irvine & Berry, 1988)? As noted in Chapter 1, simplistic claims about the relative 'intelligence' of differing groups have served to make even the posing of any question about such relationships a difficult and sensitive question, and researching it a hazardous enterprise. Nevertheless, the field of cross-cultural psychology has documented substantial relationships between differing cultural contexts and variations in individual development in a wide range of psychological domains (see e.g., Berry et al., 1997), including cognition (Berry & Dasen, 1974; Mishra, 1997; Schliemann et al., 1997; Sternberg & Grigorenko, 2004).

Cognitive Styles

In this book, we focus mainly on the relationship between ecological, cultural and intercultural experiences and the development of cognitive style. We adopt the handy definition of cognitive styles as 'one's preferred way of processing information and dealing with tasks' (Zhang & Sternberg, 2006, p. 3). They serve as ways of organizing and using cognitive information that allow a cultural group as its individual members to deal effectively with problems encountered in daily living.

This view of cognitive style follows the observation made by Ferguson (1956) in which he asserted that 'Cultural factors prescribe what shall be learned and at what age; consequently different cultural environments lead to the development of different patterns of ability' (Ferguson, 1956, p. 121). In this book, we equate these 'patterns of ability' with cognitive styles. This pattern can be observed in performances on various cognitive tasks; these performances are taken as evidence of some underlying competencies, and further down of some basic processes that are used in these performances. We will return to the 'process/competence/performance' distinction at a later point in this chapter.

As indicated in Chapter 1, the cognitive style perspective views cognition as *adaptive* to the ecological and cultural contexts in which individuals develop, without any implication of superiority or inferiority of these cognitive outcomes. It also focuses on the *style* of processing cognitive information (the *how*), rather than the *amount* (the *how much*); this allows us to avoid any suggestion of higher or lower levels of cognitive development. By using this dual approach, one can understand and interpret cognitive performances of individuals across cultures simply as differences rather than as deficiencies (Irvine & Berry, 1988; Mishra, 1998a; Witkin & Berry, 1975).

In this chapter, we outline the main theoretical issues and concepts upon which the book is based. We focus on two levels of interest: the *group* (ecological, cultural and intercultural features of a society and its population) and the *individual* (the psychological development that takes place among people living in these varying contexts). As noted in Chapter 1, we take the view that the research approach of *ecological anthropology* (e.g., Moran, 2006; Sutton & Anderson, 2010) provides a substantial guide to understanding these contexts. At the individual level, we pay particular attention to individual behavioural development in the cognitive and social domains, using the concept of *cognitive style* (Witkin & Berry, 1975). To link the ecological, cultural and acculturation features of a society to individual cognition, we employ the *ecocultural* approach (Berry, 1976a, 2011), and the related concept of *developmental niches* (Super & Harkness, 1997).

Ecological and Cultural Adaptations

A pervasive theme in cultural anthropology is that cultural variations in features of a culture may be understood as 'adaptations' to differing ecological settings or contexts (Boyd & Richerson, 1983). The line of thinking usually known as cultural ecology (Vayda & Rappaport, 1968), ecological anthropology (Moran, 2006) or environmental anthropology (Townsend, 2009) dates back to Forde's (1934) classic analysis of the relationship between physical habitats and a number of cultural features in African societies. Later, Kroeber (1939) demonstrated a covariation of cultural areas and natural areas in Aboriginal North America. A major emphasis of the ecological school of thought is on 'resource utilization' in which interactive relationships between human populations and their habitat are analysed.

Note that unlike earlier simplistic assumptions about how the environment *determined* human behaviour (e.g., the school of 'environmental determinism'; Huntington, 1945), the ecological school of thinking has ranged from the notion of *possibilism* (where the environment sets some constraints on, or limits the range of possible cultural forms that may emerge) to an emphasis on the available resources and *resource utilization* (where active and interactive relationships between human populations and their habitats are analysed in relation to the resources available (such as water, soil and temperature).

The resource utilization approach has been used in three different ways to understand human adaptation to habitat (Steward, 1955). First is the analysis of the relationship between the physical environment and the economic subsistence system. Second is the examination of shared behaviour patterns (customs) associated with a particular subsistence activity. Third is the search for any broader effects of such customs on other aspects of the culture. Of particular interest for psychologists and educators is Steward's notion of the *cognized environment*. This concept refers to the 'selected features of the environment of greatest relevance to a population's subsistence' (Steward, 1955, p. 62). With this notion, ecological thinking moved away from any links to earlier deterministic views, and towards the psychological idea that individuals actively perceive, appraise and selectively interact with aspects of their environment.

As Moran (1990, p. 10) argues, this approach has moved the field in the direction of *functionalism*: cultural activities are viewed as complex sets of interrelated activities that are collectively adapted to the ecological context, that is, how societies managed their subsistence strategies in a particular habitat. In these ecological approaches, cultural systems have been viewed as relatively stable or even permanent adaptations (i.e., as a *state*). Until recently, the study of adaptation as a *process* (and of *adaptability* as a system characteristic of cultural populations) has been limited. However, there is now a strongly shared view that cultures evolve over time in response to changing ecological circumstances, or as a result of contact with other cultures (e.g., Kottak, 1999; Sutton & Anderson, 2010).

This viewpoint has led to a more dynamic conception of ecological adaptation as a continuous interactive process between ecological, cultural, acculturation and behavioural variables. This approach has required the addition of a more dynamic conception of ecological adaptation as a continuous as well as an interactive process (between ecological, cultural, and psychological variables). It is from the most recent position that we approach the topic. It is a view that is consistent with more recent general changes in anthropology, away from a 'museum' orientation to culture (collecting and organizing static artefacts) to one that emphasizes cultures as constantly changing, and being concerned with creation, metamorphosis and recreation.

This dynamic conception has become linked to the concept of cultural evolution (Boyd, Richerson, & Henrich, 2011; Richerson & Boyd, 2005). The concept of cultural evolution is no longer considered to be one which assumes that cultural groups advance from lower to higher levels of civilization. Instead, evolution is thought of as a continuous process of adaptation to improve the fit between organisms and societies and their habitat. As argued by Boyd and Richerson (2005, p. 82):

> Our ability to successfully adapt to such a diverse range of habitats is often explained in terms of our cognitive ability. Humans have relatively bigger brains and more computing power than other animals and this allows us to figure out how to live in a wide range of environments. Here we argue that humans may be smarter than other creatures, but none of us is nearly smart enough to acquire all of the information necessary to survive in any single habitat.... We owe our success to our uniquely developed ability to learn from others. This capacity enables humans to gradually accumulate information across generations and develop well-adapted tools, beliefs, and practices that are too complex for any single individual to invent during their lifetime.

In this view, cultural evolution is very much linked to human cognition, and, in particular, to our abilities to gain the information needed to live successfully in our particular ecosystems. Thus, our cognition engages in reciprocal and interactive relationships with ecological contexts and our cultural adaptations. These complex sets of relationships are the issues that we explore in this book. Until now in this chapter, we have laid out the links between ecology and culture. In the next part of the chapter, we examine some basic features of our cognitive life that will enable us to meet the demands of living in our ecocultural contexts.

In psychology, as well as in anthropology, ecological perspectives have become more and more prominent, with the development of the field of environmental psychology. The early ecological works of Barker (1968) and Brunswik (1967) have attempted to specify the links between ecological contexts and settings, and individual human development and behaviour (see also Stokols & Altman, 1987; Werner, 1997). More recent advances (e.g., De Young, 2013; Gifford, 2007; Uskul & Oishi, 2017) have developed the field into a highly differentiated set of topics, including the study of behaviour settings, place identity and the impact on behaviour of the built environment. These advances in the ecological approach to studying individual behaviour have greatly influenced psychological thinking about the development and display of human behaviour across cultures. Werner, Brown and Altman (1997) have reviewed some of these aspects of environment–culture–behaviour links.

Cross-cultural psychology has generally viewed cultures (both one's own and with which one is in contact) as *differential contexts* for development, and behaviour as adaptive to these different contexts. Researchers in cross-cultural psychology (e.g., Berry et al., 2011) have emphasized the analysis of both the natural (ecological) and cultural (human-made) features of the environment for an understanding of human behaviour. We have long argued that ecological and cultural influences operate in tandem (Berry, 1976, 1994). Hence, an *ecocultural* model was developed by Berry and colleagues (Berry, 1976; Berry et al., 1986; Mishra et al., 1996; Georgas et al., 2006). The current version of this model (Berry et al., 2011) is presented in Figure 2.1.

The Ecocultural Approach

The ecological approach to understanding any phenomenon is to examine it in context; it is basically a relational approach in which the individuals and their situations are entwined (Bond, 2013; Gelfand & Lun, 2013; Overton, 2013). These contexts can be naturally occurring (part of the natural world) or human-made (part of the cultural world). When the concept of culture is combined with the natural-ecological context, the joint term *ecocultural* is generated. Essential to this ecocultural approach are the concepts of *interaction* and *adaptation*. Interaction implies reciprocal relationships among elements in an ecosystem; adaptation implies changes in these elements that increase their mutual fit or compatibility among elements.

The core ideas of the ecocultural approach to understanding human behaviour are that: (a) cultural and biological features of human populations are adaptive to the ecological and acculturation contexts in which they develop and live; and (b) the development and display of individual human behaviour are adaptive to these ecological, cultural and acculturation contexts. The relationships between culture and ecology have been postulated for a long time in anthropology (see Feldman, 1975). The claim that 'culture is adaptive' (see Ember & Ember, 1999, pp. 182–85) has roots that go back to Forde's (1934) classic analysis of relationships between physical habitat and societal features in Africa, and Kroeber's (1939) early demonstration that cultural areas and natural areas co-vary in Aboriginal North America. In biology, the links between biology and habitat go back at least to Darwin (1859), and continue to this day.

The linking of human behavioural development to both cultural and biological adaptation, and further back to ecology (producing the sequence ecology–culture–behaviour), has an equally long history in psychology

(Jahoda, 1995; see also Berry, 1995). Contemporary thinking about this sequence of ecology–culture–behaviour is often traced to the work of Kardiner and colleagues (e.g., Kardiner, 1939; Linton, 1939). They proposed that primary institutions (such as subsistence and socialization practices) lead to basic personality structures, which in turn lead to secondary institutions (such as art, religion and play). In this sequence, there are ecological and cultural beginnings, with psychological and then (again) cultural outcomes.

As noted earlier, the ecocultural approach is rooted in two theoretical perspectives in cross-cultural psychology. The first has become known as universalism (Berry et al., 2002, 2011). The *universalist* perspective in anthropology asserts that all human societies exhibit commonalities ('cultural universals'); in psychology, it asserts that all individual human beings possess basic psychological processes ('psychological universals'). These processes are shared, species-common characteristics of all human beings on which culture plays infinite variation during the course of development and daily activity. The second perspective, involves the processes of cultural and psychological *adaptation*. Cultures and behaviours are differentially developed and expressed in response to, and as adaptations to, ecological and cultural contexts.

With respect to cultural universals, what is the evidence for their existence? In our cognate disciplines of anthropology (e.g., Murdock, 1975), sociology (e.g., Aberle et al., 1950) and linguistics (e.g., Chomsky, 2000), there is substantial evidence that groups everywhere possess shared sociocultural attributes. For example, all peoples have tools, social structures (e.g., norms, roles), social institutions (e.g., marriage, justice) and language. It is also evident that such underlying commonalities are expressed by cultural groups in vastly different ways from one time and place to another. That is, common processes become developed and expressed differentially across groups.

There is parallel evidence, at the psychological level, for both underlying similarity and surface variation (see Berry et al., 1997, for a range of evidence of this behavioural variation). For example, all individuals have the basic processes needed to develop, learn and perform speech, technology, role-playing and norm observance. We know of no studies that reveal the absence of any basic psychological process in any cultural group. As mentioned in Chapter 1, this point of view was early captured by Cole et al. (1971, p. 233): '... cultural differences in cognition reside more in the situations to which particular cognitive processes are applied than in the existence of a process in one cultural group and its absence in another.' However, even with the existence of these common processes, there are obviously vast group and individual differences in the development and in the way of expressing these shared underlying processes.

This combination of underlying similarity with surface expressive variation (i.e., the perspective of universalism) has been distinguished by Berry et al. (1992, 2002) from two other theoretical views. First, *absolutism* denies that there are any important cultural influences on behavioural development and expression. Second, and in sharp contrast, *relativism* denies the existence of common underlying psychological processes, even suggesting that cultural experience can alter the basic processes, resulting in the transformation of the very nature of some processes. Thus paradoxically, this search for our common humanity can only be pursued by observing our diversity. And, this dual task is the essence of cross-cultural psychology (Berry, 1969, 2000).

Ecological Frameworks and Models

A number of frameworks and models have been developed over the years to provide a description of the ecological variables, their interrelationships and their probable linkages with behavioural variables. In the 1960s there began a series of articles and books that were more explicitly focused on the psychological outcomes of the process of adapting to ecological, cultural and biological contexts (Berry, 1966, 1967, 1971, 1975, 1976a; Bronfenbrenner, 1979; Dawson, 1969; Sinha, 1977; Whiting, 1977; Whiting & Whiting, 1975). There soon followed elaborations of this way of thinking, especially focused on child development using the concept of the developmental niche (Super & Harkness, 1986, 1997; Weisner, 1984; see also Keller, Poortinga, & Scholmerich, 2002).

Berry (1971) called his framework an 'Ecological-Cultural-Behavioural' model (shortened to 'Ecocultural'); Bronfenbrenner (1979) named his approach 'Ecological'; and the Whitings (1975) referred to their approach as 'Psychocultural', and introduced the concept of 'Ecological Niche'. Super and Harkness (1986) coined the term 'Developmental Niche', and Weisner (1984) continued the use of the term 'Ecocultural'. We will discuss these approaches in some detail below. For the moment, we simply point out here that all of these approaches share a common perspective: they all attempt to understand the development and display

Human Development in Ecological and Cultural Contexts 27

of human behaviour as a function of the process of individual adaptation to ecological, cultural and biological settings.

The 'ecocultural framework' of Berry has evolved through a series of studies devoted to understanding similarities and differences in cognition and social behaviours (Berry, 1966, 1976; Berry et al., 1986; Mishra et al., 1996; Mishra & Berry 2008). In this approach, ecological, cultural and intercultural variables are treated together as contexts for understanding behaviour. The basic argument is that as one crosses an ecological boundary one also crosses a cultural boundary. A major proposition of Berry's framework is that behaviour is adaptive to culture, and culture is adaptive to ecology. Because it serves as the basic framework for the research reported in this book, we will return to a detailed discussion of this framework in the next section.

The second approach is represented in the 'ecological model' developed by Bronfenbrenner (1974). In this approach, we find greater emphasis on 'experiences' embedded in ecological contexts in explaining behavioural characteristics of individuals than on 'adaptations' that develop due to the demands of ecology. In describing the enduring environment of a child, Bronfenbrenner (1974) made a distinction between outer and inner ecology. In a later elaboration of this model, Bronfenbrenner (1979) conceived of ecological environment as a set of nested structures, each embedded in the next, like a set of Russian dolls. The different systems that form the ecological environment include the microsystem, the mesosystem, the exosystem and the macrosystem. Each system contains different set of factors, although in an overall treatment, they are all interlinked.

Sinha (1977) developed an 'ecological model' for understanding the context of child development in the Indian cultural setting. In this model, ecology is viewed as consisting of two concentric layers, called 'supporting' and 'surrounding' layers. Home, school and peer groups with physical facilities, nature of social interactions and prevalent activities in each constitute the supporting layer of ecology. This layer is embedded in a larger and more pervasive setting, called the surrounding layer of ecology. Characteristics of the geographical environment, including the mode of economic pursuit and density of population, constitute the first layer of the surrounding ecology. The institutional setting of the child provided by caste, class and other factors with attendant role expectancies and interactive limitations constitute the second layer. General amenities available to individuals residing in those places (e.g., drinking water, power, municipal and civic amenities, means of entertainment, etc.) constitute the third layer of ecology. The general environment is made up of these surrounding layer factors, which combine and constantly interact with upper layer factors. These factors determine not only the economic pursuits of people and their way of life, but also their socialization processes and interpersonal relationships, which significantly influence cognitive and perceptual processes, motivation, style of coping with problems and general personality development (Sinha, 1982).

Dawson (1967a, 1967b, 1969) developed a 'biosocial' framework for understanding ecological–cultural–behavioural relationships. In a later elaboration of this framework, Dawson (1973) noted that ecology forms a fundamental basis of the biosocial system. In this context, he particularly discussed the role of factors such as physique, malnutrition, disease and hormonal changes on the one hand, and laterality and responses to Western influence on the other.

Whiting and Whiting (1975) developed an approach, which they called 'psycho-cultural'. This model recognizes the importance of ecological, cultural and behavioural elements. Ecological elements include the physical and the learning environment along with some economic and demographic features of the maintenance system. Cultural variables include the indigenous social structure and the diffusion from other cultures. Behavioural variables consist of innate and acquired behaviours as well as the 'projective expressive' systems characteristic of a group of people.

Whiting (1980) argues that the major way in which culture influences human development is by providing particular settings. Things are learned or not learned because of their availability or non-availability in the child's environment. Here, language is a good example. Biologically, human infants are able to learn any language, but will learn only the language(s) spoken around them. The impact of culture is obvious on child rearing customs and on parental ethnotheories, that is, the ideas that adult caretakers have about children and how they should be raised.

The basic idea implicated in these models is that the individual's behaviour, and particularly the child's development, occurs in interaction with contexts, which provide children with different set of experiences. Super and Harkness (1986, 1997) have discussed this under the concept of 'developmental niche'. It refers to the system formed by the developing individual, the physical and social settings in which it occurs, child rearing customs and parental ethnotheories. This is of course an open system, which in turn interacts with the wider ecological and cultural contexts.

Dasen (2003) has developed an integrated model (see Sam & Berry, 2017) by combining the elements of the various models, but specifically

Human Development in Ecological and Cultural Contexts 29

those of Bronfenbrenner, Berry and Super and Harkness. This model brings out not only the complexity of the ecological and cultural systems, but also of human behaviour, which receives inputs in different combinations from all of the elements represented in various systems. Dasen's integrated framework draws attention to the importance of studying the individuals' learning processes. These occur in interaction with the developmental niche, sometimes through observation and imitation of others and incidental immersion in what is to be learned, and sometimes through intentional interactions with a master or teacher (Dasen, 2008; Segall et al., 1999).

This framework also draws attention to the important distinction between observable behaviour and inferred constructs, as it is done in Berry's ecocultural framework. Psychologists are interested in phenomena (e.g., intelligence, personality, values, emotions or motivations, or indeed any other psychological concept) that are derived or inferred from a sampling of observable behaviour. Intelligence is a good example in this case. It cannot be observed directly; it is inferred, and depending on one's definition of the concept, inferred from very different sets of behaviours that have been observed with very different methodologies. The validity of this inference has to be assessed and questioned constantly. It is problematic at all times, but more so when one works in other cultures, and does this work in a comparative perspective. Contrary to widespread practice (e.g., Georgas et al., 2003), we do not believe that it is possible to assess children's intelligence validly through standard Western IQ tests, especially not across cultures that differ widely.

What guidelines can we take from these frameworks or models? First of all, they show that the unit of analysis has to be the 'child in context'. General psychology (e.g., experimental, developmental) largely tries to isolate the individual from outside influences in order to study intrapsychic processes in controllable conditions. Contrary to this, anthropology is typically interested in describing the wider cultural and sociohistorical contexts at the group level. What is needed, and what we are trying to do in this book, is to combine psychology and anthropology in order to study individuals in their ecological and cultural contexts (Jahoda, 1982; Mishra & Dasen, 2007).

The second lesson is that one should not feel shy of acknowledging the complexity of human life. These models indicate that human development occurs in a complex system of components, levels and processes, all interacting with each other. Of course, one cannot hope to study or measure all of them in one single research programme. We need to look at different facets of the system in a set of separate studies. Dasen and Mishra (2010) have done this in a cross-cultural study of the development of spatial language and cognition in India, Indonesia, Nepal and Switzerland, trying to combine the results of separate studies in some coherent fashion as comprehensively as possible. In this book, we are trying to do the same in our international and Adivasi children's studies by using a variety of techniques and measures.

The Ecocultural Framework

The ecocultural framework (see Figure 2.1) proposes to examine differences and similarities in human psychological functioning (both at individual and group levels) by taking into account two fundamental sources of influence (*ecological* and *sociopolitical* on the left) and a set of variables that link these influences to psychological characteristics. These

Figure 2.1
The Ecocultural Framework

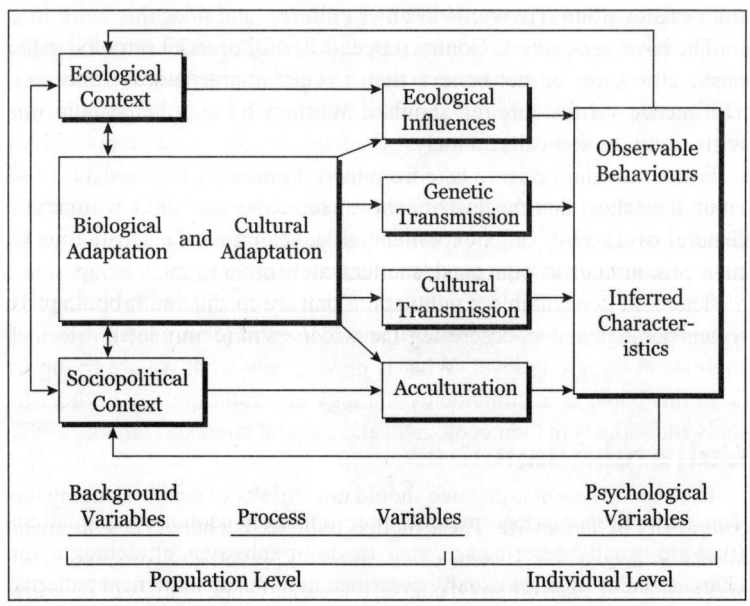

Source: Berry et al. (2011).

include *cultural* and *biological adaptations* at the population level (also on the left) and four *transmission variables* in the middle (ecological, genetic, cultural and acculturation). These transmission variables are the routes by which the population variables are inculcated into individuals' observable behaviours (their *behavioural repertoire*, on the right) through transmission processes. In short, the framework considers human diversity (both cultural and psychological) to be a set of collective and individual adaptations to context. Within this general perspective, it views cultures as evolving adaptations to ecological and sociopolitical influences, and psychological characteristics in a population as adaptive to their cultural context as well as to the broader ecological (natural environment) and sociopolitical (intercultural) influences.

This approach offers a value-neutral framework for describing and interpreting similarities and differences in human behaviour across cultures (Berry, 1994a). These different forms of adaptations to context yield different psychological phenomena, which can be understood 'in their own terms', avoiding any external evaluations. In the case of acculturation, when two cultures are involved, psychological phenomena can be viewed as attempts to deal simultaneously with two (inconsistent or conflicting) cultural contexts, rather than pathologizing colonized or immigrant cultures (Berry, 1994b).

The basic *ecology* component (upper left) of the model is rooted in the physical features of the context (such as climate and natural resources). The *ecological* features reside in the interactions of human organisms with these ecological features of their habitat, in which opportunities (affordances) and limitations (constraints) promote or limit the range of cultural practices that may evolve. These interactions take place with certain features of the physical environment in the search for the satisfaction of their primary needs (e.g., food, shelter, safety).

There are two features of populations that are considered to be adaptive to this ecological context: *cultural* and *biological* (centre left).

Cultural Adaptation

The cultural adaptations include three domains: economic adaptations (that are usually described as their mode of subsistence); demographic characteristics (that are usually described in terms of settlement patterns) and social adaptations of groups (that are usually described as ways of living together in communities, including family and marriage practices and shared norms and beliefs).

One typology of subsistence activity has been suggested by Murdock (1969). Societies have been classified as gathering, hunting, agricultural, irrigation and industrial. This classification has been used to sample societal variations for cognitive research (Berry, 1976; Berry et al., 1986; Mishra et al., 1990, 1996; Sinha, 1979). The subsistence strategies have also been found to be related to degree of food accumulation, settlement patterns and size of the local community. Hunting-gathering societies are characterized by low food accumulation, nomadic or semi-nomadic settlement pattern and small size of the community (less than 50 people living together). On the other hand, agricultural societies are characterized by high food accumulation, sedentary pattern of settlement and large size of the community (up to 50,000 or more). The ecological dimension of the ecocultural framework takes into account three variables: economic subsistence pattern, settlement pattern and mean size of local community. Hunting and gathering, nomadic and small scale groups are positioned at one end of the ecological dimension, whereas agricultural, sedentary and large scale groups are placed at the other end.

Cultural adaptation has been empirically linked to the ecological subsistence dimension, creating the ecocultural dimension. The cultural features of this dimension have been rooted in the analysis of cultural variation across habitats by McNett (1970), supplemented by the works of Nimkoff and Middleton (1960), Pelto (1968) and Barry, Child and Bacon (1959). These analyses revealed variations in 'cultural complexity', 'social and political stratification', 'tightness versus looseness' in social structure and 'assertion versus compliance' in socialization practices. These cultural variables are considered to be adaptive to the ecological demands placed on the groups. Recently, one of these features (the tightness–looseness dimension) has become a focus of cross-cultural research (Gelfand, Raver, Nishii, Leslie, Lun, & colleagues, 2011).

In developing the ecocultural dimension, four social variables have been adopted from these sources. Three of these features are the degree of political stratification, degree of social stratification and type of family. The fourth variable (socialization emphasis) examines variations in how children are raised. Political stratification has been defined as the number of levels of political authority in the society above the local community; social stratification takes into account the presence of a hereditary aristocracy and of wealth distinctions; and family-type ranges from large extended through small, further extended to nuclear independent families.

Socialization has occupied a central role in describing how features of the group (family, community) become incorporated into individuals (Grusec & Hastings, 2007). The ecocultural framework has relied on the work of Barry et al. (1959) to conceptualize and measure cross-cultural variations in the process of socialization. In that work, they rate cultures in the Human Relations Area Files (Murdock, 1969) for the degree to which the society trains children for responsibility, obedience and nurturance; these were combined into a general dimension of training for 'compliance'. In contrast, training for independence, achievement and self-reliance were combined into a dimension called training for 'assertion' (Berry et al., 1959).

The overall ecocultural dimension was created by combining these ecological and cultural features of a group to produce an ecocultural index (Berry, 1976). The ecological index (composed of subsistence strategy, settlement pattern, and size of local community) and the cultural index (composed of social and political stratification, tightness–looseness and socialization practices) were brought together to produce a single linear dimension. The reason for combining these indexes was that they were strongly correlated in early studies comparing hunting/gathering with agricultural societies. The societies high on the ecological index (i.e., societies that are hunting/gathering, nomadic and low in community size) were low on the cultural index (i.e., low in stratification, nuclear in family and emphasizing assertion in socialization). Thus, the ecocultural index was a unidimensional and bipolar index of ecological and cultural adaptation. The ecocultural model has inspired several studies. The findings of these studies form a basis for predicting not only the nature of cognitive functioning (Berry, 1976; Berry et al., 1986; Mishra et al., 1996), but also social behaviours such as conformity (Berry, 1967, 1979).

Biological Adaptation

Cross-cultural psychology has to also consider the ways in which populations adapt biologically to their habitat. An exclusive focus on cultural adaptations will miss important features of the population that are broadly biological in nature, and which interact with the cultural features. The ecocultural framework (Figure 2.1) includes biological adaptations of a population, although these features are not often explicitly examined. This is also the case in the present work, where biological aspects are not fully attended to.

Despite this lack of attention, it is necessary to have an understanding of how and why individual psychological (as well as cultural) characteristics fit into environmental conditions. This understanding is usually based on the Darwinian concept of adaptation. In its broadest sense, adaptation refers to any process in which an individual organism reacts to demands of the environment in a way that enhances its well-being, survival, or its reproduction.

However, organisms are not passively shaped by their environment; from the ecological perspective they *interact* with it. For example, the carrying capacity of the land can be reduced by overfarming or overcutting of forests; the soil can change (corrupted or fertilized) because of the excreta that are deposited. It can be said that an organism contributes to establishing its own ecological niche through the way it interacts with the environment. Over a large period of time, the environment is not constant and the ecological niche will change.

Adaptation to Sociopolitical Context

In the lower left of the ecocultural framework is the Sociopolitical Context. Cultural and biological adaptations take place not only because they interact with the physical environment and its possibilities and constraints, but they also interact with the social and cultural environments that result from contact with other cultural groups and societies from outside their own communities. These contacts initiate the process of *acculturation*, shown on the lower level of Figure 2.1.

Acculturation represents the dual process of cultural and psychological change that takes place as a result of contact between two or more cultural groups and their individual members. At the cultural group level, it brings about both cultural and biological adaptation. Culturally, it changes social structures and institutions and cultural norms. Biologically, it changes the genetic pool (through intermating) and nutrition (through the destruction of traditional subsistence strategies and the introduction of new foods). At the individual psychological level, it involves changes in people's behavioural repertoires (including inter alia, their food, dress, language, values and identities) and their eventual adaptation to these intercultural encounters. Acculturation is a multifaceted and mutual process in which these changes take place in all groups and individuals in contact with each other.

Human Development in Ecological and Cultural Contexts

The concept of acculturation was introduced by the discipline of anthropology. A widely accepted formulation of the concept of acculturation is:

> Acculturation comprehends those phenomena which result when groups of individuals having different cultures come into continuous first-hand contact, with subsequent changes in the original culture patterns of either or both groups...under this definition, acculturation is to be distinguished from culture change, of which it is but one aspect, and assimilation, which is at times a phase of acculturation. (Redfield et al., 1936, pp. 149–52)

In this formulation, acculturation is seen as one aspect of the broader concept of culture change (one that results from intercultural contact), which is considered to generate change in 'either or both groups' and is distinguished from assimilation (which may be 'at times a phase' of acculturation). These are important distinctions for psychological work and are pursued later in this chapter. In the second definition, a few extra features are added. Change can be *indirect* (not cultural, but 'ecological', due to alteration in habitat); *delayed* (there can be a cultural and psychological lag, which can result in change years after contact) and sometimes *reactive* (i.e., groups and individuals may reject the 'outside' cultural influences and change back towards a more 'traditional' way of life, rather than inevitably move towards greater similarity with the dominant culture).

Graves (1967) introduced the concept of *psychological acculturation*. This concept refers to changes in an individual, who is a participant in a culture-contact situation, being influenced directly both by the external culture and by the changing culture of which the individual is a member. At this individual level, the kinds of changes taking place might be in identity, values, attitudes and behaviour.

It is clear that both the cultural and psychological levels of acculturation and their relationships need to be studied in any comprehensive examination of how groups and individuals change following intercultural contact for two reasons. First, cultural changes in the group set the stage for psychological changes in individuals; an understanding of the cultural context is required in order to accurately describe and interpret the resultant psychological changes. Second, not all individuals who undergo acculturation in a common cultural context will have the same experiences; hence, they may have different psychological consequences. Thus, there is no simple relationship between cultural and psychological features of acculturation: neither every group nor every individual engages the process in the same way, nor evidences the same outcomes.

Although these early definitions still serve as the basis for much work on acculturation, there are some more recent additional features that have been proposed. First, it is no longer considered necessary for acculturation to be based on 'continuous first hand' contact. With growing use of telemedia, acculturation may take place remotely, in line with earlier work on *cultural diffusion* (Berry, 1980), in which aspects of culture flow across boundaries without actual intercultural contact. The second new feature is the recognition that acculturation takes place over the long term. Rather than being a phenomenon that occurs within the lifetime of an individual or in a few generations, acculturation can take place over centuries or even millennia. This phenomenon has clearly been underway in India with respect to Adivasi Peoples (Tripathi & Mishra, 2016).

A third new feature has become prominent with the increasing cultural diversity of national societies, where there is no longer one single dominant group with which ethnocultural groups can be in contact (van Oudenhoven & Ward, 2012). With multiple groups available in the larger society, the pattern of intercultural contacts becomes more complex. This multi-group exposure has clearly been underway for the Adivasi Peoples of India. As a result of these multiple cultural influences, more ethnographic research becomes necessary in order to understand this increasingly complex network of intercultural relations. We have attempted this kind of work in the present book (see Chapter 4).

As we have seen, acculturation incorporates a complex set of phenomena; it has many components and many relationships among them. Over the years, various frameworks have been proposed to identify the key components of acculturation, and they provide some structure to these phenomena. First, acculturation involves contact that takes place between cultural groups and their individual members. These contacts lead to both cultural and psychological changes. Further, these changes eventually lead to various forms of adaptation.

At the cultural/group level, we need to understand key features of the two (or more) original *cultural groups* prior to their major contact. First, the ethnographic record is a good source for understanding the cultural features that are brought to the acculturation arena; ethnographic research on their current attributes may also be needed. Second, the nature of their *contact relationships* needs to be investigated, including the purpose of their contact, such as colonization, economic and/or political domination, or migration. Third are the resulting cultural changes in the groups as they emerge as *ethnocultural groups* during the process of acculturation. All cultural groups in contact experience change; no group is immune from this culture-change process. While all groups change, the degree of change depends on the relative power (e.g., demographic, economic, political) of the groups in contact. Hence, some groups and their individual members will change more than others. These changes can range from being rather easily accomplished (such as evolving a new economic base) through to being a source of major cultural disruption (such as becoming colonized and enslaved).

At the individual level, we need to consider the *psychological acculturation* that individuals in all groups in contact undergo, and their eventual *adaptation* to their new situations. These psychological changes are the *what* component of individual acculturative changes; they can be a set of rather easily accomplished *behavioural changes* or they can be more challenging, even problematic. In the former category are surface changes in individuals, for example, in their dress, food habits and their language knowledge and use. In the latter category are deeper changes, such as in their cultural identities, cultural values and even in their personality. Second, in problematic cases, the result may be an increase in *acculturative stress* as manifested by uncertainty, anxiety and depression (Berry, 2006). These problematic aspects are at the core of concerns for the health and well-being of individuals engaged in the acculturation process. Third, because not everyone seeks to acculturate in the same way, it is important to conceptualize differing ways of acculturating, often termed *acculturation strategies*. These strategies deal with *how* acculturation takes place, and will be described in detail in the next section. Identifying these psychological changes requires sampling individuals in a population and studying those who are variably involved in the process of acculturation.

Finally, the longer-term outcomes of acculturation are various adaptations. This concept refers to *how well* individuals succeed in their own group and in the larger society. Two kinds of adaptations have been identified (Ward, 1996). First are adaptations that are primarily internal or *psychological* (e.g., a sense of well-being, or self-esteem, sometimes called *feeling well*). Second are *sociocultural* adaptations (sometimes called *doing well*). These adaptations link the individual to others in the new society, and are manifested, for example, by competence in the activities of daily intercultural living, including social relations, success at school and work and community life. A third form of adaptation has come to the fore in recent years: *intercultural* adaptation (Berry, 2015). Here, the interest is in how well individuals manage to achieve workable relationships with others across cultural boundaries. The focus here is on the achievement of positive intercultural relationships (such as mutually positive ethnic attitudes and a lack of prejudice and discrimination) and the acceptance of a multicultural ideology (a general view that places a value on both cultural diversity and equitable participation by everyone in the larger society; see Berry, 2017c; Berry, Kalin, & Taylor, 1977).

Acculturation Strategies

We turn now to the concept of *acculturation strategies* (Berry, 1980, 2017c), which refers to the *how* of acculturation. They consist of two components: attitudes and behaviours (that is, the preferences for, and actual practices of, ways of relating to one's own and other groups) that are exhibited in day-to-day intercultural encounters. Of course, there is rarely a one-to-one match between what an individual prefers and seeks (attitudes) and what one is actually able to do (behaviours). This discrepancy is widely studied in social psychology and is usually explained as being the result of social constraints on behaviours (such as norms and opportunities). In this case, these constraints lie in the social and intercultural contexts in which an individual lives, often due to differential power available to groups to pursue their preferred way of acculturating. Nevertheless, there is often a positive correlation between acculturation attitudes and actual behaviours, permitting the use of an overall assessment of individual acculturation strategies.

The centrality of the concept of acculturation strategies can be illustrated by reference to each component of the acculturation process. At the cultural level, the two groups in contact (whether dominant or non-dominant) usually have some notion about what they are attempting to do (e.g., colonial policies, or motivations for migration), or what is being done to them during the contact. Similarly, the social, cultural and political goals of the emergent ethnocultural groups will influence their acculturation strategies; how should we try to live in this new society? At the individual level, both the behavioural changes and acculturative stress phenomena are now known to be a function, at least to some extent, of what people try to do during their acculturation; and the long-term outcomes (psychological, sociocultural and intercultural adaptations) usually have some correspondence with the strategic goals set by the groups of which they are members.

As we have seen, the original definitions of acculturation foresaw that cultural and psychological homogenization (later linked to globalization) would not be the only possible or inevitable outcome of intercultural contact. This is because people hold different views about how they want to live following contact: not everyone seeks out such contact, and even among those who do engage in contact, not everyone seeks to change their culture and behaviour to be more like the other (often dominant) group.

In their 1936 statement on acculturation, Redfield et al.(1936) noted that assimilation is not the only form of acculturation; there are other ways of going about it. Taking this assertion as a starting point, Berry (1970) and Sommerlad and Berry (1970) first distinguished between the strategies of assimilation and integration, and later between these original strategies and separation and marginalization as various ways in which acculturation (both of groups and of individuals) could take place. These distinctions are based on people's and groups' orientation to two dimensions: towards one's own group and towards other groups in the larger society. A third issue included in the framework was the power of individuals and groups to choose and pursue these two orientations (Berry, 1974, 1980b).

Individual responses to these issues can be conceptualized in terms of relative preferences for: *cultural continuity* (Issue 1: maintaining one's heritage culture and identity); *contact* (Issue 2: a relative preference for having contact with, and participating in, the larger society along with other ethnocultural groups) and *power* (Issue 3: the relative power of the non-dominant group to choose how to pursue these two orientations). The unidimensional approach assumed that acculturation was a process in which individuals inevitably moved from their heritage culture towards being assimilated into the dominant culture. The first two dimensions (i.e., preference for maintaining heritage culture and for engaging in relations with other groups) have been shown to be independent of each other (Berry & Sabatier, 2011; Dona & Berry, 1994; Ryder et al., 2000); hence, the unidimensional approach has now effectively been discarded.

The current version (Berry, 2003) of the framework is shown in Figure 2.2. Orientations to the two basic issues can vary along dimensions, represented by bipolar arrows (at the top and on the left). These strategies carry different names, depending on which group (the non-dominant or the dominant) is being considered. The strategies of the non-dominant ethnocultural groups are shown on the left, those for the larger society are shown on the right.

Figure 2.2

Acculturation Strategies of Groups

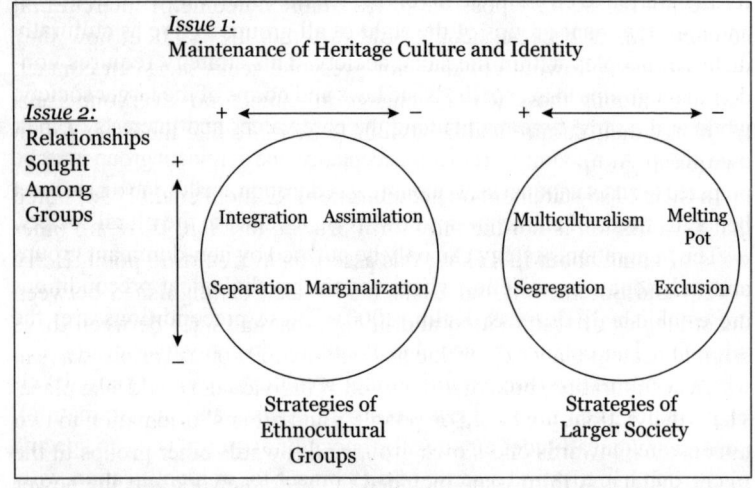

Source: Berry et al. (2011).

From the point of view of non-dominant ethnocultural groups, when individuals do not wish to maintain their cultural identity and seek daily interaction with other cultures, the *assimilation* strategy is defined. In contrast, when individuals place a value on holding on to their original culture, and at the same time wish to avoid interaction with others, then the *separation* alternative is defined. When there is an interest in both maintaining one's original culture and having daily interactions with other groups, *integration* is the option; here, there is some degree of cultural integrity maintained, while at the same time the individual seeks, as a member of an ethnocultural group, to participate as an integral part of the larger society. Finally, when there is little possibility of, or interest in, cultural maintenance (often for reasons of enforced cultural loss), and little interest in having relations with others (often for reasons of exclusion or discrimination), then *marginalization* is defined.

Of course, non-dominant groups and their individual members do not always have the freedom to choose how they want to engage in intercultural relations and acculturation. Constraints imposed by the dominant group may enforce certain kinds of relations, or limit the choices of non-dominant groups or individuals. This is most clearly so in the case of integration, which can only be freely chosen and successfully pursued by non-dominant groups when the dominant society is open and inclusive in its orientation towards cultural diversity. Thus, a mutual accommodation is required for integration to be attained, involving the acceptance by both dominant and non-dominant groups of the right of all groups to live as culturally different peoples within the same society. This strategy requires non-dominant groups to accept the basic laws and norms of the larger society, while at the same time maintaining the core values and interests of their own group. As a counterpart to this acceptance, the dominant group must be prepared to adapt national institutions (e.g., education, health, labour) to meet better the needs of all the groups now living together in the plural society.

The integration strategy can only be pursued by non-dominant groups and individuals in societies where certain psychological preconditions are established (Berry & Kalin, 2000). These preconditions are: the widespread acceptance of the value of cultural diversity to a society (i.e., the presence of a positive multicultural ideology); relatively low levels of prejudice (i.e., minimal ethnocentrism, racism and discrimination); positive mutual attitudes among all ethnocultural groups (i.e., no specific intergroup hatreds) and a sense of attachment to, or identification with, the larger society by all individuals and groups. Moreover, integration (and separation) can only be pursued when other members of one's ethnocultural group share in the wish to maintain the group's cultural heritage. When these strategies are assessed using separate scales, it is possible to observe variable degrees of preference for each strategy. For example, one could logically have a positive orientation towards both integration and separation, given that both strategies involve a preference for the maintenance of one's cultural heritage and identity.

On the right side of Figure 2.2 are the strategies that may exist in the larger society. These strategies have been referred to as the *acculturation expectations* (Berry, 2003) of the larger society and its individual members. These expectations may be manifested in public policies and attitudes regarding how they think that non-dominant groups and individuals *should* acculturate; they also include views about how members of the larger society should themselves acculturate. Assimilation, when sought by the dominant group, can be termed as the *melting pot*. When separation is demanded and enforced by the dominant group, it is *segregation*. Marginalization, when imposed by the dominant group, creates a form of *exclusion*. Finally, concerning integration, when cultural diversity is an objective of the society as a whole, and is widely accepted by its members, it represents the strategy of mutual accommodation now widely called *multiculturalism* (Berry & Ward, 2016).

Acculturation in India

In India, contact between the resident population and those from outside has been taking place since eons (Tripathi & Mishra, 2016). Although some new features of cultural contact have been added by the small influx of 'foreign' workers, immigrants, or refugees in the modern times, issues related to culture contact and change in the life of the Adivasi Peoples have been more interesting for researchers than those of the other groups.

Historical evidence indicates that Christian churches have played a major role in changing the lifestyles of the Adivasi Peoples. Considering culture as something where one feels comfortable in terms of language, food, art forms, and so on, the Christian missionaries used *inculturation* as a process of inducting the Adivasi Peoples into the Church by giving sermons in their language and by making use of cultural expressions they were familiar with. The missionaries not only weaved into the teachings of Jesus (called Good News) the metaphors, local stories, folktales, mythologies, rituals and overall sociocultural life of the Adivasi, but also went to the extent of living their Christian faith in tandem with Indian spiritual traditions (Sagayaraj, 2013).These strategies paved the way for missionaries to change religious beliefs of a large number of Adivasi people by attracting them to be a part of the Church. Although a large number of the Adivasi live in isolated forest and hilly regions, following the Christian faith system, many have moved to the urban areas in relatively recent years. Also, while a majority of the Adivasi still retains its traditional cultural features at the cost of being labeled as 'primitive' or 'backward', there are clear differences in the life of the 'traditional' and 'Christian' Adivasi groups.

Three distinct kinds of orientations towards the Adivasi groups can be noted in the recent history of India. One is that of the British, who did not bother much about the Adivasi people mainly because of the difficulties involved in the administration of remote forest areas where they lived. The second is that of the Christian missionaries who made efforts towards their assimilation into their own cultural stream so much so that in the northeast regions of India the Christian Adivasi are the *dominant* majority group today. The third orientation is that of the government, which has developed a national policy of *integration* of the Adivasi Peoples into the mainstream society. The policy seeks to preserve, strengthen and develop the Adivasi societies and nurture their cultures. The policy also seeks to enfold them within the national fabric by giving them equal opportunity to participate in political, economic, educational and other spheres of life through the creation of special quotas in educational, administrative and business organizations. This policy resembles the use of the strategy of *integration and multiculturalism* proposed earlier (Figure 2.2).

During the last century, the Adivasi populations have been subjected to other kind of influences also. Hindu reformers and right-wing political parties, who feel much concerned with the increasing number of the Adivasi turning to Christianity, have made organized efforts towards their induction into the Hindu culture. Industrialization and urbanization taking place in the Adivasi regions are other influences, uprooting the Adivasi from their original habitats and from their cultural moorings (Mishra et al., 1996).

Although the rights of the Adivasi Peoples are enshrined in the Indian Constitution, the integration of more than hundred million of the Adivasi populations with the larger society is still too far away a goal to be achieved in the near future. In many regions of the country (e.g., Assam), conflicts have been witnessed between the Adivasi and other groups so much so that they have been demanding a separate state and the expulsion of refugees or illegal migrants from their regions. Dissatisfaction of the Adivasi Peoples in other parts of the country has led to the creation of some new states (e.g., Jharkhand, Chhattisgarh), where the Adivasi population is in majority.

Acculturation Strategies of the Adivasi Groups

Attitudes of the Adivasi groups have undergone considerable change after India's independence from the British rule about seven decades ago. Early studies of change in the Adivasi focus on the impact of the government-initiated programmes on their life. Attitudinal changes among the Adivasi as a result of urban contact, industrial exposure, education and religious conversion have been studied within the framework of 'modernization' (Singh & Jabbi, 1995). In relatively recent studies of the Adivasi groups, Berry's ecocultural and acculturation frameworks have been widely used. How the Adivasi participate in the process of culture change going on in their region and how they adapt to those changes are the major questions addressed in these studies. A related question is asked about the psychological effects (e.g., changes in cognitive or health behaviours) of acculturation.

Mishra et al. (1996) studied the acculturation strategies of integration, assimilation, separation and marginalization in the Adivasi groups of Bihar (now in Jharkhand). These samples included the Birhor (nomadic hunters-gatherers group), the Asur (recent settlers pursuing a mixed economy of hunting–gathering and agriculture) and the Oraon (long-standing agriculturists). They also conceptualized and used *coexistence* as a fifth acculturation strategy. In this case, no attempt is made towards synthesis or assimilation of new cultural elements; instead, they are kept side by side without involving evaluation or using a standard of comparison for one's own or others' culture. While coexistence and integration were found to be the most preferred acculturation strategies for all the Adivasi groups, they were represented more strongly among individuals who scored higher on a contact-acculturation measure than among those who scored relatively low on it. There was a weak evidence for the use of separation, assimilation and marginalization strategies.

Mishra and Chaubey (2002) worked with the Kharwar and Agaria Adivasi groups and noted almost similar results. The Kharwar economy is largely based on agriculture with some support from forest produce. On the other hand, the Agaria engage in intensive forest activities, and they are also not in much contact with the outside world. The groups did not differ in their preference for the acculturation strategies of integration, assimilation and marginalization, but the Agaria displayed a significantly stronger separation strategy than the Kharwar. The study revealed that in both the groups contact-acculturation was a significant predictor of integration and separation strategies.

Studies of the Adivasi groups in India have more often used acculturation as a predictor of individuals' behaviour in culture-contact situations than acculturation as an outcome of contextual (e.g., historical, sociopolitical) variables. We also find more use of contact than subjective acculturation indices in the analysis of behavioural outcomes.

Acculturation Influences on Health and Well-being

Much research has been done on the impact of acculturation on health and well-being of many groups (Sam et al., 2016). Among the Adivasi populations, in this domain of health and well-being, contact experiences have been shown to be an important factor linked to the survival of the Adivasi populations (Mishra, 2015). There is some focus on how health behaviours change as a result of acculturation (Singh, 1984), but more of the research has addressed the issue of 'acculturative stress' and its relationship with certain individual variables. In their study with Birhor, Asur and Oraon Adivasi adults, Mishra et al. (1996) examined health status of the members of these groups. Marginality (a pathological condition characterized by the feelings of aggression, suspicion and ambivalence), which often results in unsuccessful acculturation situations, was also assessed. People who preferred to use integration and/or coexistence acculturation strategies reported lesser health problems, whereas those characterized by marginalization and separation orientations, and also those with high level of marginality (a stabilized condition of social disconnection) displayed greater health problems, including mental and psychosomatic ones. There was a clear evidence for the existence of acculturative stress among all the three Adivasi groups, but the stress was significantly lower among those who preferred to use integration and/or coexistence acculturation strategies.

Almost similar findings have been reported in studies in which acculturative stress of the participants at different stages of acculturation has been analysed. For example, Mishra and Kothiyal (1995) worked with adults of the Asur Adivasi group, who represented the low, transitional, moderate and high stages of acculturation. They assessed acculturative stress and marginality and reported an 'inverted U-shaped' relationship between acculturation experience and stress. The findings revealed lesser health problems in the case of low and high acculturation groups than in the case of the other two groups. The authors used the metaphor of 'honeymoon' experience to explain the low stress of the less acculturated group, and that of 'adaptation' to explain the same phenomenon in the case of high acculturated group. Greater health problems were also noted in relatively older age, less educated and Christian groups than in the younger age, more educated and non-Christian groups.

In a study with rural and urban individuals of the Oraon Adivasi group, Mishra (1997) found greater health problems in rural people, who worked in the city and commuted daily, and those who were 20–30 years old, less educated and had a field-dependent cognitive style. In the urban group, on the other hand, more health problems were found in those who were 30–50 years old, had moved to city more than five years ago and had a field-dependent cognitive style. A common finding that runs through both the rural and urban groups in this study is the greater experience of stress by people who are field-dependent than those who are relatively field-independent.

The studies of acculturation carried out with several Adivasi groups mentioned earlier indicate that the journey of acculturation is conflict-ridden, stressful and generally not smooth. The Adivasi Peoples use different strategies to adapt to the process of culture change. In general, the preference is for coexistence and integration strategies, both of which facilitate the journey of culture change and make the process of acculturation less stressful.

Conclusion

In this chapter, we have outlined two frameworks that may serve as ways of understanding ecological, cultural and acculturation influences on the development of human behaviour. In the next chapter, we present what is known about the consequences for behaviours that have been studied under these differing conditions.

3
Influences on Development of Human Behaviour

Introduction

In much early work, the ecological and cultural factors discussed in the previous chapter received considerable attention from many researchers in many disciplines. For example, in psychiatry, Kardiner (1945) argued for a relationship between sociocultural background and personality. Anthropologists and psychologists (e.g., Whiting & Child, 1953) emphasized the role of economic 'maintenance system' in the origin of cultural and behavioural variations. Whiting and Whiting (1975) later pointed out the importance of ecological and cultural factors in the development of behaviour.

Segall, Campbell and Herskovits (1966) initiated another tradition of research on ecological influences on behaviour. They studied susceptibility to visual illusions in the context of natural and cultural environment related factors. In order to determine the extent of susceptibility to visual illusions, they analysed the differential frequencies with which various geometric shapes were experienced by samples in their visual ecology. In this ambitious research scheme, the cultural products were allowed to become a part of the participant's physical environment, and there was a lack of concern for such cultural variables as socialization, social structure, social relations and language.

The general distinction between behaviour that is a function of physical environment and behaviour that is mediated by cultural influences was outlined by Berry (1976a). It was argued that cross-cultural/cross-ecology studies should consider independently two kinds of functional relationship between ecology and behaviour. One may be called a 'direct relationship' in which the focus is on behaviours in relation to the frequency with which different aspects of the ecosystem are experienced by individuals (e.g., the Segall et al. study of visual illusions). Another may be called an 'indirect relationship' in which culture is brought in, and serves as a mediating variable in the relationships between ecology and behaviour.

The latter kind of relationships can be understood only through cross-cultural studies. For example, Berry (1968) has shown how variation in illusion response is associated with cultural variables like education and socialization (in addition to visual ecology). Later work also pointed out the importance of combining ecological and cultural variables for a precise understanding of human cognitive functioning (Berry, 1986; Mishra et al., 1996; Mishra, 1997, 2001). Since it is difficult to determine empirically the extent of co-variation of ecological and cultural factors, most of the studies of cognition focus either on ecological or cultural factors in examining their influences. However, there are also a few studies in which ecology and culture have been considered simultaneously for analyzing cognitive functioning. All of these studies were inspired and guided by the ecocultural framework discussed earlier.

Ecological Influences on Cognitive Style

Much of the cross-cultural research on cognition using the ecocultural framework has been done with respect to the field dependent–field independent cognitive style. We have indicated earlier that the notion of cognitive style examines the way in which an individual cognitively deals with information in the environment. The concept of cognitive style is rooted in the *cognitive processes* that underlie any cognitive activity. The most influential conceptualization of cognitive style has been that of Witkin (Witkin, 1978; Witkin et al., 1962) who developed the dimension of the Field-Dependent/Independent (FDI) cognitive style. His starting point was a concern with perceptual and orientation abilities (spatial competencies) in air pilot trainees, but he soon noticed that a number of other abilities (including some social competencies) were related to each other in a way that evidenced an underlying pattern.

This pattern revealed itself in the tendency to rely primarily on internal (as opposed to external) frames of reference when orienting oneself in space, suggesting an underlying process. At one end of the FDI dimension are those (the relatively Field Independent [FI]) who rely on bodily cues within themselves, and are generally less oriented towards social engagement with others; at the other end are those (the relatively Field Dependent [FD]) who rely more on external visual cues, and are more socially oriented and competent. As for any psychological dimension, few individuals fall at the extreme ends, most fall in the broad middle range of the dimension. Examples of measures of FDI (the original Embedded Figures Test [EFT] and the African version; and the Portable Rod and Frame Test) are presented on the internet.

The FDI cognitive style is referred to by Witkin, Goodenough, and Oltman (1979, p. 1138) as 'extent of autonomous functioning'. The FDI construct refers to the extent to which an individual typically relies upon or accepts the physical or social environment as given, in contrast to working on it, for example, by analyzing or restructuring it. As the name suggests, those who tend to accept or rely upon the external environment are relatively more FD, while those who tend to work on it are relatively more FI. The construct is a dimension, the poles of which are defined by the two terms; individuals have a characteristic 'place' on this dimension, reflecting their usual degree of independence from the external environment. However, individuals are not 'fixed' into their usual place.

According to Witkin et al. (1962), the origins of the FDI cognitive style lie in early socialization experiences: those raised to be independent and autonomous were found to be relatively FI; those who were controlled more tightly were found to be relatively more FD. When examined across cultures (Witkin & Berry, 1975), studies revealed that societies that emphasize 'compliance' in socialization practices (Barry et al., 1959) and 'conformity to group norms' (Berry, 1967, 1979) tended to develop the field-dependent cognitive style. These are typically those societies that rely on agriculture for their subsistence, and that are hierarchical in social structure. In contrast, societies that are based in hunting economic subsistence tend to develop the field-independent cognitive style; they emphasize 'assertion' in socialization and are less conforming to social norms.

In an early study with Inuit (formerly called Eskimo) and Temne cultural groups, Berry (1966) found a strong ecocultural factor linked to the FDI cognitive style. This ecocultural factor was very important in a later study of cognitive style carried out across a wide range of societies (Berry, 1976a, see also Witkin and Berry, 1975). Members of nomadic hunting and gathering societies were found to be more field independent than members of sedentary societies living from subsistence agriculture. However, this cognitive style was also found to be influenced by acculturation; this is probably because of test-taking familiarity linked to education or employment in the 'modern' sector.

A major test of psychological differentiation theory and the ecocultural model within a single geographical area has been attempted in Central Africa (Berry et al., 1986). A comprehensive assessment of ecological, cultural and acculturation contexts was made. Male and female children and adults of the Biaka (Pygmy hunters and gatherers), the Bangandu (agriculturists with some hunting and gathering activities) and the Gbanu (full-fledged agriculturist) cultural groups were studied. The cognitive tests included the African Embedded Figures Test, Portable Rod and Frame Test, Body Adjustment Test, Sophistication of Body Proportioning Scale, Block Designs Training Test, Auditory Sequential Tones Test, Auditory Embedded Tones Test and Tactile Embedded Figures Test. These tests measured cognitive differentiation in visual, auditory and tactual domains. Evidence for differentiation in the social domain was collected by the assessment of looking, telling and sitting behaviours. Socialization emphases of the groups were studied through parent and neighbor interviews, child ratings and observation of parent–child interaction on a given task. Acculturation was measured at both the subjective and objective levels.

The results broadly supported the expectations that cognitive style would be related to ecocultural factors and to acculturation experience. Evidence for socialization emphases on independence and self-reliance in the Gbanu also corresponded to the general predictions of the ecocultural model. On the other hand, the prediction of test performance from socialization measures was not as strong as expected. The difference with respect to the experiences of acculturation was substantiated by ethnographic accounts of the groups as well as standardized test-and contact-acculturation measures, and there was clear evidence for their influence on test performance. The overall findings revealed a significant effect of ecological variables on performance even after statistically controlling the effect of acculturation.

The line of cross-cultural research on cognitive style that Berry initiated was followed in many research studies in India. For example, in an early study, Sinha (1979) worked with two subgroups of the Birhor Adivasi culture. One of these lived a nomadic hunting-gathering life; the other one had made transition to a sedentary agricultural life. A long-standing agricultural group of the Oraon Adivasi culture was also included. Boys and girls of 8–10 years, sampled from each of these groups, were administered the Story-Pictorial Embedded Figures Task (Sinha, 1978, 1984; SPEFT). This test was modeled on the Children's Embedded Figures Test (CEFT) by embedding local familiar stimuli (e.g., squirrels, snakes, and butterflies) in larger organized natural scenes (e.g., forests, and gardens) in order to ensure its cultural appropriateness. Findings revealed that children of the hunting-gathering group showed greater disembedding of stimuli in comparison to those of the agricultural group.

In another study, Sinha (1980) compared Adivasi and non-Adivasi samples, with a view to analyzing sex difference in performance of the SPEFT. The difference between boys and girls in the Adivasi sample was not significant. On the other hand, a clear gender difference (favoring boys) in the non-Adivasi sample was noted in the 4–5, 7–8 and 9–10 year groups.

The results of these studies were interpreted as supporting Berry's (1976a) prediction that hunters and gatherers are psychologically more differentiated than agriculturists, and that in complex and stratified societies, distinct sex roles are culturally prescribed, leading to differing psychological outcomes. In a later review of the findings of Indian studies on perceptual and cognitive skills, Sinha (1982) offered interpretations that were distinctly in favor of the ecocultural model.

Mishra et al. (1996) carried out an ambitious and large-scale research project, which was based in six districts of the State of Bihar (India). The districts were Gumla, Hazaribagh, Lohardaga, Ranchi, Ramgarh, and Palamau, which are now a part of the state of Jharkhand. By focusing on ecological and cultural characteristics of groups they selected children and adults of the Birhor (nomadic hunters-gatherers group), Asur (recent settlers pursuing a mixed economy of hunting-gathering and agriculture) and Oraon (long-standing agriculturists) Adivasi cultural groups. In each group, sampling variations were obtained with respect to a number of objective and subjective measures of contact-acculturation. The test-acculturation of individuals was also measured. Socialization emphases (pressure towards compliance or assertion) in the groups were assessed through a combination of observation, interview and testing. SPEFT, Tactile Embedded Figures Test (TEFT) and Kohs Block Designs Test (Kohs BDT) were used as the measures of cognitive style.

Findings again provided evidence for the existence of cognitive style; the above-mentioned measures (i.e., SPEFT, TEFT and BDT) loaded on a common factor. With regard to the effect of ecology and acculturation on cognitive performance of adults and children, results were in the predicted direction. The hunting-gathering samples scored significantly higher than the agricultural sample almost on all of the tests. On the other hand, the effect of acculturation was significant mainly for the Oraon cultural group, suggesting an interaction between ecological background and acculturation.

The findings also revealed that socialization emphasis reported by parents or children were not strong predictors of children's cognitive style. On the other hand, variables like helping and feedback (extracted from factor analysis of the House Building Task data) predicted children's cognitive style in the expected direction. K. Mishra (1996) obtained support for these results in another study with children of hunting-gathering, agricultural and wage-earning samples of the Tharu culture inhabiting the foothill region of the Himalayas.

Sinha and Shrestha (1992) examined the effect of ecology of hills and plains on the development of cognitive style in a study with 7–10-year-old children of the Brahmin and Gurung cultural groups of Nepal. Both schooled and unschooled children were administered the SPEFT. Findings revealed that schooled children generally scored higher than the unschooled. On the other hand, hill Brahmin children scored higher than hill Gurung, but plains Brahmin children scored lower than the plains Gurung. The overall findings indicated that ecology reinforced the process of differentiation by being associated with certain cultural practices of the groups.

Shrestha and Mishra (1996) later worked with boys and girls (7–10 years) of the Brahmin and Gurung cultural groups of Nepal. They found a significant gender difference in the level of psychological differentiation in the Brahmin sample, but not in the Gurung sample. On the other hand, Brahmin children appeared to be psychologically more differentiated than Gurung children in hill than in the plain ecology. Differing cultural practices of Brahmins and Gurungs in the ecology of hills and plains were held responsible for the obtained inconsistency in gender difference.

In these studies, however, the socialization practices and social structure of the groups were not assessed directly. This problem was addressed in a study (Sinha & Bharat, 1985) carried out with children reared in monogamous, polyandrous and polygynandrous families found in the cis-Himalayan region of India. The monogamous families comprised one husband, one wife and their children. The polyandrous families comprised one wife with two or more husbands (often brothers) and their joint children. In polygynandrous families, there were two or more husbands (again often brothers) sharing two or more wives and their common children. The SPEFT and BDT were administered to children of 7–9 and 13–15 years. Family experiences (e.g., mother and father involvement), disciplinary practices used with children, and mother–father dominance were observed, assessed through interviews and rated for different parameters of child socialization. While some of the socialization variables showed variations across family types, they did not significantly influence the level of psychological differentiation of children of the concerned groups.

Mishra and Singh (2008) examined the role of specific socialization variables in the level of field dependence-independence in a study in which 8–10-year-old boys and girls negotiating life in a rural ecological setting of Varanasi were tested. Children were given a house building task (Mishra et al., 1996) in the presence of their parents. Parent–child interaction during the task performance was assessed. The socialization variables included parental utterances (positive, negative and task-specific), parental help and looking up to parents and researcher (indicators of help-seeking behaviour of children). The findings revealed no significant difference in the pattern of parental interaction with boys and girls on any of the measures indicated previously. On the other hand, these variables played significant role in distinguishing FD and FI children: less parental utterances, less positive utterances, more task-specific utterances, less parental help and less help-seeking behaviour of children were associated with higher scores on the SPEFT.

Mishra (1996a) adopted another strategy for studying the influence of ecology on cognitive style among unschooled children of the Birjia cultural group in Bihar. Distances traveled away from home, either in the forest or within the village, and self-directed activities of children were assessed to develop ecological parameters. Children were administered the SPEFT and the Indo-African EFT as tests of cognitive style. The findings revealed that, in general, children moving into the forests travelled longer distances and engaged in more self-directed activities than those moving in the village surroundings. Children moving away in the forest scored significantly higher on both the measures than village children. These findings were explained in terms of greater self-exploration opportunities and high differentiation demands placed on children in the ecology of the forest than in the village ecology.

The ecocultural framework has been used in several other studies to understand sources of variation in perceptual-cognitive development (Dasen, 1975; Nsamenang, 1992; Zimba, 2002). It has also been used to comprehend the spatial orientation frames of reference used by children in Nepal (e.g., Mishra, Dasen, & Niraula, 2003) and elsewhere including India, Indonesia and Switzerland (Dasen & Mishra, 2010, 2013). These studies have clear relations to an increasing interest in cross-cultural psychology in indigenous conceptions of cognitive competence and in the cognitive tasks faced by people in daily life (e.g., Allwood & Berry, 2006;

Berry & Irvine, 1986; Berry et al., 1988). In these studies, it is argued that the indigenous conceptions of competence need to be uncovered; competencies are to be seen as developments nurtured by activities of daily life ('bricolage'), and as adaptive to ecological context. Understanding the indigenous conceptions, the cognitive values, the daily activities and the contexts is an essential prerequisite for valid cognitive assessment. Once again, as for the cross-cultural and intercultural research strategies, these indigenous (within-culture) studies need to be carried out from a non-ethnocentric standpoint (e.g., Berry & Bennett, 1992).

Ecocultural Influences on Social Behaviour

While most use of the ecocultural framework has been in the study of perception and cognition, it has also been useful to explore aspects of social behaviour. The notion of *social* or *affective style* was introduced by Berry (1973), based on studies of social conformity (Berry, 1967, 1979). In the theory of psychological differentiation (Witkin et al., 1962), the field-dependent style was associated with a number of social or affective behaviours such as conformity to social norms and susceptibility to social influence. In the review by Witkin and Berry (1975), studies showed that greater conformity to a suggested group norm is likely in cultures that are structurally tight (with high norm obligation). The relationship is robust, whether examined at the level of individuals, or by using the group's mean score as the variable related to ecology (see Bond & Smith, 1996, for a review).

A further example proposes links between ecocultural indicators and the currently popular concepts of individualism and collectivism (Berry, 1994a). It is suggested that individualism may be related to the societal size dimension, with greater individualism in a society being predicted by larger, more complex societies. However, collectivism was proposed to be related more to the social conformity dimension, with greater collectivism being related to social conformity: low in hunter-gatherer and urban/wage-earning populations, and high in agricultural populations. Berry (1994a) further suggested that when individualism and collectivism are conceived to be at opposite ends of a single value dimension, it is because data are usually obtained in societies (urban/wage-earning) where the two cultural dimensions (societal size and social conformity) are strongly distinguished; if data were to be collected in other types of societies (e.g., hunting or agricultural) where the two dimensions coincide (see Figure 3.2), then this value opposition or incompatibility may not be observed.

Research by Georgas and colleagues (Georgas & Berry, 1995; Georgas, van de Vijver, & Berry, 2004) further extends this interest in social aspects of behaviour. The first study sought to discover ecological and social indicators that would allow societies to be clustered according to their similarities and differences on six dimensions: ecology, education, economy, mass communications, population and religion. The second study further examined ecosocial indicators across cultures, and then sought evidence of their relationships with a number of psychological variables (such as values). Results showed that many of the indicators came together to form a single economic dimension (termed 'Affluence'), and this was distinct from 'Religion' in the pattern of relationships with the psychological variables. Specifically, across cultures, a high placement on Affluence (along with Protestant Religion) was associated with more emphasis on individualism, utilitarianism and personal well-being. In contrast, for other religions, together with low Affluence, there was an emphasis on power, loyalty and hierarchy values.

Most recently, the ecocultural framework has been used to guide an international study of the structure and function of families (Georgas et al., 2006). It sought to link ecological and sociopolitical contexts to family structure, family roles and some related family and personal values. Guided by both the ecocultural framework (Berry, 1976a) and by a model of family change (Kagitçibasi, 1996), the research project sought to understand contemporary families in 30 countries, representing most cultural regions of the world.

This study showed that when we examine the relationships between ecological and sociopolitical variables that were drawn from the ecocultural framework and cross-cultural features of family life, we find that there are predictable patterns, rather than random links. These patterns are consistent with the anthropological literature dealing with economic practices, and with religious belief systems. They are also consistent with, and were predicted from, previous psychological research carried out within the ecocultural tradition.

These studies bring out the role of ecological, cultural and acculturation factors in the development and display of FDI cognitive style not only in the perceptual-cognitive domain, but also in the social domain of human functioning. As far as the role of socialization in this cognitive style is concerned, the evidence is relatively less consistent to permit making any strong claim in this respect. While data obtained with various methods do not show coherence, data obtained with interview method pose challenges of reliability and predictive validity. There is some consistent evidence about the role of socialization in cognitive style across cultures, but within-culture studies do not reveal much of consistency in findings. In order to claim socialization as a factor in cognitive performance of groups across cultures, its influential role within culture also has to be established. This state of affairs calls for within-culture studies before making strong theoretical assertions about the postulated role of socialization in the development of psychological differentiation. There is also need to examine other dimensions of socialization besides the usually implicated 'compliance-assertion' dimension made available to us by ethnographic literature.

Acculturation Influences on Cognitive Style

In addition to examining the role of ecological and cultural factors in the development of cognitive style, in keeping with the full ecocultural model, the influence of the experience of acculturation has also been extensively examined. Berry's (1966, 1976a) early work on acculturation pointed out that acculturation (especially influences due to education, urbanization and wage employment) is an important factor leading to the development of a field-independent cognitive style. Inspired by this research, G. Sinha (1988) studied the role of schooling, urban and industrial experience (i.e., acculturation variables) in the development of cognitive style in children of the Santhal Adivasi culture in India. The SPEFT was used as a measure of cognitive style. The findings provided evidence for a stronger influence of industrial experience than schooling or urbanization, although all three acculturation variables were related to higher SPEFT scores.

In the large-scale study with children and adults of the Birhor, Asur and Oraon Adivasi cultural groups mentioned previously, Mishra et al. (1996) examined the role of objective and subjective acculturation in the cognitive style of children and adults. They also measured the test-acculturation (the degree of familiarity with test materials and comfort in test taking) of the participants. Tests were used to measure cognitive style and cognitive functions, such as pictorial perception, intermodal transfer, memory and classification.

Broadly speaking, a significant effect of acculturation on cognitive performance of adults and children on all cognitive measures was noted.

The effect of acculturation was mediated by the ecological background of the participants such that it contributed more to the performance of the Oraon participants than those of the other two groups. The authors used a 'threshold hypothesis' to explain the culture-bound effect of acculturation: acculturation changes the psychological characteristics of individuals only when it is allowed to penetrate into their life beyond a threshold point. Test-acculturation was also an important predictor of participants' performance on cognitive tasks, but it could not displace the effect of the long-standing ecocultural adaptation of groups.

Recent Work on Cognition and Cognitive Style

Other recent work has been devoted to understanding the relationship between the ecocultural context and the development of human behaviour. As noted in Chapter 1, in recent years, there has been work that purports to show that cognition processes are sharply different between 'Eastern' and 'Western' cultures. A strong proponent of a basic cognitive dichotomy is Nisbett (2003) who advocates a clear opposition between Western and Asian thought: 'Two utterly different approaches to the world have maintained themselves for thousands of years.' Nisbett (2003, p. xviii) denies that 'everyone has the same basic cognitive processes...or that all rely on the same tools for perception, memory, causal analysis, categorization and inference'.

These contrasting approaches include profoundly different kinds of social relations, views about the nature of the world and characteristic thought processes. In Nisbett's characterization, Western thought is analytic, whereas Asian thought is holistic. As a result, when Westerners perceive the world, they focus on objects and their attributes, whereas Asians focus on the field in which the object is located. Also, the Westerners use formal logic, whereas Asians use a dialectical approach for comprehending objects and events in their world.

To support the claim, Nisbett and his colleagues have carried out a large number of co-ordinated experiments by using American, Chinese or Japanese and Asian-American college students as subjects. Summarizing the findings of these studies Nisbett (2003) concludes, 'The research shows that there are indeed dramatic differences in the nature of Asian and European thought processes' (p. xviii).

However, Berry et al. (2011) have criticised this claim. They questioned whether these differences in performance were really qualitative, or only quantitative variations in performance on a common underlying cognitive process. In summarizing their work, Nisbett and colleagues claimed that 'Most of the time, in fact, Easterners and Westerners were found to behave in ways that were *qualitatively* distinct' (emphasis added, Nisbett, 2003, p. 191). This conclusion, that there are *qualitative* differences in basic processes, does not appear to be supported by Nisbett's own review of the evidence.

The summary provided by Nisbett (2003, pp. 191–93) of the differences in cognition between East and West all refer to *quantitative*, rather than to *qualitative*, differences in the cognitive *performance*s of participants who represent the 'East' and the 'West'. Two issues are important here. First, we see no evidence of qualitative differences in performance: apparently, all participants could perform these tasks, but to different degrees; hence there can be no claim of a cognitive process being present in one group but absent in the other. Second, even if there were qualitative differences in *performance*, this would not permit an easy claim of there being differences in underlying basic cognitive *processes*. The inferences required to go back from performance to process is a complex one, which these researchers seem not to have examined.

One limitation of two culture comparisons (such as these East–West studies) is that differences are essentially uninterpretable because other variables may be responsible for any difference found. Studies with three or more cultural groups within the same general location are required in order to deal with this problem. Such a study was the Biaka–Bagandu–Gbanu study mentioned earlier (Berry et al., 1986), as is the work reported in this book. The extension of the Nisbett-style work beyond two culture areas by Uskul, Kitayama and Nisbett (2008) is important in this regard. They sampled farmers, fishers and herders in the Eastern Black Sea Region of Turkey. This extension replicates the strategy of comparing groups within one ecological zone but who engage in different cultural ways reported in the section on cognitive styles. Based on ecocultural reasoning, and previous findings, they predicted that farmers and fishers would be more holistic than herders. They used a Framed Line Test (much like the PRFT) which presents a square with a vertical line in the centre. Participants were then presented another square of the same or different size; they were asked to draw a line that was identical to the originally shown line. There were two conditions: in one, the request was to draw the line in 'absolute' length (absolute task), or in proportion to the height of the new square (relative task). They argued that 'the absolute task would be facilitated by the ability to decontextualize or ignore the square frame and, thus, would be interfered by holistic attention. The relative task would be facilitated by the inability to ignore the square frame' (Uskul et al., 2008, p. 8554). Performance errors were calculated, with overall performance being better on the relative task than the absolute task. In keeping with their prediction, farmers and fishers were more accurate in the relative task than herders; and herders were more accurate than the others in the absolute task. They concluded that, in keeping with the ecocultural hypothesis, farmers and fishers are more holistic than herders.

As we have outlined in the previous chapter, the ecocultural framework considers that the subsistence economy of a group serves as a basis for the development of some cultural and behavioural features of a population. We have outlined variations across subsistence strategies, from hunting/gathering to agriculture to urban living. However, in societies that generally share a subsistence strategy, such as agriculture, the question arises: Does it matter what kind of crop is cultivated? Many countries have regional variations in the kind of crops that they grow, largely associated with variations in climate. For example in Europe, there is a 'wine-beer' line: south of it, grapes are grown (and wine produced); north of it, barley and wheat are grown (and beer produced). In other countries, there is also a regional division, for example, between wheat and rice agriculture: rice is grown in the south; wheat is grown in the north.

Talhelm and Oishi (2017) have examined the cultural and individual behavioural consequences of this differential agricultural practice in China. Although farming is now carried out by only a small percentage of the population in China, they ask whether there are cultural and behavioural residues that remain in a population that is modernizing. China has existed for thousands of years primarily as an agricultural society (rice in the south, wheat in the north). Can any cultural and behavioural differences still be found between regions after agriculture has become such a small part of the subsistence strategy? The authors were mainly concerned with the consequences of paddy rice farming (where rice is farmed in water in terraced plots), in contrast to dry land wheat farming.

They note that paddy rice farming requires around twice as much work as wheat farming, especially making the fields flat (to hold the water) and transplanting from small fields to the main fields when the plants reach some degree of maturity. However, the payoff is that rice produces around three times more crops per square metre cultivated than wheat. With respect to the social consequences, they argue that rice farming requires more social coordination, collective action, labour exchange and the building of social infrastructure than wheat farming. They further argue that the cultural consequence of this way of farming is that there is likely to be more collectivism in the social group. At the individual behavioural level, they found that the rice farmers make a larger distinction between 'friend' and 'stranger', and that the importance of the self was less in rice than in wheat areas.

Current Issues in Understanding Cognitive Styles

The studies mentioned in the preceding pages indicate that research on cognitive style in relation to ecological, cultural and acculturation variables has addressed many common issues during the last four decades. While earlier studies provide clear results, findings reported from diverse cultural settings in relatively recent years make the picture complex. Consequently, some theoretical advancement has surfaced in this field. These developments involve conceptualization of cultural level variables, psychological level phenomena and the relationship between them.

At the cultural level, the main concern lies with respect to specifying cultural experiences that are important for understanding psychological differentiation. In most of the studies, Berry's (1976a) ecocultural framework has been used as a guide to look for psychologically relevant variables. As indicated earlier, in this framework, the ecological (economic activity, settlement pattern, societal size) and cultural (role diversity, sociocultural stratification, socialization) variables have been combined into a single index, called 'ecocultural index'. The dimensions involved in this index are those of 'societal size' and 'social conformity' (Berry, 1987). There are now suggestions for treating these dimensions separately, because they vary differently as a function of the subsistence strategies of the groups. Relatively high field-independence reported for Western samples can be explained in terms of the importance of 'role obligation' for samples during acculturation. It may be argued that decrease in role obligation and norm imposition within a group would increase the probability of 'self–non-self segregation' and produce cultural group differences in cognitive style. We will return to a discussion of these new developments with regard to the conceptualization of cultural and cognitive dimensions in the next section.

As indicated earlier, these studies all bring out the role of ecological, cultural and acculturation factors in the development and display of FDI cognitive style not only in the perceptual-cognitive domain, but also in the social domain of human functioning. As far as the role of socialization in this cognitive style is concerned, the evidence is relatively less consistent to make any strong claim in this respect. While data obtained with various methods do not show coherence, data obtained with interview method pose challenges of reliability and predictive validity. There is some consistent evidence about the role of socialization in cognitive style across cultures, but within-culture studies do not reveal much of consistency in findings. In order to claim socialization as a factor in cognitive performance of groups across cultures, its influential role within culture has to be essentially established. This state of affairs calls for within-culture studies before making strong theoretical assertions about the postulated role of socialization in the development of psychological differentiation. There is also need to examine other dimensions of socialization besides the usually implicated 'compliance-assertion' dimension made available to us by ethnographic literature.

One problem with keeping the FDI cognitive style value-free comes from the way in which it is assessed. It would take too much space to go into details, but we can raise the issue briefly. Some tests devised by Witkin to measure psychological differentiation (e.g., the Rod and Frame Test [RFT]) are quite specific: the subjects are presented with a line surrounded by a tilted square, and they have to adjust the line so that it looks vertical. FD people are influenced by the square, so they tilt the line in the same direction as the square, while FI people set the line independently of it, according to their body perception of verticality. In this case, it is rather easy to accept that there are two ways to react to this situation, and that one is not inherently better than the other (although it is the FI people who can follow the instructions more carefully, and turn the line to the 'true' vertical).

In other tests (e.g., the EFT), where small elements have to be found in a complex drawing, field-dependent participants find the elements less easily (or take longer to solve the task, if it is timed), so it is more difficult to find their performance at par with those who are more efficient. Still a step further, some standard psychometric tasks, such as the BDT (also called Kohs blocks), or Raven's Progressive Matrices were found to correlate with RFT and EFT, and were therefore also considered to be measures of psychological differentiation (see e.g., Berry, 1976a). However, other psychologists consider these same tests as performance tests of spatial cognitive skills, and some others even consider them as measures of general intelligence. In that case, it takes a lot more cultural relativism not to consider a higher performance as better. However, from the ecocultural perspective, performances are considered as being adaptive to the local context, and cannot be judged in relation to some external (or absolute) criterion. This issue may seem somewhat abstract at this stage, but we will come back to it in later sections of the book, when we describe and discuss the results of some of these tests.

We have dealt with the notion of cognitive style in some detail, because our knowledge of cross-cultural research of cognitive functioning leads us to accept that this construct is the most appropriate way to understanding of the cognitive functioning of individuals in cultural context. Based on their studies of the development of spatial language and cognition in India, Indonesia, Nepal and Switzerland, Dasen and Mishra (2010) concluded that 'Cultural differences in cognition reside more in *cognitive styles* than in the existence of a process in one cultural group and its absence in another' (pp. 13–14). As we can see, this is a slightly rephrased version of the conclusion drawn by Cole et al. (1971) from their studies of learning and thinking in the Liberian cultural context. We think that this general conclusion is true not only for the processes of spatial cognition, but also for cognitive processes of differentiation and contextualization that we specifically address in this book.

From the selective survey of studies, it is clear that both the early and recent theoretical and empirical work on the ecocultural framework has addressed the question of the origins of similarities and differences in human behaviour across cultures, and of the relationships between culture and behaviour. It has been argued that one can go a long way to providing an interpretation of these relationships if one adopts an ecocultural perspective, which considers psychological processes as 'universal' in the species, and behaviours as 'adaptive' to both ecological and sociopolitical contexts.

Within such a framework, we can conceptualize cultural and individual behaviour as separate phenomena: culture exists apart from particular individuals, but becomes incorporated into all individuals through enculturation and acculturation processes. Hence, culture in such a framework is regarded both as an independent and as an organismic variable. Given this conception, it is possible to carry out empirical work at the two levels. Analyses can be conducted within levels (the classical ethnographic and individual difference studies). The major advantage, however, exists when cultural-level data are used to predict individual and group similarities and differences in behaviour. No longer do we need to rely on post-hoc interpretations of behavioural similarities and differences across cultures. The research strategy suggested by ecocultural framework is both 'cultural' and 'comparative', allowing for the 'cross-cultural' understanding of human diversity.

Studies on FDI cognitive style have raised certain critical issues that have emerged from the patterns of performance obtained on different tests/tasks used for their assessment. We have indicated that in the early studies of FDI cognitive style, RFT, BAT and EFT were widely used. In later studies, a portable version of the RFT, called PRFT, has been frequently employed. Several forms of EFT have also been developed and used with children and adults in various cultural groups. The CEFT, African Embedded Figures Test (AEFT), Indo-African Embedded Figures Test (IAEFT) and SPEFT have been widely used by researchers. Tests measuring FDI style in tactual and auditory domains have also been given to samples (Berry et al., 1986; Mishra et al., 1996).

A central issue of discussion in these studies relates to the consistency of test scores obtained in different cognitive domains. Gender difference in the level of FDI is another important issue. Individual and group differences at the level of FDI constitute a third major issue. The adaptability of cognitive style to ecological pressures and acculturative influences (e.g., urbanization, wage employment, education) constitutes the fourth major issue in research.

With respect to self-consistency, earlier studies, which largely explored into the perceptual domain, generally found support for consistency. Evidence for less consistency appeared between perceptual and other domains. Studies seeking sex difference found its presence in agricultural samples, but not in hunting and gathering populations (Berry, 1966; Mac Arthur, 1967; Sinha, 1980). Developmental studies revealed a shift from FD to FI from childhood to adulthood, with an evidence for the stability of the styles over time.

In order to search for individual and group differences in cognitive style, research has focused on the characteristics of family and child-rearing practices, socialization pressure on 'conformity', ecological engagements of people (hunting-gathering or agriculture) and acculturative experiences. Studies generally suggest that it is possible to predict the cognitive style of individuals and groups from the knowledge of their ecological and cultural characteristics (Berry et al., 1986; Mishra et al., 1996).

Further Conceptualizations of Cultural and Cognitive Dimensions

The ecocultural framework developed by Berry (1976a) is largely a unidimensional conceptualization. Around the same time period, Lomax and Berkowitz (1972) have proposed a bidimensional conceptual alternative to Berry's unidimensional formulation of the ecocultural dimension. Using the same cultural database as Murdock, they found evidence for two independent factors of cultural variation over the ecological range. These were referred to as 'differentiation' and 'integration'. The first refers to the number and kind of role distinctions made in the society, while the second refers to the 'groupiness', i.e., the degree of cohesion among members of a society. However, over the middle range of subsistence activities on this 'evolutionary culture scale' of Lomax and Berkowitz, the two dimensions were positively correlated. This formulation seems to be more general in approach because its data were obtained from a large number of societies representing a large range of cultures.

In a series of papers, Boldt and his colleagues (Boldt, 1976; Boldt & Roberts, 1979; Roberts, Boldt, & Guest, 1990) further examined the possibility of the existence of these two independent dimensions. Similar attempts have been made by Gamble and Ginsberg (1981). It has been argued that 'structural complexity' and 'structural tightness' need to be distinguished. The first refers to the degree of 'role diversity' encouraged in a culture. Since it expands the range of activities available to an individual, it should enhance choice and individual autonomy (Roberts et al., 1990, p. 69). The second refers to 'social conformity', which is the degree to which social expectations are imposed on individuals. This should reduce an individual's autonomy by narrowing the opportunities for negotiating a preferred course of action (Roberts et al., 1990, p. 69).

This distinction is similar to the differentiation-integration distinction proposed earlier by Lomax and Berkowitz (1972). It breaks the more general indexes such as 'cultural complexity' (McNett, 1970), 'tightness-looseness' (Gelfand et al., 2011; Pelto, 1968) and the 'ecocultural index' (Berry, 1976a) into two components. In the case of ecocultural index, it places the ecological variables (of settlement pattern, mean size of the local community) and the cultural variable of political stratification into one construct (structural complexity), whereas other cultural variables of social stratification and socialization emphases into another construct (structural tightness).

In view of the evidence collected in favour of two dimensions of cultural variation across different subsistence level groups, a new operationalization has been developed. The two new terms proposed for these two dimensions are *societal size* and *social conformity* (Berry, Bennett, & Denny, 1995). The first is defined and operationalized as comprising four components: (a) settlement pattern (nomadic, transitional, sedentary), (b) mean size of local community, (c) political stratification (number of levels above local units) and (d) occupational specialization (crafts, religion, etc.). The second (social conformity) consists of three variables: (a) social stratification (relatively permanent distinctions based on heredity, wealth, class, or caste divisions), (b) socialization emphases (responsibility, obedience, nurturance or self-reliance, achievement and independence, called compliance-assertion) and (c) social obligation (degree of role and norm obligation placed on individuals to conform to the standards of the group).

Researchers have reported high degree of egalitarianism, individualism and atomism among people living as hunters-gatherers (Honigmann, 1968; Ridington, 1988; Woodburn, 1982), which are less valued qualities among agriculturalists. Members of hunting and gathering societies enjoy greater freedom of choice in matters such as residence, personal relationship, marriage, and qualities such as independence, self-reliance and flexibility are admired. In agricultural societies, on the other hand, many of these elements are reversed. Individuals are dependent on groups to which they are bound for the whole life, senior members regulate the necessities and exercise control over juniors by limiting access to food, land, marriage partner, etc. There is also a distinct hierarchy of authority, which demands compliance from children and from persons lower in age and hierarchy in family.

Thus, the two new dimensions of societal size and social conformity seem to vary considerably as a function of subsistence strategies of groups. These correspond to Lomax and Berkowitz's (1972) differentiation and integration dimensions. Our hypothesized relationships are presented in Figure 3.1 (based on Lomax & Berkowitz, 1972). It may be observed that while societal size appears as a linear function of subsistence economic strategy, social conformity seems to present a curvilinear relationship (relatively low in gathering, hunting and industrial societies, but higher in rudimentary and irrigation agricultural societies). In view of such a pattern of relationship, different cognitive consequences for different subsistence strategy groups can be predicted. There is already some empirical evidence to indicate the existence of these two cultural dimensions and their differential relationship with the ecological engagement of groups

Figure 3.1

Hypothesized Relationship between Two Cultural Dimensions of Societal Size and Social Conformity and Subsistence Strategies

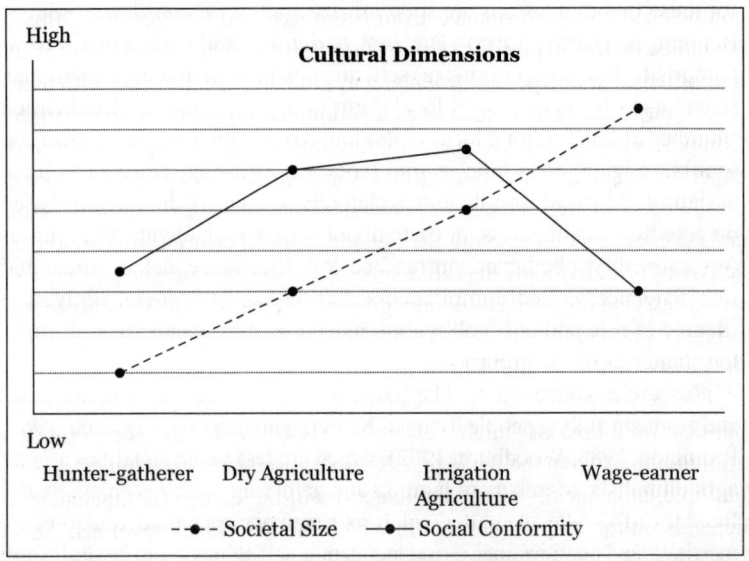

(see Mishra, 1996, 2011b; Mishra & Berry, 2008). Before discussing these studies, we will discuss the individual-level psychological issues involved in these relationships.

Individual Psychological Issues

In this section, we present in some detail the notion of cognitive style, and outline some of its core features. Although less frequently examined in recent years (Berry, 2000), there has been a call to reinstate the concept by Sternberg and Grigorenko (1997). In essence, the notion of cognitive style examines the way in which an individual cognitively deals with information in the environment, rather than how successful this activity may be in relation to some fixed criterion. In this way, we seek to 'neutralize' the issue, by considering the *quality*, rather than the *quantity* of any cognitive activity.

The concept of cognitive style seeks to identity the underlying *cognitive processes* that permit any cognitive activity. Only the *cognitive performances* may be observed, and such performances can only be carried out if there is a developed *competence* on which it may be based. We adopt this well-established distinction in psychology between process, competence and performance from Sternberg and Grigorenko (2004). As indicated in Chapter 1, processes are those psychological features of individuals that are the fundamental ways in which people deal with their day-to-day experiences, such as perception, learning and categorization. Competencies are those features of individuals that develop with cultural experience, such as abilities, attitudes and values. They are developed on the basis of the interaction between the basic underlying processes and peoples' encounters with the outside world. Performances are those activities of individuals that are expressed as behaviour, such as skilled work, carrying out projects, or engaging in political action. They are those expressions of competencies that are appropriate to, or are triggered by, the need to act in a suitable way in a particular context.

The actual performance will depend, not only on the competence, but also on a host of situational factors (Berland, 1982). For example, all individuals have the basic processes required to learn a language (or multiple languages). Which language(s) will be learned (competencies) depends on the cultural context in which the individual develops. And, in a situation where there is a choice of language, the performance will depend on the language of the interlocutor and the requirement to speak a particular language in any specific situation (such as at work, or in one's cultural community).

Our approach to cognitive style is rooted in the *universalist* perspective that assumes that all human beings everywhere have these basic capacities, regardless of culture or experience. This assumption is widely held (Berry et al., 2002; Mishra, 1997, 2001); it is supported by the fact that no evidence has yet been found for the absence of basic processes in any cross-cultural study of cognition (or indeed of any other behavioural domain).

The concept of *cognitive competencies* refers to cultural knowledge about how, and the ability to carry out daily activities. These can range from some rather mundane abilities (such as knowing how to use eating utensils) to much more complex sets of knowledge (such as the laws pertaining to taxation). Competencies are built up on the basis of the interaction of underlying processes and peoples' encounters with the outside world. For example, the competence to speak a language will depend on a number of factors, including opportunities to learn it (through formal instruction or informal social interaction).

Not everything a person is capable of doing is actually carried out; the stage needs to be set appropriately for any competence to be performed.

As a result, *cognitive performances* are those expressions of competencies that are appropriate to, or are triggered by, particular contexts. Cognitive performances may or may not be expressed if they are not appropriate to the situation.

In some cases, speaking a language in front of others who do not understand it may be considered by them as an affront or insult. As indicated earlier, all people have the process available to learn the language of their own society and the language of another society. The actual performance will depend not only on their competence, but also on a host of situational factors, such as the language of the interlocutor and the requirement to speak a language in any particular situation.

We acknowledge that any assessment of cognitive style requires the observation of some *performance* (either on a specific task in a controlled setting, or in daily life). We also acknowledge that any such performance requires the prior development of the *competence* to carry it out. However, our main concern is to use the performance and the presumed underlying competence as a basis for inferring the process that is at the base of these overt behaviours. We turn now to a description of four of these basic cognitive processes.

The Cognitive Style Dimensions

We have indicated earlier that the notion of cognitive style examines the *way* in which an individual cognitively deals with information in the environment. The concept of cognitive style is rooted in the *cognitive processes* that underlie any cognitive activity. In the present book, we note that any cognition consists of certain units and parts. For example, a syllogism (unit) may consist of a major premise, a minor premise and a conclusion (parts), just as a Block Design (unit) may comprise several blocks (parts). The units and parts may have two basic relations. One is 'distinctiveness', which refers to the recognition of parts and units as distinct from one another. The second is 'connectedness', which refers to the recognition of relationship among parts and units. These relationships can occur at two places: (a) among different parts within a unit, called Intra-unit, and (b) among different units themselves, called Extra-unit. When these notions are combined, we get four cognitive functions, which are presented in Figure 3.2. Two of these, *Intra-unit Distinctiveness* (ID) and *Extra-unit Connectedness* (EC), are of main interest in research on cognition in a cross-cultural perspective.

Figure 3.2

Four Cognitive Processes

Cognitive operations	Relations	
	Intra-unit	Extra-unit
Distinctiveness	Recognition of parts as distinct: *Differentiation*	Recognition of units as distinct
Connectedness	Recognition of connections among parts of units	Recognition of connections among units: *Contextualization*

Intra-unit Distinctiveness (Differentiation)

Intra-unit distinctiveness is defined as cognition, which emphasizes differences among the parts inside a cognitive unit. It is reflected in attending to, conceptualizing and labeling the parts in a figure or an image. In previous research on cognition, it was called 'differentiation' (Witkin & Berry, 1975). Extra-unit connectedness, on the other hand, refers to a cognition, which emphasizes connection of a thought unit with other thought units, e.g., when a word is understood only by its relation to other words in a sentence. In previous research, this variable was referred to as 'contextualization' (Denny, 1991). Making more distinctions within a cognitive (thought) unit provides evidence of higher differentiation, whereas making more connections to other cognitive (thought) units provides evidence of higher contextualization.

Research has tried to explore the existence of the 'differentiation' and 'contextualization' cognitive style dimensions among individuals across different ecocultural contexts. There is some evidence to suggest that these cognitive style dimensions vary systematically across cultures with variations in subsistence strategies of groups. The hypothesized relationship of subsistence strategies with cognitive styles reported in different studies is summarized in Figure 3.3.

A curvilinear relationship between subsistence economy and the level of differentiation of individuals is clearly in evidence: The tendency to emphasize distinctions among parts of a cognitive unit is high among hunters, low among rudimentary agriculturalists, medium among irrigation agriculturalists and high among the members of urban societies.

This relationship is largely based on the research findings carried out in different parts of the world (Berry, 1976; Berry et al., 1986), including

Figure 3.3

Hypothesized Relationship between Two Cognitive Styles of Differentiation and Contextualization and Subsistence Strategies

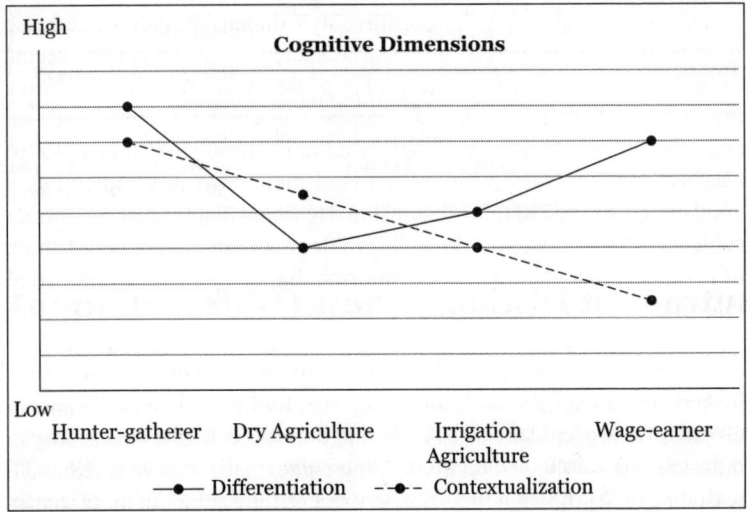

India (Mishra et al., 1996). As indicated earlier, these studies have focused on the process of 'differentiation'. For a number of samples representing three of the subsistence types, it has been found that hunting-gathering and the urbanized groups show greater differentiation than agriculturalists on psychological tests in which the tasks involve making distinction within a cognitive unit (e.g., perceiving a simpler visual design as part of a more complex whole such as in the EFT). Studies also suggest differentiation to be a characteristic feature of irrigation agricultural people in the middle levels of societal size (Bishop, 1978) and relatively higher levels of acculturation (Berry et al., 1986, Mishra et al., 1996).

Studies with exclusively gathering samples are relatively few and not very current. In an early study, McIntyre (1976) found that traditional Aboriginal children in Australia were the lowest in differentiation on the EFT than white Australian or Westernized Aboriginal children. Similarly, Reuning and Wortley (1973) found that Bushmen gatherers in South Africa had difficulty with the EFT. In irrigation societies, on the other hand, studies have shown medium to higher levels of differentiation on the EFT (Iwawaki, 1986; Iwawaki & Vernon, 1988). Taken together, these results indicate a curvilinear relationship of intra-unit distinctiveness (ID) with the subsistence strategies of individuals or groups.

Extra-unit Connectedness (Contextualization)

As indicated in Figure 3.3, this cognitive style dimension shows a decrease from hunters and gatherers to industrial society. This conclusion seems to find support in psychological studies of deductive reasoning on tasks involving syllogisms. Such tasks can be done without dependence on any other information beyond that stated in the problem. Luria's (1976) classical study of farmers in Soviet land mentioned in Chapter 1 is a good demonstration of this relationship. He found that the peasant farmer subjects either refused to do such problems because they could think of no appropriate context for the information, or they added contextual information before reasoning.

Similar evidence of contextualization has been reported by Greenfield (1972), Scribner (1977) and Hutchins (1980) among agricultural groups in Africa and Papua New Guinea. In a study with indigenous groups in Canada, Denny and Davis (1989) found that subjects assessed as low in industrialization showed relatively high contextualization in a deductive reasoning task. Although again not very recent, the findings of these studies lead us to speculate that hunting and gathering groups demonstrate a high level of contextualization on cognitive tasks.

There are some studies carried out in a non-psychological testing tradition, which throw light on this relationship. In a study, Denny (1986) has shown that hunting societies (e.g., Inuit and Oji-Cree in Canada) carried out mathematical thought in a highly contextualized manner. On the other hand, Goody (1977) has reported a partial decontextualization for the literate irrigation agricultural group. Although the evidence is not very compelling, these studies do indicate the existence of cognitive style dimension of contextualization among groups.

Studies of Differentiation and Contextualization in Relation to Cultural Dimensions of Societal Size and Social Conformity

From the studies mentioned earlier it is clear that they have focused either on the process of 'differentiation' or of 'contextualization' in relation to the cultural dimensions of societal size and social conformity. However, there are three of our studies in which the possibility of the existence of cultural dimensions of societal size and social conformity, of cognitive dimensions of differentiation and contextualization and of their differential pattern of relationship with ecological features of individuals has been examined. It might be noted that in these studies the hunting-gathering groups were not distinct from each other. Members of these groups were neither exclusively hunters, nor were they exclusively gatherers. Two such studies (Mishra, 1996b; Mishra & Berry, 2008) were done with people from four subsistence level strategy groups (hunting-gathering, dry agriculture, irrigation agriculture, wage-earning). These groups were drawn from the Adivasi regions of Bihar (now in Jharkhand) in India. Measures of societal size, social conformity, social-connectedness, individual connectedness and socialization behaviour were used for the assessment of cultural dimensions. SPEFT, Hidden Words Test (HWT), Locating Objects Test (LOT), Syllogistic Reasoning Test (SRT), Unknown Words Test (UWT), Visual Closure Test (VCT) and Object Enumeration Test (OET) were used for the assessment of cognitive dimensions of differentiation and contextualization. The relationship between the two cultural and cognitive dimensions was also examined.

With respect to cultural dimensions, the findings revealed that societal size showed a progressive increase from the hunting-gathering to wage-earning through agricultural groups, whereas social conformity was low in the hunting-gathering and wage-earning groups, but high in the agricultural groups. Social as well as individual connectedness was highly placed in the agricultural than in hunting-gathering and wage-earning groups. The cultural variables (societal size, social conformity, social and individual connectedness) formed a cohesive cluster, indicating that the variables were highly interrelated.

With respect to cognitive dimensions, the analyses revealed that the level of differentiation in hunting-gathering and wage-earning groups was higher than that of the agricultural groups. On the other hand, the level of contextualization in the hunting-gathering group was lower than that of the agricultural and wage-earning groups respectively. Differences between boys and girls in all test performances were less evident in the hunting-gathering than other groups. There was also evidence for 'task specificity' with respect to gender effect on performance across different subsistence level groups. Multiple regression analyses revealed that 'years of school education' was the strongest predictor of children's performance on various measures. Subsistence economy and urban contact also made significant contribution to a number of measures.

These findings have been confirmed in a third study carried out with Birhor (hunting-gathering) and Kharwar (agricultural) groups (Mishra, 2011b). The cultural dimensions were assessed by using the same instruments as in Mishra (1996b) and Mishra and Berry (2008) studies. The cognitive dimensions of 'differentiation' and 'contextualization' were assessed with the help of SPEFT and LOT respectively.

As predicted, societal size in this study was found to be the lowest in the hunting-gathering group with evidence for linear increase from hunting-gathering through dry and irrigation agriculture to wage-earning groups. On the other hand, social conformity was found to be low in hunting-gathering and wage-earning groups, but high in dry and irrigation agricultural groups. Social connectedness and individual connectedness were found to be low in hunting-gathering and high in agricultural groups, showing a curvilinear relationship with ecological engagement of groups. Analysis of performance on cognitive tasks revealed differentiation to be high in hunting-gathering and wage-earning groups, but low in both the agricultural groups. In contrast to this, contextualization was found to be low in hunting-gathering and wage-earning groups, but high in both the agricultural groups. The study suggested differentiation and contextualization as two independent cognitive processes showing a variable relationship with ecological and cultural dimensions.

The Current State of Knowledge

The anthropological literature suggests the existence of 'societal size' and 'social conformity' dimensions. Cognitive research provides evidence for the existence of 'differentiation' and 'contextualization' dimensions. Some research on cognition suggests a predictable relationship between the two cultural and cognitive style dimensions. However, the way these relationships have been examined in research presents a number of weaknesses. The major problems are as follows:

1. Societal dimensions have been identified by anthropologists, and cognitive style dimensions have been spelled out by psychologists, but they have not been combined in cross-cultural research in any systematic way. Studies in which they have been examined together are all 'within-culture' studies. The generality of these findings needs to be tested cross-culturally.
2. Studies have been carried out around the globe (northern Canada to Australia) often drawing different kinds of samples from different

places. For example, gatherers have been sampled from South Africa, hunters from Arctic Canada, irrigation agriculturalists from Japan and industrial people from the USA. Such widely varying samples create certain problems of comparison and interpretation of data, and raise doubts about the validity of inferences drawn from various studies. Thus, there is a need to examine the relationship of cultural and cognitive dimensions by analyzing their patterning both within and across-cultures.

3. There is very little work to relate these dimensions in research in the multicultural setting of India, where ample opportunities exist for doing cross-cultural research at the next door. One can easily locate and work with samples ranging from hunting-gathering to industrial wage-earning activities within a relatively narrow geographical region to get rid of many confounding variables that cannot be easily handled in studies of geographically widespread samples.

4. There has been little attempt to comprehend the wider implications of the study of the relationship between culture and cognition for education or development of a given population. Potentials of such research studies for handling the problem of education of Adivasi children in India in relation to these cultural and cognitive variables have been pointed out (Mishra, 2007, 2008; Mishra et al., 1996). The evidence suggests that culturally emphasized cognitions are more likely to develop and to be highly placed among groups than those cognitions, which have no cultural significance for people (Mishra, 2005, 2007; Sinha & Mishra, 1997). Thus, while cognitive achievements of children need to be analysed in these terms, they have not been so treated in research, at least in the Indian cultural setting.

Our Expectations

In view of the propositions made in the conceptual and empirical work reported in this chapter, we expect that:

1. Social conformity would be lower in hunting-gathering and industrial groups than in rudimentary and irrigation agricultural groups.
2. The level of contextualization would show a decrease from hunting-gathering to agricultural to industrial groups.

Influences on Development of Human Behaviour 75

3. Differentiation would be higher in hunting-gathering and industrial groups than in agricultural groups.
4. The cultural dimension of societal size would be negatively correlated with the cognitive dimension of contextualization, whereas social conformity dimension would be negatively correlated with the cognitive dimension of differentiation.
5. The educational achievements of children in various subsistence strategy groups assessed with our tasks would show considerable variations: the wage-earning group would show greater achievement than agricultural group, who would show greater achievement than hunting-gathering group.

It may be pointed out that none of the predicted relationships is considered to be deterministic; at best, they are all probabilistic. In view of this, only the direction (not necessarily the magnitude) of differences and correlations may be considered as the evidence of support for our expectations. Yet, attempt will be made to test statistically the predicted relationships against the assumptions of a null hypothesis. We shall come back to these issues later when the cultural groups (with whom we have worked) and the various tasks and methods employed in the assessment of the variables of interest have been introduced in the following two chapters.

4
The Cultural Groups

Introduction

In this chapter, we describe the cultural groups with which we worked at various places around the world. We describe the ecological, cultural and acculturation conditions of the groups, focusing particularly on their economic subsistence strategies, daily life activities, social structure, family settings and child socialization processes. We also describe the changes taking place in the life of groups in recent years as a result of their acculturation which is due to education, urbanization and industrialization. The description is presented in a sequence such that the hunting-gathering groups are described first followed by those groups whose livelihood is based on agriculture. The description of the wage-earning group is presented at the end.

The Hunting-gathering Groups

The work with the hunting-gathering groups was carried out in India (Birhor hunter-gatherers), Ghana (Vagala hunters) and Canada (Oji-Cree hunters). We now describe each of these communities.

India Hunters-gatherers: The Adivasi Birhor

The Birhor group is a traditional Adivasi group of Jharkhand state in India still living largely as nomads. Some decades ago, very few of them had fixed habitation. They moved about from one forest to another in small bands in search of game animals, fruits, roots, nuts and other forest produces. These were their primary means of subsistence. Collection of fibers, honey and bees wax were their other economic activities.

The Birhor believe that their descent is from the sun. According to a legend, seven brothers came down to their country from the Kaimur Hills. Four of them went to the east, and three remained in Ramgarh district (presently situated between Ranchi and Hazaribagh). One day, when the three brothers were going out to fight against the chief of the land, the headdress of one of them got entangled in a tree. He considered it a bad omen and decided to stay behind in the jungle. When his two brothers came back after defeating the chief, they found their third brother cutting off the bark of a tree. They decided to call him 'Birhor', which in the local language means 'woodman' or a 'chop cutter'. This brother preferred to live in the jungle. Thus, the Birhor became the king of the forests.

The Birhor live largely on forest resources through hunting and gathering activities (Mishra et al., 1996; Sinha, 1979; Vidyarthi & Sahay, 1976). When the resources in one area are diminished, they move on to another area. They have very little contact with other Adivasi groups in their region as well as with the outside world.

On the basis of the degree of nomadism present in their life, the Birhor have been divided into two classes: the *Uthlu* (wanderers) and the *Jaghi* (settlers). The *Uthlu* Birhor frequently move from one forest to another except for the rainy season (July to September). On the other hand, the *Jaghi* Birhor live at a fixed place, usually on a hilltop or on the outskirts of a forest. The Tribal Welfare Department of the government has now built houses in those places. As a result, many traditional settlements of the Birhor have now turned into colonies. The distinction between *Jaghi* and *Uthlu* Birhor, however, has not been very rigid. Even today, the *Uthlu* turn into *Jaghi* by taking on a relatively permanent habitation, and the *Jaghi* become *Uthlu* by abandoning their settlement and moving into the forest.

The shifting camps of Birhor are known as *tanda*. Each *tanda* consists of five to eight families, which generally have a common lineage. A *tanda* is the largest unit for food quest and for social and religious activities. The Birhor group is divided into a number of exogamous clans named after animals, plants, fruits or flowers. These clans generally do not hang together. So much so that different families of the same clan living apart hardly ever meet each other. On the other hand, the families belonging to different clans, but constituting a *tanda*, show great cohesion and solidarity. Each *tanda* has a headman (*Naya*), who also works as a priest.

Each family in a *tanda* lives in a separate hut made of tiny branches and leaves. The huts have a conical shape and these can be erected within a few hours. A hut generally has two compartments. One of these serves as a storeroom for pots and pans, axes, hunting nets and mats, etc. The other part is used for cooking and sleeping. The entrance of the hut is so small that one can hardly crawl through it. When the family moves into the forest, the entrance is covered with a fence of tiny branches and leaves.

The Birhor economy is largely based on hunting and gathering. The daily routine of a Birhor is to leave the settlement soon after sunrise. Women and children also join in this endeavour. Old or sick people stay back and take care of young children. Older children often go for fishing in nearby ponds or rivulets, or trapping wild rats in the nearby bush, and gathering fruits, roots, yams, tubers, caterpillars and firewood. Men generally engage in hunting and trapping animals and birds. Once the hunting/trapping plan has been organized and the nets have been spread, women get involved in gathering activities. The game is often shared and eaten up by the group, but sometimes these are sold to outsiders, and the money is shared by all involved in hunting/trapping activities. The hunting schemes differ according to the season and the needs of the community.

The Birhor believe in continuous progression of life. To acquire strength to combat supernatural evil influences that surround them is a major quest of their life. Death represents the highest stage of existence wherein one is transformed into a spirit and is capable of influencing others for good and bad. Such a belief system forces parents to protect the mother and the child from the very beginning stage of conception.

A child is highly valued in the Birhor society. From birth onwards, the child remains in the mother's lap and sleeps in mother's bed. Breastfeeding is carried out until the next child is born. While performing various chores, the mother carries the child on her back by wrapping her/him in a piece of cloth. The infants are never kept away from mother's contact. Later, children enjoy enormous freedom during the early and late-childhood stages. Basic life skills are acquired by observing others.

A number of changes have taken place in the traditional life of the Birhor during the last few decades. Some of them have been brought about by the developmental schemes of the government, while others have occurred as a result of their contact with outsiders. During the post-independence period, some Birhor settlements were developed by the government. This initiative did not meet success. In the absence of technical and practical knowledge of agriculture, the Birhor families could not grow enough food, and they looked back to forests. Despite having a house in the settlement, many Birhor families have continued with their nomadic lifestyle.

While the cherished life for the Birhor is still wandering in forests, the legislation regarding forest and wildlife conservation has denied them free access to the forest. This has forced many nomadic Birhor families to move into government settlements. Some of them have also learnt a rudimentary form of agriculture. The poor quality of land, however, provides them with food barely for 2–3 months. For the rest of the year, they depend on forest resources in spite of the government legislation against their exploitation. Massive cutting of trees by government contractors has led to deforestation and reduction in the prospects of hunting and trapping. Consequently, a large number of Birhor families now engage in rope-making, or work as labourers in coalfields.

Many non-governmental organizations (NGOs) are also actively involved in the settlement of the Birhor. Tata Industrial Steel Company (TISCO) established some settlements in which the Birhor families were provided with life skills training and children with primary education. However, these efforts did not make any long-lasting impact. The spread of Christianity has been a major event to take place in the lives of the Birhor. Over the years, many Birhor families have accepted Christianity. In spite of their religious conversion, the Birhor identity has remained very strong.

Increasing contact of the Birhor with outsiders over the last few decades has introduced some major changes in their life. Industrial development in traditional Birhor areas has been the most powerful influence. Ban on the exploitation of forest resources by the government, uncertainties about the availability of food in the dwindling forest around them and the opportunities created for wage employment in the local industries have worked together to force many Birhor families to settle in small town-like habitations coming up around the industries and work on wages. The children of these families also attend schools run either by the government, or by the NGOs with the support of the industry authorities.

The effect of industrial participation can be observed in several domains of the Birhor's life. For example, the Birhor children have picked up Hindi and/or English language so much so that many hardly speak their own language. Their furniture, ornaments, pots and pans, clothes and clothing styles have changed. While modern technological gadgets (radios, bicycles and motorbikes) are now part of the Birhor life, many families also travel to nearby cities and/or to the state capital for tourism and watching movies. These influences are also gradually penetrating into the lives of those, who stay in the forest engaged largely in traditional subsistence economic activities.

A doctoral student of psychology at Ranchi University assisted us in carrying out the work with the Birhor group. He belonged to a family that lived in a village situated in the area where the Birhor settlements were developed. Many Birhor families would also camp at the edge of the forest, close to the Birhor settlements. The assistant had a good knowledge of the field and of the Birhor settlements and camps. He also had a well-established connection with people of the forest region.

Ghana Hunters: The Vagala

The Vagala are a small cultural group in the Damongo district of the Northern Region of Ghana. They are located about 50 miles directly south of the main town of Wa. They number between 12,000 and 15,000 people. While formerly mostly hunters, nowadays they are occupied primarily with farming. Their customs and traditions, however, accentuate the central importance of hunting in their culture. While culturally significant, hunting has diminished in importance as a food resource. This is due to continuously accelerating population pressure on the land throughout the north of Ghana, which has made game increasingly scarce over the past century. The one exception to this trend is the Mole Game Reserve where wild animal populations are protected. Many Vagala villages are located directly to the east of the reserve; hunting continues to be a rewarding activity in these areas because of spillover. Complaints by Game Wardens, however, open suspicions about possible poaching as well.

It is not possible to assess the extent to which hunting has fallen off over the last few decades. Elderly men seldom hunt these days, but this has more to do with the infirmities of age than lack of desire. Like all hunters, the elderly enjoy boasting about animals taken in former times—particularly buffalo and elephant. Middle-aged Vagala men continue to hunt and appear to go after game fairly frequently (about twice a month), particularly in the dry season when farming activities are at a minimum and when game is easy to locate around the contracting number of water holes. They hunt any animal in the bush but talk primarily about the larger animals they have taken, primarily bushbuck, antelope, warthog and buffalo. They say they enjoy hunting as well as the prestige attached to bringing home quantities of meat.

Hunting appears to be falling off in popularity with younger men in their late teens and 20s. Schooling and the widespread accoutrements of modernization probably account for this change. It is hard to find a young man who hunts, despite the fact that it is men of this age who formerly went out with their fathers and brothers (sometimes just with friends) to bring game back to the village. Normally, men hunted in small groups of two or three individuals although there were very large communal hunts in the dry season. Men also hunted alone. Vagala women do not hunt.

When asked what makes a man a good hunter, Vagala reply is: 'Killing an elephant.' What kinds of abilities does a good hunter have? 'The ability to vanish.' Hunting, they say, is something that is taught, usually by father to son. But there is also hunting magic. Like hunting skills and practices, this is handed down from father to son, but good magic may also be obtained from special practitioners.

The Vagala live in villages ranging in size from fifty to five hundred individuals. Farms line out from the village. Primarily yams, cassava, sorghum, maize, beans and groundnuts are grown. Yams and cassava are more important here than in areas farther north; guinea corn (sorghum) and millet are less so. The men undertake the heavy work of clearing the fields, weeding, raising yam mounds and staking yam vines, etc. Women help with sowing and harvesting. They also cultivate crops such as tomatoes, pepper and okra on their own. Bush plants are also collected, both for medicine and food.

Within the family, age and maleness reign supreme. Land and cattle are inherited through males. On marriage, women move to their husband's compound. The oldest male in a compound is usually recognized as its head and has authority over all its members, particularly young men and women. While women have considerably less authority than men, there are limits to what women will put up with and a wife's option to leave her husband and return to her natal village acts as a brake to the arbitrary exercise of power. Age bestows its benefits everywhere. Even among children, older siblings or cousins can order younger ones around.

These days every Vagala village has a chief. The Vagala say they have always had chiefs. Recently, the office of Paramount Chief has been created, each Paramount having a kind of administrative jurisdiction over a certain number of village chiefs. Although the Vagala live within the area claimed by the vast Gonja kingdom, they do not currently recognize the Gonja Paramount as having any say over them. This certainly would have been otherwise before the arrival of the British at the end of the 19th century. At that time, the Gonja maintained their influence by force of arms, in particular, the use of armed and mounted warriors. Warfare between Gonja and neighbouring kingdoms was frequent, and for security reasons the Vagala would have aligned themselves with one group or the other, at least for paying lip service to the 'king' and probably rendering some kind of tribute even if only token. Today nearly every Vagala village has a school but the majority of these are of recent origin, most of them erected within the last ten years.

The work with the Vagala was carried out at a village called Jang, in the Damongo district of the Northern Region. Jang lies a short distance east of the main Bole–Sawla road.

Canada Hunters: The Oji-Cree

Between the Ojibway inhabitants of the more southerly areas of northwestern Ontario and the Cree, who are located along the coasts of the James Bay and Hudson Bay, there lives a widely dispersed group of people who refer to themselves as 'Oji-Cree'. Their spoken language and much of their culture is a mesh of Cree and Ojibway. Their traditional way of life is also something of a blend of the two cultures. Viewed through another lens, their way of life can be seen as perhaps the only possible response to the incredibly harsh realities of their environment. They experience brief often surprisingly hot summers and long punishing winters, when temperatures can fall as low as minus 50°C. These conditions are exacerbated by the wind that pushes down from the north-west, with not a hill or a mountain for a thousand miles in any direction to moderate its bite.

The Oji-Cree were traditionally hunters. They farmed no crops of any kind. Even the pious example of the missionaries, who came to proselytize among them, could not persuade these stubborn northerners to till their own soil. In any case, the growing season is phenomenally short, the soil mostly poor and the cultural support for cultivation notoriously absent. Even the gathering of wild plants is minimal. Extremely few wild plants are cooked and eaten, but the greater part of gathering revolves around teas and medicines. The exception of course is berries, which are available in many species and in abundance, but only for a limited number of weeks, primarily in late August.

Traditionally, everyone hunted: men, women and children. Men were the primary providers of game and it was usually the men who ranged far afield in the hunt for larger animals. But there were no restrictions on women taking game. It was more a matter of opportunity; women tended to employ themselves in the hunting camps, making clothing, preparing meat, curing skins and looking after children. Both women and children set and checked snares along the runs of smaller animals such as rabbits, hares, etc. There are plenty of stories of menfolk returning to camp empty-handed to find the women waiting to feast them with caribou or moose they had killed in their absence. The women, of course, love to tell these stories. Nevertheless, it was boys who were taken along with the older men on the hunt, boys whose hunting skills were honed in the bush, and boys whose first large kill was considered a particularly momentous event.

Hunting camps tended to be small, kin-based and temporary. People followed a seasonal migration along routes used and established by their forebears. This movement was dictated by the weather and the presence of game. The most difficult periods were the annual 'freeze up' in autumn and 'break up' in spring. At these times, it was impossible to move freely across the land. Northern Ontario is a mosaic of rivers, streams, lakes, ponds and muskeg (swamps/bogs). Viewed from height, water appears to comprise half the landscape. The open waters of summer and the deep, rock-hard ice of winter enabled easy travel by canoe or sled, and these days, of course, by skimobile. During freeze-up and break-up, however, with ice half formed or perilously thin, people were effectively marooned in whatever area they found themselves. It was of the upmost importance that they set up camp at these times in locations where the supply of fish and game would be sufficient to tide them over until they could move out again by boat or by snowshoe. Fishing and the hunting of migratory birds played a prominent role in survival at these times, which were always potentially grim. The French term for break-up, *debacle*, captures well the nature of this seasonal event.

Traditionally, Oji-Cree spent most of the year in small hunting camps centered around a man and his son(s), or two or more brothers and their families. Arrangements were flexible, however, and camps based on relationships through women or even through non-kin relationships were not uncommon. Camps normally comprised some half dozen to a dozen people. Higher numbers were difficult to accommodate because of the low carrying capacity of the land.

Annually, at the height of summer, Oji-Cree would gather in particular areas where an abundance of game, and in particular an abundance of fish, allowed one or two hundred people to live together for a couple of weeks. These times were highly anticipated as a chance to exchange news, to renew friendships and to trade for the few items people did not make for themselves. They were also a time for young men and women to check out possible mates. With the advent of the commercial fur trade, trading posts were established in these traditional gathering places. Missionaries followed later. Today, most Oji-Cree are at least nominal Christians, although efforts have been made recently to rehabilitate pre-Christian religious/spiritual traditions.

Starting in the 1950s, a concerted effort was made by governments to bring native Canadians into the larger Canadian society and its culture. Schools were among the foremost emissaries of this deliberate attempt at acculturation. Treaty money and other government payments, which had automatically gone out to people in the Treaty Nine area, were now withheld if the recipients had children of school age who were not in attendance at school. This tactic had the effect of bringing most Oji-Cree people into year-round residence on reserves, in settlements of several hundred to over a thousand inhabitants. This process of urbanization brought about further acculturative changes, including those in governance and in interpersonal and intergroup relations. Little in their repertoire of cultural values was available to support Oji-Cree people in their attempts to become entangled in such large groups for extended periods of time. Unsurprisingly, the reserves became dysphoric examples of poor nutrition, sub-standard housing, non-existent sanitation, unsafe drinking water, astronomic unemployment rates (over 80 per cent on many reserves) and the subsequent social ills such as alcoholism, substance abuse, high suicide rates, etc. Today, Oji-Cree typically live in houses on reserves in something approximating a slightly extended nuclear family—husband and wife, a few children (some of which may be nieces, nephews, or grandchildren) and perhaps one extra relative, a grandchild, an uncle, a widowed brother and a mother-in-law.

Oji-Cree society traditionally recognized no legitimate authority outside the individual himself/herself. Orders and commands are abhorred. Instead, people adhere to a fierce egalitarianism that reigns even within the family. However, with increasing contact with Euro-Canadian society and its institutions over the past decades, they have had to endure directives from government, police, missionaries and teachers. Before these acculturative influences, Oji-Cree parents are loathe to discipline even the youngest children, believing that children learn best from direct interaction with the environment and that the lessons learned from mistakes are learned better than any instructions others can supply. Thus, a group of adults will sit around with white knuckles attempting to carry on a 'normal' conversation while a pair of toddlers open their father's tackle box and play discovery games with the fishhooks.

Adults' verbal demands on children are at a minimum. Warnings are low key. Parents will say, 'The ice is thin', not 'Don't go out on the ice, you could fall in.' Direct orders are felt to be odious. Even direct questions—demanding, as they do, a reply—are considered coercive and more often than not remain unanswered. It is only in extremis that mothers can be heard to cry out, 'Don't do that!' These occasions are usually marked by children putting other children at risk, e.g., when a four-year-old is whirling around on the woodpile with a heavy axe while his two-year-old brother approaches admiringly. Similarly, assertiveness in children is much admired and parents fondly relate stories of their children's exploits that Euro-Canadians might find appalling, such as furniture broken, young children wandering off into the bush alone to hunt, equipment 'borrowed'. Many of these stories have a 'boys-will-be-boys' feel to them and as such are not totally foreign to the Euro-Canadian ear. Unfortunately, Oji-Cree parenting styles have often been considered neglectful by visiting non-native social workers with disastrous results for all concerned.

Children are raised to be able to look after themselves, not to be a burden on anyone else. Competence and self-reliance are emphasized. They are qualities expected in all adults. People are reluctant to ask for help, though this is almost always given when requested. Conversely, offers of assistance are seldom proffered as these (theoretically) impugn the ability of the person in need to look after their own affairs.

When questioned about the past, elders invariably stressed the paramount importance of 'survival'. In one way, of course, this is obvious. But 'survival' would not be the item to take first mention in most societies. It is indicative of the harshness of traditional Oji-Cree life that the process of staying alive was so present in their minds so much of the time. The qualities of self-reliance, assertiveness and respect combine with an unarticulated stoicism to give a particular nuance to the native Canadian outlook. The notion of 'respect' is helpful here (see Berry & Bennett, 1992). Among the Oji-Cree respect is a complex of attitudes approaching something like admiration and nurturing care. Notions of fear and intimidation are foreign to it. One Big Trout elder explained, 'Look, you know the Bible says: When God made the world, he had *respect* for his creation.'

The work with the Oji-Cree was done in the communities of Big Trout Lake (population approximately 1100 people at the time), Angling Lake (roughly 350 people) and Summer Beaver (about 300).

The Agricultural Groups

The study with agricultural groups was based in Ghana (with the Wala), China (with the Han) and India (with Oraon and Hindu farmers).

Ghana Farmers: The Wala

Wa is a small, traditional West African savanna kingdom consisting of a central town (population now close to 30,000) and more than a hundred surrounding villages varying in size from a couple of dozen people to more than 1500 in the larger settlements. The land around Wa comprises gently rolling savanna grasslands with various densities of woodland or orchard bush as well as thicker riverine vegetation. To the south and east of the town, the human population steadily declines and the land grows more heavily wooded. Traditionally, most Walas have been farmers, though often with some craft or other part-time specialization occurring on the side, such as tailoring, healing, weaving and blacksmithing. The soil around Wa varies, but is nowhere particularly fertile. Traditional farming practices call for three to four years of cultivation followed by a lengthy fallow period of up to eight or 10 years to allow the soil to regain its fertility.

The climate permits an abundance of staple crops to be grown, such as yams, guinea corn (sorghum), maize and millet as well as groundnuts, rice and cassava. Several kinds of pulses, vegetables, melons and gourds round out the diet. A number of local wild fruits are available, although much fruit is now ported from the south. Cattle are raised and are surprisingly abundant. Goats, sheep, chickens, guinea fowl, turkeys and even ducks can be found in any village. Non-Muslims also keep pigs. None of these animals are fenced in or penned.

Men perform the heavy fieldwork of clearing land and preparing it for sowing. Women help with planting and hoeing. The entire family (including children of all ages) works together to bring in the harvest. Small herds of cattle are looked after by the boys of the family. Larger herds are put into the care of Fulani, who can be found on the outskirts of almost any large village.

Not all food is cultivated. Bush trees and plants supply fruits, oil nuts, medicines, seasonings, flavouring and some ceremonial foods. Fish are netted in rivers and ponds. Wild game is also available, though no longer nearly as abundant as in earlier times.

Wa climate is marked by distinct dry and rainy seasons. The rains commence in late March–early April, becoming heavier through May and June, and then dropping off somewhat before recommencing in earnest throughout August and September. Temperature varies from around 10°C to 40°C, the maximum temperatures occurring from February through April. The lowest figures are reached during the nights of the Harmattan season in December and January, when night-time temperatures can fall below the single-digit centigrade mark.

Wala settlements are fairly dense, people living in close proximity to one another in collections of large clan or sub-clan households, the inhabitants of which trace relationship through males. Farms are located in the area surrounding settlements, some farms abutting the village directly, others located at a distance of two miles or more. In the town of Wa, this pattern persisted until the middle of the 20th century when the town simply grew too large. Today, with a population of 30,000, there is little available farmland within walking distance of Wa town. Nevertheless, a number of town residents continue to maintain farms in outlying villages to which they normally travel by bicycle, motorbike, or car. Many people in Wa, however, now earn their living through wage labour or salaried positions, either directly with the government (Wa being both a district and regional capital), or in the service economy the government positions support.

The Wala state has existed in something close to its present form for several hundred years during which time its sphere of influence has expanded and contracted repeatedly. The current kingdom was established approximately 300 years ago by members of royal families from neighbouring states who were forced to flee from their own kingdoms because of dynastic rivalries. These 'royals' arrived in the area of Wa as armed, mounted warriors; they imposed the stamp of kingship upon not only the autochthonous peoples living there, but also several clans of Muslims of diverse origins, some of whom had sought refuge in the area from imperial disruptions in Mali to the north.

At the end of the 19th century the British, as part of the scramble for Africa, established treaties of 'friendship and protection' with Wa. The arrangements they worked out with the traditional state both augmented and undermined the authority of the *WaNaa*, the king of Wa. It is impossible now to reconstruct exactly the range and extent of his authority prior to the arrival of the colonial power. Certainly, he had claim to tribute of various kinds as well as mandatory labour for a number of days on his farms. Many claim that formerly the king had powers of life and death over his subjects. Other research, however, suggests that the king's powers never approached that of European monarchs, but have always been severely limited by the need for wide public assent. In other words, the Wala king has always had to rule with the consent of the governed.

Several 'royal' families are eligible for the office of king and these families take it in turn to sit on the 'skins' (*gbanga*). Such an arrangement introduces an element of flexibility into a system, which might otherwise have calcified into a much stricter hierarchical structure. Below the WaNaa are six divisional chiefs, and below them, dozens of chiefs and sub-chiefs. Village chiefs are responsible for dispute settlement (usually concerning land or women) as well as certain administrative functions. Local chiefs hand along directives from the WaNaa as well as from various levels of national and regional government. Disputes, which village chiefs cannot resolve, are sent on to the courts of divisional chiefs who, in turn, hand problem cases over to WaNaa and/or to the national court system, either criminal or civil.

There are a series of offices in the king's traditional court, each of which is hereditary within a specific non-royal family. Three of these offices are of particular importance. The *Tendaana* is the senior representative of the autochthonous groups in the area. He is literally the 'landowner' or steward of the land, responsible for the fertility of the land and its ritual purification. He is also held to have important spiritual powers. The Imam and the *YeriNaa* (chief of the Muslims) together represent the interests of the large Muslim establishment in Wa. In one sense, authority in Wa can be seen as diverse, resting among the heads of what have been called the three 'estates' of Wa: the royals, the landowners (autochthons) and the Muslims. This tripartite structure greatly encourages the development of skill in the areas of negotiation, persuasion and charm.

Like many northern kingdoms, the traditional Wala state maintains an uneasy coexistence with regional and national governments. The relationship is further complicated by the desire of those successful in the wider national arena to exert what is perceived to be undue and inappropriate influence on the traditional system.

The typical Wala compound (*jaga*) consists of all the living male descendants of a common male ancestor together with their wives and unmarried daughters. Compounds may comprise only one or two generations, but many trace ancestry back to a deceased ancestor in the distant past. The most senior man in the compound (not always the oldest in years) is the head of the compound and as such exerts considerable authority over everyone who lives there as well as over absent family members. Age is extremely important in Wala families. By the age of two or three, every Wala child knows precisely where he fits into the family hierarchy. Those older than him can order him to run errands, perform small tasks, hand over possessions, etc. This authority exists within the child's own generation. However, the position of each generation vis-à-vis its preceding and succeeding cohorts is also strictly monitored, with seniority always apportioned to the older generation. For example, say that Generation A comprises a group of brothers. The children of these brothers form Generation B and their children form Generation C, etc. But Wa is a polygamous society. Men take wives and continue to have children well into their sixties and seventies. It quickly transpires that members of the senior Generation B may be decades younger than some members of the junior Generation C. This leads to all sorts of variations on the theme of age, seniority and authority. Nevertheless, small children easily master the complexities of family politics and quickly learn who they may and may not boss around.

Within the family, the authority of the father is paramount. Walas say that no man can consider himself an adult until his father has died. Formerly, decisions about a child's schooling, marriage and career were all made by the father and were considered irrevocable, though, of course, the father would already have consulted with the senior head of the compound. This practice continues in the villages. In the town of Wa, the position of fathers and compound heads has begun to weaken.

In former times, there was little opportunity for any full-time pursuit apart from farming. The exceptions prove the rule. There were a few families of blacksmiths in Wa town, though there were many part-time smiths in the villages as well. There were a small number of full-time Muslim scholars. However, even the Imams of Wa often worked on their own farms. Some Muslims depended on trading for a living. But for most people, the specialized occupations they followed were strictly part-time and reserved for the dry season when the pressure of farm chores was absent. There were weavers, tailors, smiths, musicians, brewers, horse trainers, mid-wives and curers of various kinds.

With the introduction of western education, which only came to Wa in a serious way after the Second World War, the variety and number of job opportunities has mushroomed to include teachers, clerks, mechanics, construction workers, seamstresses, hotel workers, and so on, i.e., the full panoply of jobs that accompanies development.

In tandem with this explosion of opportunity, the size of families has begun to shrink. Younger men move out of the traditional family enclave to build their own homes for their own nuclear or polygynous families. The physical distance from the head of the family mirrors a growing social distance from the authority the older man can expect to exert.

Nevertheless, the old values persist. Children are expected to be seen and not heard. Obedience and compliance are still universally expected. One of the worst epithets that can be applied to a child is 'troublesome'. The assertive behaviour of Western children (what little is known or seen of it) is generally condemned as appalling.

The values inculcated in childhood carry on into adult life. Young men and women frequently display a fawning desire to serve those above them in age/seniority as well as an exasperating inability to do anything on their own initiative. Many Western teachers admire the docility of Wala students and speak fondly of the diligent, tractable nature of their students in classrooms without disruptions of any kind. However, it is also true that children (and adults) can gravely exhibit convincing signs of consent when asked to do something, only to run off as soon as they are out of sight. Conflicting loyalties are a frequent excuse for an errand not performed—'Oh, I couldn't do it, because grandfather/uncle/aunt came along and asked me to …'

Young people with degrees from secondary school or university often literally squirm when asked about the choice of their career path. Only directives from their elders can put them at ease.

In the wider society, interdependence is strongly encouraged, while self-reliance tends to be viewed with suspicion; in many minds it is associated with witchcraft. When someone behaves notoriously, others will say of him, 'Such people will die alone in the bush.' To live and to die on one's own is regarded as the ultimate failure. The few people who do so are imagined to have unmentionable connections with the spirit world. The US American Peace Corps and the Canadian University Service Overseas (CUSO)[1] volunteers are occasionally criticized because they 'never ask for help'.

The work with Wala people was done in both Wa town and in the village of Busa, eight miles to the east, a community of some 1200 souls and the seat of one of Wa's six divisional chiefs.

China Farmers: The Han

The Han people of contemporary China represent an old dynasty of China, which was founded by Emperor Gaozu of Han. At the present time, the Han constitute the largest population in China (over 90 per cent of the total population). In the early days, the philosophy of Confucius guided the life of the Han people. This period represents an age of great economic,

---

[1] CUSO is a development organization that works to reduce poverty and inequality through the efforts of highly skilled volunteers, collaborative partnerships and compassionate donors.

technological, cultural, and social progress in China. The Han had a hierarchical social structure in which nobles, officials, farmers and artisan-craftsmen enjoyed a higher social status than ordinary merchants and slaves.

The typical Han Chinese household in early days represented a nuclear family, which generally consisted of four to five members. In the later phases, multiple generations and extended family members often shared the same household. Families were patrilineal, arranged marriages were the norm and sons were preferred over daughters. Women engaged in various activities in and outside of the home. Farming was considered as a decent profession. Wealthy nobles, officials and merchants could own land, but they mostly relied on poor tenant farmers (*diannong*) for cultivation. Wage labourers (*gunong*) and slaves were also employed on the estates of the wealthy. On the other hand, the landowners, who had small to medium-sized estates, often acted as the managers of the land. Their sons tilled the fields and daughters weaved clothes and engaged in the production of silk for use in home or sale at the market.

The Han had rulers from western as well as eastern parts of China. In the Western Han period, the majority of farming peasants were conscripted by the government to perform labour or military duties. For the labour service, males would be drafted for one month out of the year to work on construction projects and other activities. For the military obligation, all males aged 23 were trained for one year of military service, and they were expected to perform one year of active service as troops until they reached age 56. Significant changes in this system took place during the Eastern Han period. Peasants who wanted to avoid the one-month labour obligation or the military service had to pay a commuting tax.

Artisans and craftsmen enjoyed a social status between that of farmers and merchants. The merchant class was viewed as lower in the social hierarchy than the farmers. Registered merchants, even if small shopkeepers, were obliged to pay commercial taxes, whereas the farmers were not taxed. Registered merchants could also be forced to join armed forces or resettle in malaria-prone lands.

In spite of a relatively low status, the merchants engaged in several private trades and industries. A single merchant often combined several trades to make greater profits (e.g., animal breeding, farming, manufacturing, trade and moneylending). In the early Western Han period, powerful merchants could employ more than a thousand peasants to work in salt mines and iron industries. Another profitable industry for merchants was brewing wine and liquor. Medical practice, sorcery, physiognomy, pig breeding and butchery were other occupations of the Han people.

Han society has followed, both for commoners and nobles, a socio-economic ranking system in which there was a provision for promotion in ranks. This promotion brought to individuals a more respectable place in seating arrangements of the hamlet banquets, a greater portion of hunted game at the table, less severe punishment for certain crimes and exemption from labour service obligations to the state. Since a longer lifespan meant more opportunities to become promoted, this system apparently favoured the elderly. In addition to an increase in salary, the newly promoted men were also granted other privileges (e.g., wine and ox-meat in banquets). Sometimes these ranks were sold to collect more revenues for the state. Thus, anyone who presented a substantial amount of agricultural grain to the government could also be promoted in rank.

Largely based on agriculture, the Han people harvested many crops from farming. They grew all foods one can think of, but the rice, paddy and wheat were the most important agricultural produce. They were grown in big amounts and stored safely in order to feed large families. Farmers also made their own clothes, built their houses and worked as unpaid labour to the government.

The life of a Han farmer in earlier days was hard and full of challenges. Many consider the Cultural Revolution and the 'reforms' of the post-Mao era as well as the reaction of the overwhelming mass of the peasantry to these movements in the earlier decades as an outcome of the hardships faced by the farmers in China. Although the revolutionary movements put rural populations and intellectuals in significant hardships for some time, they led to impressive gains in agricultural production and change in people's lives. The post-Mao era 'reforms', on the other hand, led to huge inequality in China and enhanced the suffering of the rural population by dismantling public support for health care and education. The officials also sold some farmlands for development purposes without paying adequate compensation to the farmers. This resulted in massive unrest in rural areas and led to thousands of incidents of protest by the farmers in relatively more recent years.

The second five-year plan of the Chinese revolution (called The Great Leap Forward) signifies a period of rapid development of industry and agriculture in China. During this period, communes were formed and many 'backyard' small-scale steel industries were set up all over the country to fulfill the needs of local people. Several irrigation projects were also started in which farmers showed interest and active participation. To deal with the problem of food shortage, the government paid attention to rural areas so much so that the local government, office and factory workers, teachers, army personnel and college students were asked to come forward to help farmers during the busy seasons. Although such initiatives are often regarded as 'persecution of intellectuals', the initiatives have certainly led to a sense of importance of farming and enhancement of farmers' self-esteem.

An important goal of the Cultural Revolution in China was to empower ordinary villagers so that they could effectively participate in all spheres of village life (e.g., economic, social, political). The central, provincial, regional, county and commune governments paid great attention to rural areas, agriculture and farmers. Not only were the farmers selected to participate in all levels of government, officials were urged to work with them, and the urban people to support them. In the early 1980s, the Chinese media was filled with success stories about rural reform. Crop yields increased dramatically, and farmers' income also rose significantly. Yet, several rural protests have been witnessed during the last three decades. There has been a major shift in farmers' perception of the government policies. They believe that the government wants only money instead of doing anything positive for them. As known about many developing countries, malpractices, corruption and crime have shown phenomenal increase during the last decades in China also.

During the Great Leap Forward and Cultural Revolution periods, Chinese society was relatively poor. People had barely enough to eat and wear, but there was a general equality in the conditions of people's life. While most people in rural China have become more affluent today, the gap between the rich and the poor has also become wider. The Chinese government today faces a number of problems with regard to rural areas, agriculture and farmers. Scholars and government officials have started to discuss these problems openly. A major outcome of open discussion is the elimination of agricultural taxes by the Chinese government for the rural population. While this step has brought relief to farmers and is widely appreciated, it has weakened the presence of government in rural areas, which is strongly needed for education, medical care and overall development.

As noted earlier, the Han people today comprise over 90 per cent of the population of China; hence they are very representative of the majority. The others (10 per cent of the population) are made up of over 50 other nationalities, and are not represented in our work. The vast majority of Chinese is living in villages and engages in agriculture, although there has been rapid urbanization to provide workers for the industrial expansion of China. Like any other agricultural society, contemporary Han society is hierarchically organized in which the elderly and senior people have power to control young people and children. Children are expected to be responsible, obedient to elders and nurturant to the young.

The Han people in Guangdong province (population over 100 million) still represent these agricultural villages; however, about 30 per cent of this population are migrant workers from the surrounding villages. The rural people of Guangdong live in close proximity to the urban and industrial cities of Guangzhou (formerly called Canton) and Hong Kong, and are inevitably influenced culturally by them.

The work with Han farmers was done in the villages around the city of Zhaoqing, which is located in the west-central region of the province, about 90 kilometres from Guanzhou. The terrain is mainly mountainous, but with a large valley suitable for farming. A colleague who was originally from this area worked as an assistant in our research programme.

India Farmers: The Adivasi Oraon

The Oraon represent a settled Adivasi group. They live in different parts of Jharkhand as well as in the states of Odisha, Madhya Pradesh, Assam and West Bengal. In this group, we worked with children whose parents were engaged in economic activities based on dry agriculture, irrigation agriculture and wage-earning.

The history of the Oraon group is mainly derived from legends. It appears that they migrated to North India from the West Coast, and settled down as agriculturalists in the state of Bihar. Successive hordes drove them to places such as the Rohtas plateau, Rajmahal hills, Palamau and Ranchi, which are now part of the Jharkhand state. They settled in these regions some 1800 years ago. With their agricultural knowledge and hard-working nature, they soon became a dominant Adivasi group in the Chota Nagpur region. The word 'Oraon' in Mundari language means 'hardworking' or 'unwearied'. They made extensive clearance of forests for cultivation and forced other groups (e.g., the Mundas) to move to the southern and eastern parts of the plateau.

The areas of Jharkhand, in which the Oraon are settled, consist of undulating mountains and hills divided into several sections by numerous streams and small rivers. Between the hills, the Oraon have cut the land into terraces for cultivation. While in the uplands, millet, oil seeds and coarse varieties of rice are grown, the low lands are used for producing finer rice.

The Oraon villages are generally located on highlands. The houses are made of mud walls and tiled roofs. There is usually a big room in the central part of the house with closed verandahs built all around this room. These verandahs are used for cooking, living and sleeping purposes, and also for sheltering animals. Cows, bullocks, pigs and chickens are their main animals. The Oraon are mainly agriculturists. They can distinguish a variety of soils based on their quality. A system of crop rotation is followed. Farmers use a variety of indigenous manures prepared from cowdung, *karanj* flowers and leaves mixed with ashes. Since water resources are insufficient and the soil has very poor water retention, a successful harvest depends on adequate rainfall. Only in some areas can the crops be irrigated by using tanks, wells, streams and rivulets as water sources. Vegetables such as potato, tomato, cabbage, cauliflower, brinjal, green pepper, cucumber and some gourd-like vegetables, along with pulses and rice generally form part of a typical Oraon diet.

The Oraon are divided into several clans. Each clan derives its name from a bird, fish, animal, vegetable, plant, or mineral. These serve as totems, and are regarded as sacred. The Oraon will not eat or harm the object from which the clan has got its totem name. Wooden or brass emblems of the totems are maintained in the Oraon villages, where they are worshipped, and sacrifices are offered for achieving success in different spheres of life. Marriage within the same clan is not permitted. Each clan is associated with a *parha*. Each *parha* has a particular territory of agricultural land, forest, grazing land, water supply and fishing pool. All villages belonging to a *parha* are subject to authority of the *parha panchayat* (congregation), which is constituted by four villages of the *parha*. The *panchyat* decides the cases of infringement of a variety of taboos related to marriage, sex, theft, assault, witchcraft, and matters of eating and drinking, disputes regarding precedence at the festivals and the right to hunt. All villages of a *parha* collectively participate in hunt and dance at festivals.

A typical lineage system prevails among the Oraon. The main lineage is known as the *bhuinharikhunt*. This is the lineage of the pioneer families who cleared the forest and brought that particular area under cultivation. The oldest member of the lineage was called *pahan* who had full authority over the settlement. In performing his duties, he was assisted by another senior member of the lineage, called *mahto*. Both *pahan* and *mahto* commanded great respect and status, which is still maintained. As religious and secular heads, they share many responsibilities of the village community.

The Oraon also used the services of other caste and craft groups. These included cattle tenders, blacksmiths, potters, musicians, basket makers, and cloth weavers. Some of these families can be found in almost all Oraon villages.

Fairly complex rules of inheritance are observed in the Oraon society. The father's land is divided among his sons. The elder son gets a larger share. The son born from the first wife also gets a larger share than the one born from a second wife. A widow cannot inherit property, but can get maintenance allowance until her death. Sons adopted formally from the same clan can inherit all of a father's property, but one belonging to another clan has restricted inheritance rights. A person excommunicated has no inheritance rights unless he is readmitted into the community. There are also well-developed rules for rights over unoccupied land and the forest tracts.

Rules of marriage in the Oraon society are well defined. Monogamy is the first rule. Marriage within the same clan is not permitted. Marriage between brother and sister or near relations is also not permitted. Marriage between boys and girls of the same village is not sanctioned. Marriage with a girl of other Adivasi group leads to excommunication. Widow marriage is widely practiced. Divorce is accepted in the community and is permissible in a number of circumstances.

A child is highly valued in the Oraon community. Every effort is made to protect the mother as well as the child from evil spirits before and after childbirth. The mother is not allowed to go out alone. Sacrifices to the principal village deity are made soon after the birth of the child. The initial 8–9 days are considered critical. All children stay in the lap of their mother. They are breastfed for about three years, or until the birth of the next child. While carrying out various domestic activities the mother carries the child on her back wrapping him/her in a piece of cloth. Older children often look after babies, while they move in the village and play with other children. They build models of animals and carts from clay, and use old containers, bottles and several other things as play materials. Wealthy parents also buy some toys. A strong tradition of storytelling exists in the community; they are intended to encourage cultural activities, traditions and values among children. Some people in each village are expert in riddles.

The Oraon also had a traditional institution, called *dhumkuria* (youth dormitory), which was supervised and controlled by some selected boys and girls of the village. *Dhumkuria* boys performed many social activities such as cooking at weddings, attending visitors to the village, running errands, thatching houses and serving people during illness or epidemics. The girls performed activities such as pounding rice, making cakes at weddings, helping people in transplanting and reaping rice and preparing palm-leaf mats for dormitories. Children learnt necessary skills for playing domestic, economic, educational and other roles through participation in various activities organized by *dhumkuria*. During the last decades, this institution had become weaker, but there are symptoms of its revival in recent years.

The Oraon have faith in a number of deities and unseen forces. They also believe in mystical powers which, when offended, bring disease, death or natural calamities. Many religious activities are directed to the propitiation of their deities, unseen spirits and mystical powers by offering prayers, worships and sacrifices to them.

With an agricultural economic pursuit, fixed habitation, highly stratified society, complex religion, well-defined rules for inheritance of property and well-developed institutions for child socialization, the Oraon have lived a happy life in the Jharkhand region for almost 2000 years. They still live largely as agriculturists, but a number of changes have taken place in their lives due to contact with the outside world. The Christian missionaries took great advantage of certain political and economic instabilities prevailing in the Oraon region (see Mishra et al., 1996; Tripathi & Mishra, 2016) and were successful in placing them under the influence of missions during the last 100 years. This led to loss of many of the Oraon cultural traditions, including the most valuable *akhara* (community dance) activities.

Christian missionaries also played a major role in educating Oraon children. The educated Oraon were employed in local schools, offices, hospitals and government industries. The popularity of education in this group has gradually increased over the years. Government schools opened in villages do attract Oraon children, but many of them drop out soon and stay home to help parents in subsistence activities. Grazing cattle, weeding crops, guarding and plucking vegetables and collecting seasonal flowers and fruits are the major activities of children.

The pressures of economic changes and migration of the Oraon people to towns and cities have significantly influenced their traditional institutions. Several industrial plants set up in their region have also brought changes in their life. Participation in the commercial economy is one of them. The loss of land due to industrialization has led many Oraon to migrate and work in tea gardens in the states of West Bengal and Assam. There are instances of periodic migration too. In these cases, people leave home after the harvest, work in brick factories in adjoining states, and return when the rains have set in and the brick factories are closed. In the present days, the Oraon economy is no longer based on agriculture alone. Since decades, both government and voluntary organizations have been running developmental programmes for the welfare of the Adivasi society. Among others, agricultural development and cattle rearing have been the main focus of such programmes. The Oraon families are encouraged to use new and improved variety of seeds, chemical fertilizers and sophisticated agricultural implements. New breeds of buffaloes and cows have been distributed to encourage dairy production. Concerted efforts are being made to improve irrigation facilities in the region. Small scale industries are also being encouraged. These efforts have been aimed at improving the economic level of the Oraon and preventing their migration, but the response has not been encouraging.

As a result of these acculturative experiences, the Oraon nowadays witness a variety of changes in their traditional life. They have lost their original language and have picked up a contact language (Chotanagpuria) spoken in that region by the members of other Adivasi groups also. In schools, children learn Hindi and English as languages to connect with the mainstream society. In towns and big cities (e.g., Ranchi, the capital of Jharkhand), a number of English-medium schools are available for the Oraon children who can afford the cost of education. The Oraon use new kinds of ornaments, pots and pans, furniture, dresses and modern electronic gadgets. Many also move out with families to big cities for tourism and recreations.

The foregoing discussion shows that as a group the Oraon exhibit considerable variation in terms of socio-economic and cultural parameters. We can find among them people who follow traditional as well as highly modern agricultural practices, and also those who have taken to full-time employment. The forces of socio-economic change are still in operation. In spite of many influences, many of them have continued to live the Oraon lifestyle that has been practised throughout the ages. They still enjoy their *handia* (rice beer) at all festivals and ceremonies. Their drums still beat in the evenings, and the melodies of songs let them forget many miseries of life.

For working with the Oraon group, we took the assistance of a doctoral student of psychology at Ranchi University. He belonged to a family that lived in a village situated in the heart of the Adivasi area. Having been born and brought up in the same village, the assistant had a good knowledge of the field and had well-established contact with people in villages.

India Farmers: The Hindu

In addition to working with the agricultural group of the Adivasi population, we also worked with an agricultural group of the mainstream society. We chose to work in Bandipur village, which is located in Jaunpur district in the state of Uttar Pradesh at about 58 kilometres west of Varanasi. The city became an important place during the second half of the 16th century when one of the Afghan kings, who ruled over Delhi for some time, made it the centre of his political activities. A large number of Muslim families moved to the city to serve their ruler. The city still represents a high concentration of Muslim population. For centuries, the city has been famous for manufacturing and distributing good quality perfumes, hair oil and a variety of floral concentrates. Even today, the perfume industry forms a very significant part of the economic activities of people in this city and its surrounding areas.

Bandipur village is situated on the side of the highway, which connects Varanasi (the cultural capital of India) and Lucknow (the political capital of Uttar Pradesh). The village has been in existence for almost last 200 years with a dominant population of Hindus. The land around the village is flat with rectangular fields in which a variety of crops are grown all around the year. Towards the south of the village, the human population is less dense, and the trees are also lesser in number until one reaches the basin of a river approximately 2 kilometres from the village. In the northern side of the village the population is relatively dense, and trees are also taller and more numerous. Plenty of mango trees can be seen all around, especially in the northern part of the village.

There are well marked dry and rainy seasons in this region. The rains generally commence in the middle of June, reach a peak in August, and fall off sharply around mid September, although there have been evidences of an early as well as late rains. The temperature normally varies between 5°C and 45°C, the maximum temperature recorded in the months of May and June. At this time extremely dry winds come down from the deserts of Rajasthan bringing with them a fine pale dust that fills the sky with 'haze' during day hours. This season is no good for agricultural activities. However, some vegetables and fodder are grown in the fields where irrigation facilities are easily available. The lowest temperature is recorded during December and January when the winter crop season is at peak, and fields are covered with yellow flowers of mustard plants.

Agricultural activities are seriously undertaken during rainy season (July–September) when paddy, millets, corn and rice are especially grown.

During the winter season (October–January) wheat, peas, chickpeas, potatoes, sweet potatoes, lentils and a variety of oil seeds are grown. In fact, the latter months represent the main harvesting season, which culminates in late April or early May. The beginning of the season is marked by the celebration of the great festivals of Dussehra (when big fairs are organized) and Deepawali (when thousands of lamps are lighted in houses as well as outlying fields). The end of the season is observed by celebrating another great festival, Holi, when people sing, dance, throw coloured water and talc on each other and organize great feasts. This day also marks the beginning of the New Year for the Hindus (as per lunar calendar).

Traditionally, the people of this area have been farmers pursuing crafts or other specializations as part-time activities, especially during the time when there were very few agricultural activities. In recent years, however, full-time occupational specialization has been possible for a handful of village people. A great variety of staple crops are raised around the village. There are a few tractors in the village to do most of the agricultural cultivation, but farmers with small landholdings also use a plough, which is pulled by a pair of bullocks. Lift pumps are used for irrigation of crops during dry seasons. The production of staple foods is generally the responsibility of men, although women help in most of these activities (barring those which are considered heavy). The whole family may come forward to help when the work is very intensive (e.g., plantation of rice or harvest).

In addition to staple foods, a variety of vegetables and fruits are also grown. Tomato, onion, garlic, pepper, pumpkin, beans, lady's finger (okra), brinjal (egg plant), radish and spinach are grown by all families in different amounts. Melons and watermelons are grown during the summer. A multitude of leaves and condiments have no English equivalents. Trees of mangoes and guava, and the plant of papaya and banana can be found in great numbers in the village surrounding.

The livestock of people primarily consists of bullocks, cows and buffaloes. A few families also rear sheep, goats and chickens. The animals are generally kept penned. It is mostly in the summer that they are untied during day hours, but herd boys keep an eye on them. The quality of cattle is a prestigious measure of wealth of any family.

There is a marketplace at a very close distance (less than 1 kilometre) from Bandipur. Some permanent grocery stores, general stores, tea and betel stalls, tailoring shops, bicycle repair shops and restaurants exist in the market. On two of the weekdays, this place is filled with a noisy crowd of buyers and sellers of foodstuff, clothes, kitchenware and hardware.

Traditionally, men tended to dominate the market, but now there are a number of commodities in which women traders specialize.

Considerable occupational specialization has now taken place in the village. About three decades ago, all families had agriculture as their main source of livelihood. The pattern has witnessed a change over the past years. While most of the families still depend on farming, some have taken to full-time business or wage employment. Some wealthy men employ others in farm activities, while they themselves engage in business or in salaried jobs.

The people of the village generally live close to each other, but a number of small hamlets of houses also exist there. Each represents a particular community (e.g., of barbers) in terms of its occupational specialization. Most of the houses have mudwalls and tiled roofs, but a few have brickwalls with tiled roofs, while other few have brickwalls with cemented roofs. The size of the houses varies considerably, and so does the number of rooms in those houses. The general pattern is to build a rectangular house with an outward projected courtyard (verandah) in the frontal region of the house. The living and stores rooms are built on the back and the two sides of the house, each having its entry from a large open space left in the central part of the house (called *Aangan*). A separate house facing the main house is built for the cattle. The number of houses in various hamlets varies between 5 and 20. The size of the family also varies from 5 to 40 members per family. The village is characterized by the existence of nuclear, extended and joint families. The Bhar and Mushar (the low caste groups) houses are widely separated from the main village habitation, but their relationship with other groups is harmonious. They generally work on wages for the higher caste groups. There is a village head and a village *panchayat* (local court to settle disputes) with representative members from all communities living in the village. In case of break of joint families, the same house may either be divided among all families, or families may decide to build new houses from the compensation received from the person who retains the old house.

All people living in the village speak and understand Hindi language. In day-to-day interaction, they speak Bhojpuri, a regional dialect of Hindi language. Educated families use a mixture of colloquial and standard Hindi languages. While there is considerable impact of Urdu language on older people, the younger generation exhibits more impact of English language. Frequent intrusion of English words in the use of local dialect can be easily noted in the conversation of common people.

Bandipur represents a case of a plural society. Most of the families have come from many different places, and have arrived at different times.

The first people to come there were the Kshatriyas (traditionally a warrior caste group) some 200 years ago. Other groups came later and settled on the land provided by the Kshatriyas to which they got legal claims later. At the present time, the village is inhabited by high caste (e.g., Brahmin, Kshatriya), backward caste (e.g., Ahir, Kurmi) and low caste (e.g., Bhar, Mushar) groups. Different groups have their own hamlets of houses. The bond within families of a group seems to be stronger than in the families across the groups. However, they all participate in the wider sociocultural and political life of the village. There has been no evidence of caste tension in the village. Economically, the Mushar and Bhar have been in weaker positions than other groups, but they are better off now as a result of their participation in wider economic activities, including employment in salaried jobs (e.g., as teachers or office-bearers).

In spite of these plural social characteristics, the political dominance of Kshatriyas still continues. Their landholdings are large and they are highly educated. They have high status jobs in schools, government offices and industrial organizations, and also enjoy good administrative and political connections. Earlier, almost all village headmen and *panchayat* chiefs were elected from this group alone, but this pattern is now changing due to the new government policies framed for these positions. Their political and social dominance is also now diminished in the sense that they can intervene but cannot impose any decisions on people even in the matters of small local disputes.

In earlier times, all foodstuff was locally produced and stored. These were generally supervised and managed by the eldest person in each household. The senior person (called *maalik* [owner]) had full authority over foodstuff produced by all members of a household. The preparation of meals was a collective activity of women, and people would take food, often in a group, in the open space available inside the house in its central part. Children were served first, then the male members were called in, and finally the women got their turn. The meals would generally consist of home-made patties (*chapati*), rice, a soup of lentils, a seasonal vegetable, and yogurt or milk. The food items and the manner of their serving have remained largely unchanged over the years. However, commercial food products (e.g., sliced breads, biscuits, cookies) are now widely used in families, and tea with milk and sugar has become the most popular drink.

Human labour is of great importance in an agricultural society. The ability to command the labour of others had been, and still continues to be, an important symbol of high status in Indian villages. Respect and obedience are instilled in and demanded of children from a very early age.

Children carry messages to members within a family or neighborhood, and run errands of minor kinds. No child is expected to refuse request from an adult of the family or neighbourhood. In extreme cases, the lack of compliance on the part of a child may result in the withdrawal of food. The kinship terminology is complicated; many broad classes of people are classified as siblings who would not be done so in Western societies (e.g., a father's father's brother's son's son).

Relationships of seniority are remembered through generations, which are often tracked in families in general conversation. Since the society is monogamous, tracking generational links is not difficult. Respect for elders is marked not only by linguistic usage (e.g., polite words), but also by many behavioural courtesies (e.g., not speaking in their presence, leaving a chair or cot on their sight, fetching water for them, giving bath, and washing and spreading their clothes to dry, etc.). These are highly valued qualities in a child signifying the importance and value of authority in the village.

A number of changes are taking place in the village in recent years. Education, urban contact and industrial exposure are most important factors responsible for these changes. Expansion of education in the country and its perceived value has encouraged many villagers to seek higher education, including professional and technical education. A primary school exists in the village. Colleges of higher education and universities, located at Jaunpur, Varanasi, Lucknow and Allahabad, have been catering to the people's needs of education for the last several decades. Frequent movement of people to cities in the pursuit of education and employment has greatly exposed them to an urban industrial lifestyle. Thus, day by day families are getting nuclear, older authority structure is being replaced by the authority of parents and immediate family members, community and fraternity bonds are weakening, families are becoming more self-centred, and lifestyle is becoming more materialistic, mechanical and monotonous. An urban style of life with the possession of electrical and electronic gadgets has become a status symbol. People's participation in these spheres is highly variable, and there are still families that barely reflect these changes.

Our work at Bandipur was facilitated by a doctoral student of psychology at Banaras Hindu University, who came from the same village and had earlier worked for his own research study in this very area. He had collected some useful background information about a number of villages, including Bandipur. These prior contacts and field relationships led us to decide to work in this village, and take the advantage of the long-term contact with local people.

The Urban Industrial Group

Canada Urban: The Euro-Canadians

Canada has been a culturally diverse society since its formal establishment as a nation state in 1867. Canada has become an even more diverse and pluralistic society in the past 50 years as a result of immigration from other parts of the world. When European explorers arrived on the east coast of Canada in the 1500s, they found a land populated by around half a million Aboriginal Peoples living throughout the territory that is now Canada. As the population of French and British colonialists grew, many settlers expanded westward and northward. Following the American Revolution of 1776, those loyal to Britain fled from the United States of America; these refugees settled in eastern and southern Canada.

The 18th and 19th centuries saw a continuing flow of British immigrants, as well as Ukrainian, Chinese, Italian and Irish settlers. In the early 20th century, many eastern and southern Europeans came to farm in the Canadian Prairies. Between 1946 and 1954, 96 per cent of the immigrants came from Europe. Since the 1980s, the majority of immigrants have come from Asia, Africa and the Caribbean. Due to this shift, those who are not of European descent accounted for 19 per cent of the population in 2011, making Canada even more diverse. The self-declared ethnic origin is highly diverse, with over 10 million indicating that they are Canadian, and another 12 groups with over 1 million: English, French, Scottish, Irish, German, Italian, Chinese, Aboriginal, Ukrainian, Indo-Pakistani, Dutch and Polish. Aboriginal Peoples account for 3.8 per cent of the population.

This ethnic mix varies by region and province. For example, in Newfoundland 95 per cent of the population are of British origin, while, in Québec, 85 per cent are of French origin. The Province of Québec and the territory of Nunavut have social institutions and policies (including language, education, laws) that reflect their respective French and Inuit cultural origins. The majority of Canadians are Christian (67 per cent), among them Roman Catholics are the largest (39 per cent, professed mainly by those of French, Irish and Italian origin). Various groups of Protestants account for 28 per cent, while Asian religions are 7.2 per cent of the population.

At present, most (57 per cent) of the annual flow of between 250,000 to 300,000 immigrants comes from Asia (including East, South, South East and West Asia). Other regions of origin are 13.7 per cent from Europe,

12.5 per cent from Africa (including North Africa) and 12.3 per cent from South and Central America and the Caribbean. With respect to specific countries of origin, the Philippines was the leading source (around 150,000 persons, or 13 per cent of all arrivals), followed by China and India (10 per cent each). Other source countries (in order) were the United States, Pakistan, the United Kingdom, Iran, South Korea, Colombia and Mexico. Since the 1980s, the number of Asian immigrants and Aboriginal Peoples in the country has increased, and the relative proportion of British and French origin has decreased. As a result, Canada is now one of the world's most diverse countries.

The population of the Province of Ontario (where the sample for the study was drawn) is 13 million. Of these, around 5 million are of British origin, 1.5 million are of French origin, and 3 million are of other European origins. Thus, the European-origin peoples represent the largest portion of the population, and are often called Euro-Canadians. The sample in the present study was drawn from the city of London, Ontario, in the southwest of the province. The community is located in the centre of a large and prosperous agricultural region. Many of those living in the city have recent roots and still have family in the surrounding farms. The main occupations are in the service industries (mainly retail, insurance and banking) and in light industry.

The city has a population of 475,000, out of which around 21 per cent are immigrants to the country (mainly from the UK, Poland and Columbia). The ethnic composition of the city is around 75 per cent of European origin (mainly British), with the largest other groups originating in Latin America and South and East Asia. Over 80 per cent speak English as their mother tongue; around 2 per cent speak Spanish and another 2 per cent speak Arabic at home. The population of London is thus characteristic of the long-standing population found in English Canada and serves as a suitable comparison group.

At this location, we worked mainly with parents of children, attending two schools in middle-class neighbourhoods. A schoolteacher working in a school in the city assisted us in all our research-related activities.

5
Capturing Cultural and Cognitive Dimensions

Introduction

From the discussion in Chapter 1, it may be recalled that our intention in this book is basically to examine the relationship between certain ecological, cultural, acculturation and cognitive dimensions in adults from Canada, China, Ghana and India, and children from Birhor and Oraon Adivasi groups in India. The work with adults from four different countries was done in order to provide an international perspective and context to the work with the Adivasi children in India. A related goal of the work with the Adivasi children was to gain insight into the educational challenges faced by children in schools. The following pages present a brief description of various measures we employed in our work. First, we describe the ecological contexts and the measures of cultural and acculturation dimensions, which are followed by a detailed description of the measures of the cognitive style dimensions.

While much progress has been made in psychology with respect to the assessment of cognitive behaviours, the assessment of contextual factors, including cultural variables, has been attempted less systematically (Irvine & Berry, 1988). The dominant tendency has been to treat features of culture globally by providing their status largely as nominal variables. In the present work, we attempt to operationalize them more precisely, and to quantify them along two dimensions.

It may be noted that the international study was carried out with a reduced number of tasks as compared to the Adivasi study. Also, while some of the tasks were common between the two studies, some were developed and used only in the Adivasi study. Although the basic parameters of the tasks used in the two studies were common, the language, content and situations of the tasks were selected and adapted according to the local cultural contexts of the populations.

In the following pages, we first describe the contexts (ecological, cultural and acculturation) of the lives of the Adivasi children. Then, we provide details of the various tasks and measures that were used with the Adivasi children. In a later section, we will describe the alternative tasks that were given to participants only in the international study. We will also mention the variations, if any, in the structure and use of the tasks between the work done with international and the Adivasi cultural groups.

Ecology Dimension

The ecological contexts of Adivasi children included in this work varied from hunting/gathering to agricultural (dry and irrigation), to urban settings. These have been described in Chapter 4, and will not be discussed further here. However, we should note that these are categorical descriptions for the groups as a whole, even though there are certainly variations in how individuals may participate in these contexts, and in how they cognize and understand them.

Measures of Cultural Dimensions

We consider that the cultural contexts of the Adivasi children are adaptive to these four ecological contexts. As indicated earlier (Chapter 1), a major goal of our work was to explore the relationship between these ecological contexts and two cultural dimensions of 'societal size' and 'social conformity'. Then, we seek to relate these cultural dimensions to the two cognitive style dimensions of 'differentiation' (intra-unit distinctiveness); and 'contextualization' (extra-unit connectedness). Although these cultural and cognitive dimensions were implicated in the international work also, they were assessed at the individual level only in the case of the Adivasi children in India.

There are many ways to operationalize the cultural dimensions of societal size and social conformity. The one developed for use in this work is largely based on the parameters derived from ethnographic studies of the Birhor and Oraon Adivasi groups in India. Hence, it deviates to some extent from the parameters used in studies carried out in other cultural settings (e.g., Berry, 1976).

Societal Size

This variable is defined and operationalized as comprising four elements:

1. Population size
It refers to the number of persons living in a settlement. It was rated on a 5-point scale in which 1 = Less than 100 persons, 2 = 100–199 persons, 3 = 200–299 persons, 4 = 300–499 persons, 5 = 500 persons and above.

2. Settlement
It refers to the settlement style of individuals or groups. It was rated on a 4-point scale in which
1 = Nomadic, 2 = Semi-nomadic, 3 = Semi-sedentary, 4 = Sedentary.

3. Political stratification
It refers to the political hierarchy prevailing in a group. It was rated on a 4-point scale in which
1 = Only local unit, 2 = Single unit above local unit, 3 = Two units above local unit, 4 = Three or more units above local unit.

4. Religion
It is conceived of in terms of beliefs and faiths of the members of a group, and rated on a 3-point scale in which: 1 = Animism, 2 = Sarna (a traditional religious faith), 3 = Hindu, Muslim or Christian faith.

The total score range on this cultural dimension of settlement size is 4–16. A lower score on this dimension is indicative of 'smaller societal size', whereas a higher score indicates 'larger societal size'.

Social Conformity

This variable consists of the following four elements:

1. Hereditary social distinctions
It refers to permanent social distinctions based on heredity, wealth, caste or class that prevail in a society. It is rated on a 2-point scale in which 1 = Low distinction, 2 = High distinction.

2. Socialization for compliance
It refers to the degree to which children are expected to be obedient, responsible and nurturant by the members of a community. It is rated on

a 5-point scale in which 1 = Very little, 2 = Little, 3 = Moderate, 4 = Much, 5 = Very much.

3. Role obligation
It refers to the degree to which age, or gender-specific norms for performing various roles are well-defined and strongly emphasized in a community. It is rated on a 4-point scale in which 1 = Little, 2 = Moderate, 3 = High, 4 = Very high.

4. Freedom from parents
It refers to the degree to which children are allowed freedom by their parents. This element is rated on a 5-point scale in which 1 = Very much, 2 = Much, 3 = Moderate, 4 = Little, 5 = Very little.

The overall score range on this cultural dimension of social conformity is 4–16. A lower score on this dimension represents 'low social conformity', whereas a high score is indicative of 'high social conformity'.

It should be noted that indices of both societal size and social conformity dimensions were collected at the community level, using both participant observation and interview techniques. Ratings were made by mutual agreement of two judges. The reason for using different point rating scales (1 to 5 points) was the degree of fineness exhibited in a variable, that is, a degree with which it could be conceived of meaningfully.

While the societal size variable did not present any major challenge in its assessment, the social conformity variable has always been found to be problematic. Even in Western folk models, the farmers (agriculturalists) have often been described as conformists. They stay in one place; they have little adventure in their life; they are beset by endless responsibilities and obligations; and they bring up their children to be obedient, responsible and nurturant. These qualities of a society are generally not admired in the Western cultural model.

While working with the Oraon people, we noted that all these qualities were present among them to a considerable extent. However, an attempt was also made to articulate what was felt to be the strength of the Oraon society. Many of them were discovered: people's kindness and generosity, cheerfulness, sense of good humour, unassailable sense of identity, sense of security, high morality and tolerance.

In view of these observations, it appeared that besides conformity, it was worthwhile to measure how people were, and how they perceived themselves to be, tied to other members of their family, clan, or community. That is, how enmeshed they felt themselves to be with other members of their family or group. Hence, a new scale was developed to assess the 'social connectedness' of persons in both the Birhor and Oraon groups.

Social Connectedness Measure

This measure consisted of eight items which probed into issues like the selection of spouse, decision for marriage, choice of child's work, naming of a child, matters related to residence, raising children, kinship orientations and social supports. For assessing the position of a community on each of these aspects, 5-point rating scales were used. The overall score range on this measure was 8–40. A higher score on the scale represented greater social connectedness in a community, whereas a lower score indicated lesser connectedness.

Individual Connectedness

Besides measuring connectedness at the group or community level, an attempt was made to assess it at the individual level. It was felt that all individuals of a particular community would not reflect the same level of social connectedness that characterized their community, and that in all communities there might be differences in the level of connectedness of individuals depending upon their level of education, exposure to urban or industrial life and many other general features of acculturation. Hence, another 6-item scale was developed to assess the individual level of connectedness. It probed into the extent of an individual's participation in *akhara* (collective dance), birth, marriage and death ceremonies, and the frequency of visit to relatives and sick neighbours. A 5-point scale was used for rating an individual on each of these items. The score range on this scale was 6–30. A higher score on the scale indicated greater individual connectedness, whereas a lower score was indicative of lesser connectedness of individuals.

Acculturation Measures

In this work, we have considered that the cultural features of the Adivasi children have been influenced not only by features of the ecological context, but also by their contact with other cultures through the process of acculturation. These influences have come mainly from interactions with, and sometimes domination by Hindus or Christians. To estimate the influence of acculturation, we include measures of media exposure, urban contact and formal schooling. These are essentially a measure of 'contact acculturation', as earlier used by Berry et al. (1986) and Mishra et al. (1996).

Measures of Cognitive Style Dimensions

A number of tasks were employed for the assessment of the two cognitive style dimensions. Some of these were the standard tasks. For use with Adivasi children, these were adapted by using local contexts and local language to make them suitable with children of these cultures. In addition to adapting some tasks, some tasks were also locally developed or selected from those already developed in India and used with Adivasi children in previous research studies (e.g., Mishra & Berry, 2008; Mishra et al., 1996; Sinha, 1988). A brief description of these tasks is presented in the following pages.

Broadly speaking, the cognitive tasks are intended to assess the two different processes describe earlier, called 'differentiation' and 'contextualization'. For assessing differentiation, Story-Pictorial Embedded Figures Task (SPEFT) and Hidden Words Task (HWT) were used. For assessing contextualization, Verbal Reasoning Task (VRT), Unknown Words Task (UWT) and Locating Objects Task (LOT) were used. Because our focus was on the understanding of the cognitive performance, we prefer to call all measures as 'tasks', although in previous research, some of these measures have been labelled as 'tests'.

The tasks of differentiation measure the level of ID among children, whereas the tasks of contextualization measure the level of EC. A description of these tasks is given in the following pages.

Differentiation Tasks

Story-Pictorial Embedded Figures Task (SPEFT)

This task was developed by Sinha (1984) to measure differentiation in the visual domain. The task consists of three practice sets and eight task sets. Each set consists of one card containing some simple stimulus (object), and one complex card containing a drawing of a familiar setting in which the simple stimulus are embedded. The subject locates the simple stimulus in the complex card. A story is related to stimulus on each card, which creates the necessary motivation for disembedding the hidden objects. The participant is asked to locate the stimulus in the complex card after listening to the story. Ninety seconds are allowed for this purpose on each card. Time taken and the number of stimulus (objects) correctly located are noted. This task has been used in a number of studies conducted with the Adivasi children and adults in India (Mishra et al., 1996; D. Sinha, 1979; G. Sinha, 1988).

Hidden Words Task (HWT)

This task was developed especially for use in this particular work along the line suggested by Berry, Bennett and Denny (1995). It represented a verbal counterpart of the Visual Embedded Figures. The task consisted of 11 sets of words. Three of the sets are used for practice purpose, whereas the remaining eight sets constitute the task series. Each set consists of three real words presented with three nonsense words. The child listens to the series, and then repeats only the words. The series of real words and nonsense words is presented through a tape recorder. The child listens to a series and says the real words that were played. All words reported by the child are recorded. The number of real words reported correctly is the child's score on this task. Each nonsense word repeated by the child is counted as 'error'. A lower error score indicated higher differentiation.

Contextualization Tasks

Syllogistic Reasoning Task (SRT)

This task was modeled on Luria's (1976) work to measure contextualization in verbal reasoning. It consists of six syllogisms, two of which are used for practice and the remaining four for task purposes. Two of the syllogisms of the task series present problems, which are familiar to children; the remaining two syllogisms pose problems that are unfamiliar to children due to not being in the normal range of their experiences. Each problem consists of a premise, a factual statement, and a question to which the answer requires an inference based on previously provided information.

The children are presented with the syllogisms one at a time, and asked to answer the questions. The answers are recorded and evaluated as 'correct' or 'incorrect'. Any request for repeating syllogisms is also recorded and scored. Greater discrepancy in reasoning of familiar and unfamiliar problems and greater number of requests are indicative of more contextualization.

Unknown Words Task (UWT)

This task was developed for measuring contextualization in a familiar descriptive situation, such as in a story. Eight stories were developed around the themes, which were highly familiar to the Adivasi children. In each story, an unknown (meaningless) word is used to describe a person, object or activity. The stories are presented through a tape-recorder. The child listens to the story, and is asked at the end of each story to tell the meaning of the unknown word. The meanings told by the child are noted, and are evaluated for their 'appropriateness' or 'relevance' in the context of the concerned stories.

Two judges were asked to discuss these words and agree upon their contextually appropriate meanings. Their judgements were used to score the child-reported meanings as correct or incorrect. Each correct meaning is given 'one' point. More number of correct meanings and more number of requests for the repetition of story are indicative of more contextualization.

Locating Objects Task (LOT)

This task was developed by Berry et al. (1995) for use in a cross-cultural study of cognitive style. The task consists of 13 snoopy pictures. Three of these are used for practice; the remaining ten pictures constitute the task series. The child is presented with the name of an object and is required to point to the same object in a picture as quickly as possible. The time taken to point out the picture and success/failure are noted.

The task series comprise two sets of pictures. In one set, the objects are placed in appropriate contexts (such as an axe on a man's shoulder). In the other set, the objects are placed in inappropriate contexts (such as a fish in the sky rather than in the river). Responses on each set and time taken to respond to items are noted. Discrepancy in the performance of the two series of pictures in terms of time (appropriate context minus inappropriate context) is taken to provide evidence of contextualization.

Other Measures

Besides these cognitive style tasks, some other measures were developed for understanding personal, social, demographic, acculturation and other features of the participants. In particular, these measures included a Personal Information Sheet, an Interview-cum-Observation Schedule, a Socialization Questionnaire and a Parental Strictness and Interference Rating Scale. These measures are briefly described further.

Personal Information Sheet

This sheet was used to record some personal details of children such as their name, age, years of education and their parents' name. It was also used to record some details of their parents, such as their means of livelihood, income and measures of contact-acculturation, degree of urban contact and the amount of exposure to media.

Interview-cum-Observation Schedule

This schedule was developed to record the sociopolitical parameters of the Birhor and Oraon Adivasi groups. It included such details as the number of people of the community living in a village, their lifestyles (whether it was nomadic or sedentary, or a combination of both), social hierarchy prevailing in the group (i.e., distinctions among the members in terms of their age, sex, wealth, power position, etc.), occupational specialization and any other special features of the groups.

Socialization Questionnaire

It intended to measure the behavioural dimensions of socialization that were emphasized by parents of different subsistence groups during their children's socialization in the respective communities. It was developed and used by Mishra et al. (1996) in a research carried out with Adivasi children and adults in India. The questionnaire consists of 39 items, but there is also a shorter version of the questionnaire, which is equally useful. In our work, we used this shorter version. The questions covered those features of socialization that were related to the fostering of FD or FI cognitive styles. The questions probed into the actual behaviours of parents, not their attitudes, in four behavioural settings in which the children usually engaged either alone or in the presence of their parents. These settings included sweeping, sitting around the fire, going to toilet and cutting grass. There were also questions relating to socialization for conformity, opportunity for environmental learning, social sensitivity and salience of parents.

One of the parents was asked the questions. The interview was informal, more like a general chit-chat with parents about their children. Each question sought information from parents about some behaviours of the child, activities in which the child is often engaged, demands made by parents from the child, and the manner in which the child was handled or treated, especially when he/she refused to do something the parents asked for. The overall purpose was to assess whether parents emphasized independence, autonomy and achievement (called 'assertion') or obedience, responsibility and nurturance (called 'compliance') on the part of children in their socialization, as noted by Barry et al. (1959). Similar scales were used by Berry (1966) and Dawson (1967a, 1967b).

Parental Strictness and Interference Rating Scale

This measure consisted of two 5-point ladder rating scales, one for assessing 'parental strictness' and another for assessing 'parental interference' in child's day-to-day activities. Two simple questions were asked to the child: 'How strict do you consider your parents for you?'; 'How much freedom do your parents allow you in day-to-day activities?' The child had to rate parents on a 5-point scale ranging from 'very much' to 'very little' with the help of a real five-step wooden ladder provided for this purpose. The scores range from 1 to 5 on each scale.

Measures of Educational Achievements

Originally, these measures were intended to assess the classroom achievements of children in language, mathematics and general sciences on the basis of examination records and teacher ratings. During the initial survey of these groups, it became evident that such records would not be available for children of the hunting-gathering Birhor and dry agricultural Oraon groups, because children of these groups were generally not attending schools despite some of them being enrolled in schools. Also, in many schools, such records were not prepared, and teachers had difficulty rating a child's level of competence in the requisite areas of achievement. Hence, a new task was developed. This task was also necessary in order to ensure the 'comparability' of groups in respect of these achievements.

Based on the observation of what children experienced in day-by-day life in their respective cultural contexts, the tasks for the assessment of language, mathematics, and general science were developed. These tasks were very similar to those that children would be given in examinations at the primary school levels. Hence, we call them Educational Achievement Tasks (EAT).

Language Tasks

It consisted of tasks of word meaning, sentence meaning and story comprehension.

In the *word meaning task,* a set of four pictures is given at a time, and the child is asked to point out a picture named by the researcher. Four such series are given. One point is given for each correct response. The score range is 0–4.

In the *sentence meaning task,* a set of 12 pictures is presented to the child. Each picture depicts an event or activity. The action of one of these pictures is described, and the child is asked to point out the picture corresponding to the described action. A series of four trials is given. One point is given for each correct response. The score range is 0–4.

In the *story comprehension task,* a small familiar story is told to the child. Then a series of four questions are asked, each related to an important event described in the story. The child's answers to these questions are recorded. One point is given for each correct answer. The score range is 0–4.

Mathematics Tasks

Four series of problems were given to children to assess their mathematical competence. These included the recognition, counting, sequencing and use of coins.

In the *coin recognition task*, the child is provided with six different coins, and is asked to tell what those coins are. The number of correct recognitions is recorded. One point is given for each correct recognition response. This part is used as a preparatory item, and not scored.

In the *coin counting task,* a number of coins are placed before the child. The child is asked to count them. Four series of counting are given. The number of correct counts is recorded. One point is given for each correct counting. The score range is 0–4.

In the *coin sequencing task*, the child is given the six coins used in the coin recognition task, and is asked to arrange them in terms of their increasing values. The number of coins arranged correctly is recorded. For each coin arranged in the correct sequence, one point is given. The score range is 0–6.

In the *coin use task,* the child is asked three questions related to the use of coins. The number of correct answers is recorded. While the first two questions require verbal answers, the third one requires actual manipulation of coins. Each correct answer is given one point. The score range is 0–3.

Science Tasks

In this task, a series of eight events, which occurred in day-to-day experiences of children and involved scientific principles, were sampled. The events are described, and the child is asked to tell why those events could happen the way they were (e.g., 'We get more hurt when we fall down from a place higher up from the ground. Why?'). The reasons given by children for the occurrence of various events are recorded.

Two university professors of the Faculty of Science, Banaras Hindu University, were requested to judge by mutual agreement whether or not the reasons given by children were based on any scientific principles. Thus, each answer was categorized as 'scientific' or 'non-scientific'. Each 'scientific' answer is given one point. The score range is 0–8.

On the whole, the selection and development of culturally sensitive tasks/measures corresponding to the cultural background and cognitive life of Adivasi children were challenging exercises. A number of discussions were held with parents and children of the respective Adivasi communities, with primary school teachers working in Adivasi areas, and with experts who had undertaken such exercises with task-naive people in order to ensure the appropriateness of tasks for different groups.

Preliminary Trials

The research tools were initially tried out on a group of 25 children in Varanasi with a view to work out the instructional and procedural details of the work. A field manual describing procedural details of work was also prepared. Then the tasks were given to 100 Adivasi children in Ranchi City and in five villages around it, including some Birhor settlements in Hazaribagh. Because the tasks were time-consuming, not all of them were given to all children.

The work with the Adivasi children revealed a number of difficulties with the tasks and tasking procedures. The main problem was related to language. Adivasi children, especially of the remote villages, did not generally feel comfortable with the use of Hindi language (i.e., the language in which we were comfortable). The difficulties were realized to a greater extent when the work progressed with the Birhor children. These difficulties led us to take the following decisions regarding our tasks and tasking procedures in the field:

1. Tasks should be carried out only by an assistant who could speak the language of the concerned Adivasi peoples.
2. A lengthy task or questionnaire should be avoided as it tended to produce a loss of interest among children.
3. The verbal tasks/scales should be rendered in the local dialect to promote communication and comprehension. Further, these tasks should be carried out in the form of informal conversations, instead of being used like tasks in a formal setting.
4. While administering various tasks, the time factor should be underplayed, as it had little importance in the lives of the Adivasi children.
5. The tasks should be carefully guarded against diffusion in the child population.

These insights obtained from the initial work with the Adivasi children were specifically used at later stages of the work. These changes in the procedure made task administration go smoothly, and the tasks were generally enjoyed by the children.

Although some of the tasks were standardized, a further check on the structure of their items as well as on the items of the newly developed tasks was considered desirable. Of the 100 Adivasi children with whom the preliminary work was done, we could identify 46 children who had completed all items of the tasks. Using the data of these children, inter-item and item-to-total correlations of task items were computed to examine their internal consistency. Broadly speaking, the scores tended to show moderate to high correlations (both inter-item and item-total) on the LOT. Similar patterns of relationship were noted on the HWT, RT and UWT.

On the basis of these analyses, the task items which showed less consistency (low item-to-item total correlation) were eliminated. This exercise led to a reduction in the length of the tasks (and tasking sessions), which was strongly desired to minimize the burden of work for children. The tasks finally used in the work are given in Table 5.1. The number of items in the task and the measures on which the performances were scored are also mentioned. The score range on each measure is also indicated.

Table 5.1

Questionnaires, Tasks and Measures Used in Work with the Adivasi Children

Measures	No. of Items Originally Included	No. of Items Finally Used
Cultural dimensions		
1. Societal Size Measure	4	4
2. Social Conformity Measure	4	4
3. Social Connectedness Measure	8	8
4. Individual Connectedness Measure	6	6
5. Socialization Questionnaire	20	20
Cognitive style dimension: differentiation		
1. Story-Pictorial Embedded Figures Task (SPEFT) a. Disembedding b. Time	8	5
2. Hidden Words Task (HWT) a. Correct Real Words b. Nonsense Words	11	7
Cognitive style dimension: contextualization		
1. Syllogistic Reasoning Task (SRT) a. Reasoning b. Request	6	4
2. Unknown Words Task (UWT) a. Meaning b. Request	8	5

(Table 5.1 Continued)

(Table 5.1 Continued)

Measures	No. of Items Originally Included	No. of Items Finally Used
3. Locating Objects Task (LOT)	13	13
a. Time (appropriate context)		
b. Time (inappropriate context)		
c. Time discrepancy		
Educational achievement		
1. Language		
a. Word Meaning	6	4
b. Sentence Meaning	6	4
c. Story Comprehension	4	4
2. Mathematics		
a. Coin Recognition	6	6
b. Counting	4	4
c. Sequence Arrangement	1	1
d. Coin Use	3	3
3. Science	14	8

It may be pointed out that socialization and educational achievement measures were not subjected to item analysis. The socialization measure was developed and already used with the same populations. For the educational achievement measures, on the other hand, the expert ratings for the appropriateness of items were considered adequate. In this way, the tasks were finalized. It may also be pointed out that snoopy pictures (cartoons) on the LOT, although apparently looking unfamiliar, were greatly enjoyed by children due to their novel and amusing features.

Having made the necessary changes in the tasks and tasking procedure (consequent on the pilot study), we set out to work with boys and girls belonging to the four subsistence activity groups. The tasks were given to children (200 boys and 200 girls) in a random, instead of predetermined, order. The only violation of random administration of tasks was to start either with the LOT or with the SPEFT. These tasks were not only greatly liked by children, but they also motivated them to take other tasks.

While there were hardly any refusals for participation in the study, there were some dropouts. Since the tasks were time-consuming (3–4 hours per child), they were given in three to four sessions. In 36 out of a total of 400 cases, the assistants could not get back to the same child for whom a part of the work had been carried out. Most of these dropouts were in the Birhor sample, where children left the settlements/camps for subsistence activities early in the morning and could not be traced in the forest. All tasking was carried out by an assistant who belonged to the Adivasi area and spoke the local Chotanagpuria language. The other assistant of non-Adivasi background rendered help in administering the tasks and recording the responses. Many a time these field activities were closely supervised by the one of the authors.

As a team we had very pleasant interactions with people in the field. Invitations to participate in cultural activities of groups were often extended to us. All possible kinds of help were rendered to us by people of the settlements or villages in which we worked. Collective dances were organized for us in most of the settlements/villages, and people gave us a very warm send off when we finished our work there. All these represented good positive indicators of our acceptance in settlements/villages where the work was carried out. On the whole, working in the Adivasi settings has been a very pleasant and memorable event.

International Studies

As indicated earlier, there were certain tasks/measures, which were used in our work with the Adivasi children in India and the adult participants internationally. These common measures included the HWT, SRT, UWT and LOT. Because we worked with adults in the international study, instead of using the SPEFT, or any other version of the EFT (e.g., CEFT or AEFT) meant for children, we used six items of the Witkin's Embedded Figures Test (EFT), which assesses field dependence-field independence, and has been used in many studies globally (see Witkin & Berry, 1975; Witkin & Goodenough, 1981).

Each set of the EFT consists of a simple geometrical shape (e.g., a triangle) drawn on a card. The shape is also embedded in a complex figure. The colour and form of the figure create a complexity of the figure within which the shape is hidden. The participant is first presented with the simple shape for inspection. Then the complex figure is presented. The participant has to spot out and show the simple shape within the complex camouflaged figure. Good performance on the EFT (i.e., greater number of shapes disembedded in the complex figure) is taken as a marker of field independence, that is, the ability to disembed information from the context or surrounding gestalt.

The participants were given six items of the EFT, which were selected from the whole set on the basis of a careful preliminary work. Thus, a maximum of six scores were possible for any participant on this task if all shapes were correctly disembedded. A higher score indicated field independence or higher psychological differentiation.

The HWT, SRT, UWT and LOT, described in the previous section, were used almost in the same manner as in the case of the Adivasi children. The differences were mainly in terms of the language and the number of items used in the tasks. These minor variations will be explicit in Chapter 6 when we present the findings of our work carried out with cultural groups internationally.

At each location where we did the international part of the work, local assistants were employed to administer the tasks. The field activities were closely supervised by the one of the authors (Ramesh Mishra in India) along with some of our good colleagues (e.g., Jo-Anne Bennett in Ghana and Canada and Zheng Xue in China), who were associated with us for quite some time. Working in cultures other than one's own is always a challenge and the work is full of difficulties and limitations in the absence of strong local support. We were privileged to have good colleagues at each location to help us with field activities (e.g., selection of participants, task administration, etc.) including the day-to-day supervision of the fieldwork to ensure procedural adequacy and quality of observations. Working in such culturally diverse settings has indeed been a great learning experience for both of us and our colleagues.

In this chapter, we have presented a description of the various tasks that were used with the Adivasi children in India and with adult participants internationally. We have also described the manner in which the tasks were selected, developed and conducted in both studies. In the next two chapters, we will describe our findings from the international and Adivasi studies and examine the similarities and differences between the findings of these two studies.

6

Cognitive Styles in International Context

Introduction

As mentioned in Chapter 1, one goal of our book is to examine the distribution of cognitive styles in some societies around the world that vary in their ecological engagement. To achieve this goal, we worked with groups in Canada, China, Ghana and India with adult members of cultural groups that differed in their subsistence strategy and their related cultural adaptations and acculturation. They represent groups that engaged in four kinds of subsistence: gatherers (from India), hunters (from Canada and Ghana), farmers (from China, Ghana and India) and urban/industrial (from Canada). These cultures were selected to provide a range of subsistence strategies across the theoretical range outlined in the previous chapter. They are intended to provide a broad context for the interpretation of the findings with the Adivasi children. Some basic information about participants of these subsistence groups is provided in Table 6.1.

In addition to variation in their subsistence strategy, the groups clearly differ on their level of years of formal schooling, which serves as an estimate of their degree of contact-acculturation. There are thus two important kinds of differences in context that need to be considered in this study, while examining the performance of the groups on differentiation and contextualization tasks.

Table 6.1

Participants in the International Study

Subsistence	Culture	Country	Years of Schooling	N
Gatherers	Birhor	India	4.1	60
Hunters	Oji-Cree	Canada	6.0	62
Hunters	Vagala	Ghana	0	76
Farmers	Han	China	4.2	60
Farmers	Wala	Ghana	4.9	90
Farmers	Hindu	India	9.7	60
Urban	European	Canada	11.4	49

Differentiation Tasks

As mentioned in Chapter 5, differentiation was assessed by two tasks: Embedded Figures (Hidden Pictures) and Hidden Words.

Embedded Figures Task

The findings on EFT are shown in Table 6.2. They replicate the classic findings in the literature: the mean number of hidden figures found (out of a possible 6) was highest for hunters (5.94 and 5.91 for Canadian and Ghanaian hunters respectively), followed by European Canadians (4.60),

Table 6.2

Differentiation: EFT (Max. Score = 6)

Subsistence	Culture	Country	Mean	SD
Gatherers	Birhor	India	3.73	1.7
Hunters	Oji-Cree	Canada	5.94	1.0
Hunters	Vagala	Ghana	5.91	0.7
Farmers	Han	China	1.71	1.7
Farmers	Wala	Ghana	2.07	1.7
Farmers	Hindu	India	2.46	1.6
Urban	European	Canada	4.60	1.7

Figure 6.1

Mean Scores of Groups on the EFT

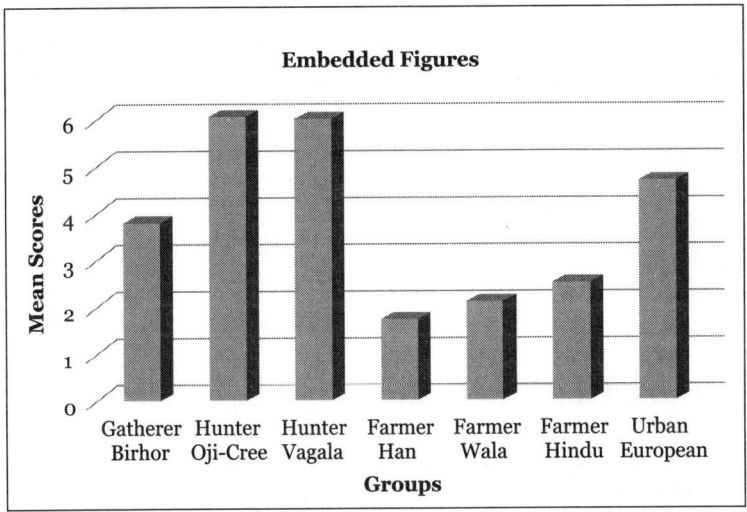

Indian gatherers (3.73) with Indian, Chinese and Ghanaian farmers having the lowest scores (2.46, 2.07 and 1.71 respectively).

The variation across cultures is significant [$F(3, 216) = 50.1$, $p<.01$]. The hunters had higher scores than other groups (except Canadian Urban), and the latter had higher scores than the others; the farmers did not differ from each other (Figure 6.1). This pattern supports our main hypothesis that the hunting subsistence strategy leads to higher differentiation skills than farming. Analysis of covariance, using years of schooling, did not change this pattern.

Hidden Words Task

The findings on the HWT (correct and error scores) are shown in Table 6.3. Our main innovation in the differentiation domain was to develop this new task that was based on verbal, rather than pictorial, material. Participants were read a list of real words (in their language) and nonsense words in a mixed order. They were scored for the number of real words they could repeat correctly. It was predicted that the hunters and urban

Table 6.3

Differentiation: HWT (Max. Score = 16)

Subsistence	Culture	Country	Correct		Errors	
			Mean	SD	Mean	SD
Gatherers	Birhor	India	11.17	2.5	0.36	0.83
Hunters	Oji-Cree	Canada	9.48	3.6	0.55	0.56
Hunters	Vagala	Ghana	13.92	2.9	0.84	0.80
Farmers	Han	China	6.08	2.1	2.95	2.40
Farmers	Wala	Ghana	8.08	2.4	0.23	0.64
Farmers	Hindu	India	8.11	1.8	0.66	0.97
Urban	European	Canada	12.56	2.4	1.14	0.08

groups would be able to differentiate the real from the nonsense words better than the other groups.

We notice again that the highest scores are indeed for these groups (Ghanaian hunters, followed by Canadian urban and Canadian hunters: 13.92, 12.56, and 9.48 respectively). However, Indian gatherers also scored high (11.17) contrary to expectation (see Figure 6.2). As predicted, the three other farming groups scored lowest (Indian, Ghanaian and

Figure 6.2

Mean Scores of Groups on the HWT

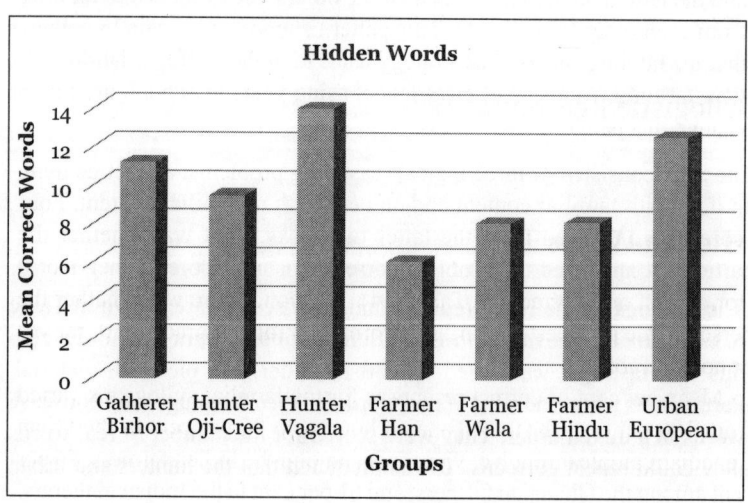

Chinese with 8.11, 8.08 and 6.08 real words repeated respectively). The overall variance was significant [F= 62.8, p<.0] and all groups differed significantly from each other (<.01).

We conclude that the HWT is a successful verbal task for assessing differentiation, and that differentiation is a general cognitive style that applies to verbal as well as visual tasks. However, the pattern is not exactly as predicted: the Chinese farmers (who were expected to be in the mid-range) had the lowest score, and the Canadian hunters were only slightly better at the task than the Ghanaian and Indian farmers. When the analysis of covariance (using schooling) was conducted, the order remained the same, but the difference between the three latter groups lost significance (p = 0.10).

The analysis of errors (last column of Table 6.3) shows the number of nonsense words that participants claimed were real words. Most participants made only a few errors (out of a possible 16), with the Chinese farmers making the most such claims (2.95). We made no hypotheses regarding errors, and there is no interpretable pattern to them; it may reflect some variation in a tendency to make guesses.

Contextualization Tasks

Contextualization was assessed with three tasks: Syllogistic Reasoning; Unfamiliar Words and Locating Objects.

Syllogistic Reasoning Task

The SRT consisted of three logical reasoning problems: a practice item, an item with familiar content and an item with unfamiliar content. Four scores were derived from the latter two tasks. First was whether the participant answered the problem correctly or not, scored either 1 or 0 (for correct or incorrect see Table 6.4). A second score was whether the person made a request for further information (also scored 1 or 0, for yes or no see Table 6.4).

Mean per cent of correct responses for the familiar syllogisms varied from 100 per cent for the Ghanaian hunters to 95 per cent in the urban Canadian sample through to 93 per cent among the Indian farmers, 76 per cent among the Ghanaian farmers, and 61 per cent in the Indian gatherers.

Table 6.4

Contextualization: Syllogistic Reasoning (per cent correct)

Subsistence	Culture	Country	Familiar		Unfamiliar		Difference
			Mean	SD	Mean	SD	
Gatherers	Birhor	India	0.61	0.54	0.43	0.56	0.18
Hunters	Oji-Cree	Canada	0.86	0.39	0.37	0.47	0.39
Hunters	Vagala	Ghana	1.00	0	0.40	0.49	0.60
Farmers	Han	China	0.87	0.34	0.78	0.22	0.07
Farmers	Wala	Ghana	0.76	0.43	0.73	0.45	0.03
Farmers	Hindu	India	0.93	0.46	0.69	0.37	0.24
Urban	European	Canada	0.95	0.95	0.78	0.22	0.17

There was a significant effect for culture [$F(3, 210) = 4.31$, $p < .05$], but only the Ghanaian farmers and Indian gatherers scored lower than the Canadian urban sample. Scores were somewhat lower for the unfamiliar syllogisms, but still generally above chance level, except for Canadian and Ghanaian hunters and Indian gatherers (see Figure 6.3).

The variation by culture was significant [$F(3, 210) = 7.06$, $p < 0.01$]; the only significant group difference was between the Canadian hunter

Figure 6.3

Mean Per cent of Correct Responses on the SRT

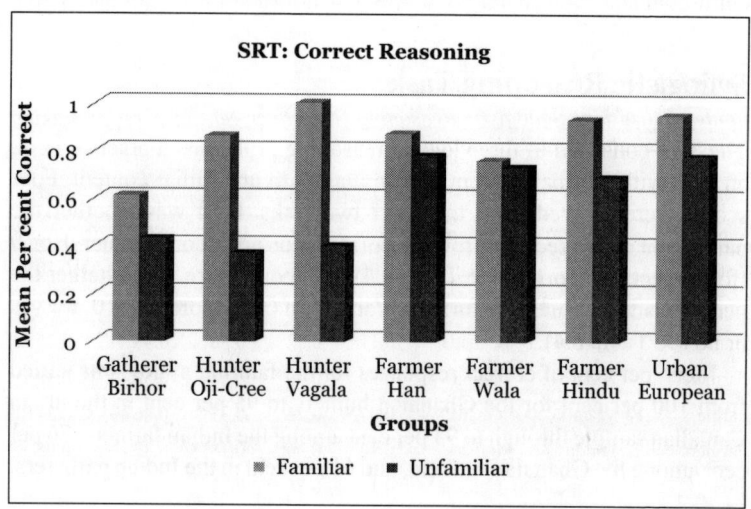

and urban samples. Since the items had contents dealing with farming, and the Canadian hunters had little familiarity with farming, they were at a disadvantage; other hunting and gathering groups live in areas where farming took place, but the Canadian hunters did not. Using schooling as a covariate did not substantially change these results.

A second score was for the number of requests made for additional information in order to work out the answer. The score is the mean percentage of people who made such requests, scored for familiar and unfamiliar content of the syllogisms (Table 6.5). We expected that contextualizing groups would make more such requests (first column of Table 6.5), and that they would do so more for the unfamiliar syllogisms (i.e., there would be a greater difference in the percentage requests; see last column of Table 6.5).

In a MANOVA (which treated familiar vs. unfamiliar syllogism contents as a repeated measures variable), there was a significant difference between familiar and unfamiliar contents [$F (3, 210) = 35.4$, $p<0.01$]; this confirms the main premise of the procedure. There was also a significant difference across cultures as expected [$F (3, 210) = 6.03$, $p<0.01$]. The simple main effect between cultures was mainly present to the unfamiliar items [$F (3, 210) = 6.01$, $p<.01$]. The large main effect for familiarity was mainly due to the large number of requests from the Chinese farmers (58%). Overall, the number of added requests was greater for the unfamiliar items for the Chinese and Ghanaian farmers and for the Canadian hunters (Figure 6.4).

The major difference is as expected: people in the three contextualizing cultures made more calls for additional information in this deductive

Table 6.5

Contextualization: Syllogistic Reasoning (Mean per cent of persons making requests for additional information)

Subsistence	Culture	Country	Familiar		Unfamiliar		Difference
			Mean	SD	Mean	SD	
Gatherers	Birhor	India	0.05	0.28	0.15	0.49	0.10
Hunters	Vagala	Ghana	0.00	0.00	0.28	0.48	0.28
Hunters	Oji-Cree	Canada	0.11	0.32	0.36	0.48	0.25
Farmers	Han	China	0.20	0.40	0.58	0.50	0.38
Farmers	Wala	Ghana	0.07	0.26	0.31	0.46	0.24
Farmers	Hindu	India	0.13	0.36	0.18	0.42	0.05
Urban	European	Canada	0.15	0.36	0.22	0.42	0.07

Figure 6.4

Mean Percentage of Participants Requesting Additional Information

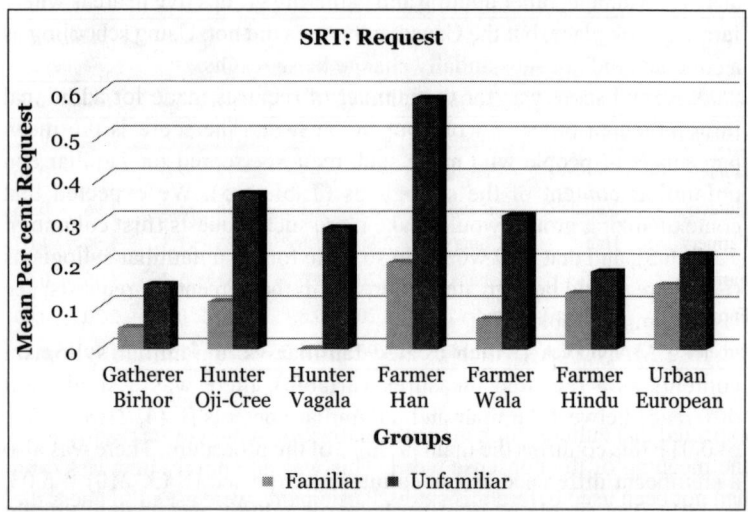

reasoning task than did those from the decontextualizing urban industrial society, but only when the content was unfamiliar. Furthermore, among people in the urban sample, there was no difference in these requests between familiar and unfamiliar items.

Taken together, the results with the SRT are important for three reasons. First, this is the first time that a study has verified (using tasks) the contextualizing nature of hunting societies. Second, the data generally support the predicted relationship between subsistence strategies and cognitive contextualization. However, it needs to be noted that the Chinese farmers requested the most information on the unfamiliar task, while we predicted that they would be in the mid-range of scores. And third, these results show that samples with little formal schooling can score well (above chance) on logical (deductive reasoning) tasks.

Unfamiliar Words Task

Contextualization was assessed by a second verbal task, using unfamiliar words. The findings are presented in Table 6.6. In this task, participants were asked the meaning of a nonsense word whose meaning could be inferred from a short story in which the nonsense word was used. It was

Table 6.6

Contextualization: Unfamiliar Words

Subsistence	Culture	Country	Guess		Correct		Adjusted Requests	
			Mean	SD	Mean	SD	Mean	SD
Gatherers	Birhor	India	2.00	1.2	1.10	1.8	1.12	0.00
Hunters	Oji-Cree	Canada	3.19	1.9	3.12	2.0	3.37	0.96
Hunters	Vagala	Ghana	4.35	1.1	1.86	1.2	1.96	0.55
Farmers	Han	China	2.80	1.6	1.26	1.3	1.50	1.02
Farmers	Wala	Ghana	3.20	1.6	2.81	1.3	1.46	0.93
Farmers	Hindu	India	4.20	0.8	0.30	0.6	2.20	0.00
Urban	European	Canada	4.90	0.6	2.24	1.0	1.79	0.12

expected that cultures high in contextualization would more readily infer the meaning of the nonsense word. This was an entirely new task, and had not been used before this study. Participants were asked to guess the meaning; the scores presented in the table (first two columns) are the number guessed and the number correct.

The highest correct scores were obtained by the Canadian urban and hunter samples and Ghanaian farmers (Figure 6.5), and this does

Figure 6.5

Mean (guess and correct meaning) Scores of Groups on the UWT

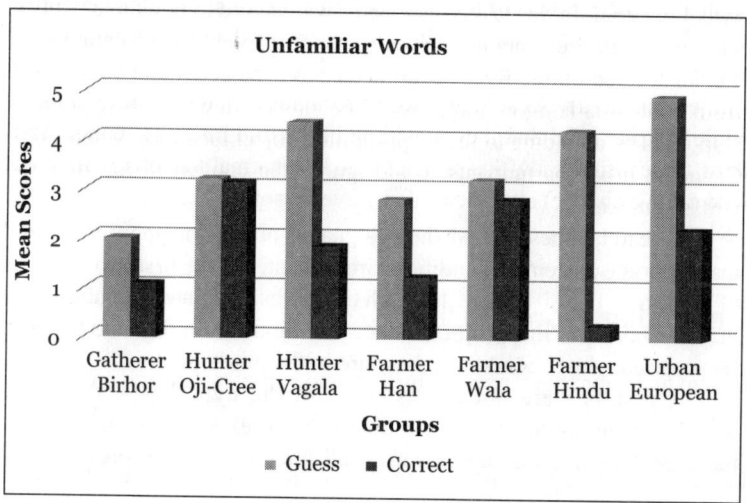

not correspond with our expectation. Since Canadian schools often ask students to figure out the meaning of a word from its context, we calculated the correlation between a person's years of schooling and the number correct; it was +.32. To take the effect of formal schooling into account, an adjusted score (column three) was calculated using years of schooling as a covariate. With this adjusted score, the Canadian urban and Ghanaian farmer group means drop to a mid-range score (from 2.24 to 1.79 and from 2.81 to 1.46 respectively), while the Canadian hunter group score is minimally affected (rising from 3.12 to 3.37). The adjusted scores for the other groups also increase. However, the rank orders of the adjusted means still do not correspond to our expectation.

When results using a new task do not correspond to expectations, it is difficult to decide whether the task or the theory is at fault. So, we considered using a fourth score, similar to the one we used with syllogistic reasoning: the number of times a participant requested more information in order to carry out the task (which could range from 0 to 5). The rank order of the means on this score for the groups does correspond with our expectations: the Canadian urban group was the least contextualizing (.12). Since this score was not part of the original design, these findings should be treated with caution.

Locating Objects Task

Contextualization was assessed with a third task, the LOT, which uses visual material. In this task, participants were asked to point to objects in a picture that were either in an appropriate or inappropriate location (e.g., a chair located on the floor or in the air). We expected that participants from contextualizing cultures would be slowed down in their pointing responses by attending to the inappropriate object locations, whereas the Canadian urban participants would ignore the context of location and will be quicker.

The search times to find the designated object for appropriate and inappropriate placement conditions are presented in the first two columns of Table 6.7. The difference in search times was calculated by subtracting the time taken in 'inappropriate place' condition from the time taken in 'appropriate place' condition; these are in the third column.

The results were not consistent with the hypothesis: the mean differences in speed of locating objects were expected to be least for the Canadian urban group; however, all the groups had scores that did

Table 6.7

Contextualization: LOT—Mean Search Time (in seconds)

Subsistence	Culture	Country	Appropriate Place		Inappropriate Place		Difference	
			Mean	SD	Mean	SD	Mean	SD
Gatherers	Birhor	India	22.7	19.1	23.5	16.9	0.8	13.4
Hunters	Oji-Cree	Canada	6.3	4.3	10.2	6.4	3.9	4.5
Hunters	Vagala	Ghana	8.0	30.7	25.4	24.7	3.0	17.2
Farmers	Han	China	7.8	25.6	28.9	12.3	8.9	20.1
Farmers	Wala	Ghana	21.6	18.3	23.3	17.9	1.7	18.3
Farmers	Hindu	India	13.7	0.4	22.4	30.7	8.7	13.0
Urban	European	Canada	2.7	2.4	6.6	2.7	3.9	1.9

not differ from each other, except for the Chinese farming group (which differed from all the others).

It is important to note that the time used in the search for objects both in appropriate and inappropriate places differed greatly: the two Canadian groups had very low search times compared to the other groups (approximately one-third to one-half the time, see Figure 6.6).

Figure 6.6

Mean Search Time Score of Groups on the LOT

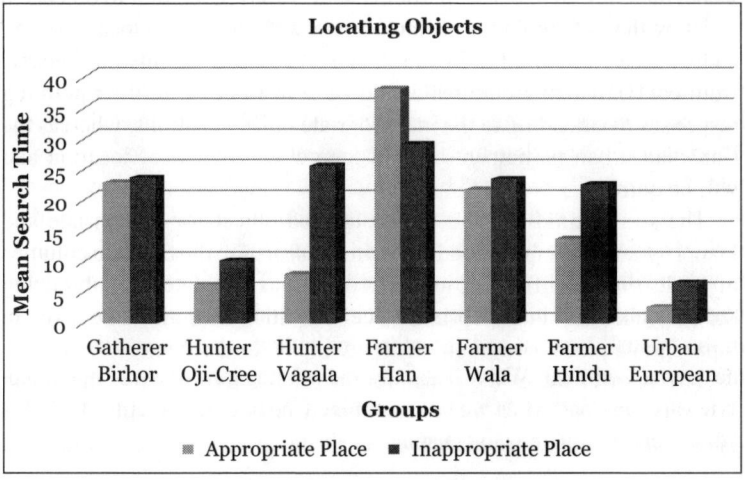

It is possible that this task is one of perceptual speed, rather than one of contextualization. An analysis using schooling as a covariate did not change these results in any substantial way. We thus conclude that this new task cannot be interpreted as a visual task for assessing contextualization.

To summarize the findings with respect to contextualization, we may say that the results from the one 'proven' contextualization task (SRT) support our expectation that people from contextualizing cultures do make contextualizing responses on a familiar and unfamiliar deductive reasoning task. This corresponds to findings from previous research. Moreover, we have extended the range of findings with this task: for the first time, this result has been found with hunting societies, as predicted. However, our efforts to find new contextualizing tasks seem to have failed: neither the verbal task (UWT) nor the visual task (LOT) produced results that could be interpreted in terms of contextualization.

Factorial Structure

A pan-cultural factor analysis was carried out in an attempt to discover the dimensions underlying performance on these tasks. There were three factors found, with 45.7, 13.4 and 9.6 per cent of the variance accounted for respectively. The first factor loaded the EFT and HWT (both used as measures of differentiation). A second factor loaded one contextualization task (LOT), while a third factor loaded the other contextualization tasks (SRT and UWT).

These findings provide evidence for the presence of three clusters of cognitive style variables. The first factor, indicating the 'differentiation' cognitive style, presents us with a structure that is similar to the one we have noted in our previous studies (Berry et al., 1986; Mishra et al., 1996). This factor corresponds to the 'field–dependent/independent' cognitive style that was originally proposed by Witkin et al. (1962) and found by Witkin and Berry (1975) in their review of cross-cultural studies of this cognitive style. The new cognitive style proposed in this study ('contextualization'), however, did not reveal a unitary structure. Tasks to assess this new cognitive style are split into two groups—one indicating contextualization in the 'visual' domain and the other one indicating contextualization in the 'verbal' domain. We will discuss the implications of these cognitive style variables later when we have examined the findings obtained with the Adivasi children in the next chapter.

7
Cognitive Style and Educational Achievement of Adivasi Children

Introduction

In this chapter, we focus on our work with the Adivasi children, first describing the participants from two groups, namely the Birhor hunting-gathering group and the Oraon, who are a farmer group, but with three different ecological engagements: dry agriculture; irrigation agriculture and urban wage-earning. We also describe how we worked with these groups and what we found. Towards the end of the chapter, we will examine our findings with respect to the patterning of relationships between the cultural, acculturation and cognitive styles dimensions.

As we have indicated earlier, the Adivasi peoples for a long time were known as 'tribals' because they belonged to different 'tribes' living in the forest and hilly regions of the country. The term 'tribe' is usually used to refer to a group of people who share a common and distinct name, an in-group sentiment, and a common and specific territory (Prasad, 1961). In India, the social, economic, political and cultural traditions of tribes are so different that each tribe seems to represent a distinct cultural group. For centuries, the state of Bihar, particularly the Chotanagpur region (now a part of the state of Jharkhand), has been the 'homeland' of some 29 distinct tribes. In keeping with their status as indigenous peoples, in official language they are now called Adivasi (meaning 'original inhabitants').

According to the 2011 census, there were about 104 million Adivasi people in India constituting 8.6 per cent of the total population of the country. In Jharkhand, they constituted about 28 per cent of the population of the state. In Gumla district, where we did most of our work, they constituted more than 70 per cent of the total district population.

In Chapter 4, we have described the ecological and physical features of the Adivasi region and the sociocultural and acculturation characteristics of the Birhor and Oraon groups with whom we have worked. In this section we present some details of the participants, and of the procedures we used in our work. Since procedural difficulties and constraints of work in the Adivasi settings are not much known, we will describe in some detail the strategies that we used in this work.

The work reported in this chapter was carried out with the Adivasi children, aged between 9 and 12 years old. They belonged to four groups, which varied in subsistence activities ranging from hunting-gathering to industrial wage-earning. At each level of subsistence strategy, we worked with samples of both boys and girls. Thus, there were four subsistence-level groups crossed by male and female gender. This design yielded eight groups, formed on the basis of four subsistence activities (hunting-gathering, dry agriculture, irrigation agriculture, wage-earning) and two genders (boys, girls). There were an equal number of participants in each group (50).

The work was carried out with 400 children (200 boys and 200 girls) of 9 to 12 years of age. They were selected from the Birhor and Oraon Adivasi groups living in Gumla and Hazaribagh districts of Jharkhand state. The reason for organizing our activity in these districts was the availability of children of all kinds of groups (i.e., hunters-gatherers, dry agriculture, irrigation agriculture, industrial wage-earners). Easy accessibility to both places from Ranchi (the state capital), their geographical proximity and heavy concentration of the Adivasi population were other practical considerations in order to decide to work in these places.

The original plan was to work with four groups of children by selecting them from different Adivasi groups that were engaged in different subsistence strategies (i.e., hunting-gathering from the Birhor group, dry agricultural from the Birjia or Asur group, irrigation agricultural from the Oraon group, and industrial wage-earning from the Munda group). Our initial visits to the Adivasi settlements and villages revealed that with respect to subsistence strategies, the Oraon represented a very diverse population, and that except for participants of the hunting-gathering subsistence, all other kind of participants could be drawn from the Oraon group alone. The decision to work with these other kinds of participants from the Oraon group resulted not only in the minimization of 'costs' of our work (e.g., time, money and energy), but also in the maximization of 'comparability' across groups, which is one of the most important issues of consideration in studies undertaken with diverse cultural groups such as those involved in the present one. Despite being predominantly agriculturalists, the Oraon presented a good probability of providing us with children of 'industrial wage earning' background from the outskirts of Gumla and Hazaribagh cities, as well as from the peripheral regions of coal mines of Hazaribagh.

Thus, the eventual decision was to work with children of the Birhor and Oraon Adivasi groups. The Birhor group provided the hunting-gathering participants, whereas the Oraon group provided the other three kinds (two agricultural and one industrial) of participants. In each group, we included an equal number of boys and girls. The details of these groups along with some background characteristics of participants are given in Table 7.1.

The initial work began by selecting children from primary schools located in the Oraon villages, but this strategy did not work well. Two serious problems were encountered in this approach. First, there was quick diffusion of knowledge about our tasks among village children, which resulted in stereotypical responses. Second, irregular attendance of children in schools did not allow the work to proceed by random selection of participants. Hence, the decision was taken to work in villages by selecting participants at the family level.

The 2001 census of villages was available at the time when our work began, but many irregularities were found in it. The seasonal migration of the Oraon people from villages and a wanderer's lifestyle of the Birhor also presented difficulties in working with census data. These necessitated an innovation in the procedure of working. In each village, where the work was to be carried out, we prepared a list of all families, which happened to have at least one child of 9–12 years of age. Parents were contacted

Table 7.1

Ecocultural Groups and Participants: Number, Gender, Age, Acculturation

Groups	N	Boys	Girls	Mean Age	Mean Years of Schooling	High Urban Contact	Non-traditional Occupation
Hunter-gatherer Birhor	100	50	50	10.14	1.97	00	68
Dry Agriculture Oraon	100	50	50	10.30	2.86	01	27
Irrigation Agriculture Oraon	100	50	50	10.71	5.06	01	85
Wage-earner Oraon	100	50	50	10.88	5.51	76	69

and their willingness for allowing the child to participate in the study was ensured. Then we randomly selected participants (one out of three) from the list using the robust and popular 'chit lifting' technique. Thus, from each house selected randomly, we worked with one child. This strategy worked successfully even with the Birhor group. With previous commitments made by parents, the children were easily available for working with us.

We encountered great difficulty in determining the age of children, especially those belonging to the Birhor group. The child's age was generally not recorded anywhere, and in many cases, the year of birth was also not known to parents. In such cases, the age was determined either by associating the birth of child with some significant local events (e.g., killing of a tiger, the arrival of elephants in the settlement, the construction of school or road, etc.), or by matching the births with those of other children in the village for whom some record or knowledge of age was available. This approach was used in some previous studies (Berry et al., 1986; Mishra et al., 1996) and was found to be valid. Since we did not intend to make comparison across different age groups, a wider age-range (9–12 years) was used. The decision to begin from 9 years of age was governed by the suitability of our tasks not before the age of 8 years, as revealed in their preliminary tryout. It was generally not difficult to identify children of this age range on the basis of their physical appearance barring some extreme cases where physical appearances were, of course, deceptive.

The decision with respect to selection of villages was primarily governed by the availability of children of different subsistence strategies we were interested in. Geographical accessibility of the area, our social contact with people in that region, and willingness of village chiefs to cooperate in work were the practical considerations in the selection of villages.

Participants from the hunting-gathering group were selected from 14 settlements; the dry agricultural group was selected from 13 settlements; the irrigation agricultural group was selected from 11 settlements and the wage-earning group was selected from 7 settlements. The major sites of our work are shown in Figure 7.1, which represents a part of the map of Jharkhand. The places mentioned on the map are the major cities or towns of the Chotanagpur region around which the settlements or villages of the Birhor and Oraon Adivasi groups were located. The dotted lines show the major roads that connect these different places.

It may be observed that the groups we worked with are not widely spread geographically; they are separated maximally by 200 kilometres

Figure 7.1

Map of the Major Sites of Work

(by road connections). Despite this geographical proximity, their position on the ecocultural dimension (hunting-gathering to wage-earning) is widespread. This spread is essential not only for the quasi-manipulation of the ecocultural variables, but also for the appraisal of ecocultural effects on behaviour in any reliable manner.

We spent almost a full year in the selection of settlements, and in the preparation, development and selection of tasks and questionnaires, and in the preliminary tryout of the tasks. The actual work took almost a year and half, but some interviews of parents had to be conducted in a second round of work. With respect to the sequence of work, first we worked with the two agricultural Oraon groups, then with the wage-earning group was approached, and finally the work with hunting-gathering Birhor group was completed, although part of this work (in Gumla district) was accomplished prior to moving on to the wage-earning group of the Oraon.

Working in a different cultural setting requires great support from local people. While we had good knowledge of the Birhor and Oraon peoples through our previous engagement in two major research projects (Mishra et al., 1996; Mishra & Berry, 2008), the work was greatly facilitated by the support of Dr Azariah Hans, former director, Adult and Continuing Education at Ranchi University, and Principal, Saint Columba College at Hazaribagh. He had previously assisted us in the earlier project (Mishra et al., 1996). His knowledge of the local areas and of the Adivasi languages, and his close contact with government officials and many 'headmen' of the Adivasi villages made our research activities a smooth sail. Yugant Kumar, one of our assistants, who came from a family that lived in an Adivasi village of Gumla and commanded great respect locally, also proved to be of great help. Not only were the consents to work in villages easily managed with the help of these two persons, but the work was also guarded against many resistances of the community and the influences of local politicians, which often work as barriers. Thus, our previous familiarity with the land and our contact with people there were of great help in managing work with children of the agricultural and hunting-gathering groups.

Empirical Findings

In this section, we present the analyses of data and our findings on different measures that were employed for the assessment of cultural and cognitive style dimensions as well as of educational achievement in Adivasi children. First, we present the analyses based on mean scores and use of analysis of variance. These are followed by correlational analyses. Integrative analyses based on stepwise multiple regression analyses are presented at the end of the chapter.

Cultural Dimensions

Table 7.2 presents the mean score of various groups on cultural dimensions of societal size and social conformity. The mean scores are pictorially depicted in Figure 7.2. It may be observed that the scores show different trends on these dimensions for the groups under consideration. On the

Table 7.2

Mean Scores of Groups on Cultural Dimensions

Groups	Societal Size Score Range: 4–16	Social Conformity Score Range: 4–16	Social Connectedness Score Range: 8–40	Individual Connectedness Score Range: 6–30
Hunting-gathering				
Mean	6.11	6.51	10.47	12.33
Standard Deviation (SD)	0.74	0.98	1.49	2.16
Dry agriculture				
Mean	8.82	13.10	30.12	22.85
SD	0.74	1.34	4.25	3.43
Irrigation agriculture				
Mean	11.79	12.14	25.85	21.63
SD	0.81	1.95	4.10	3.74
Wage-earning				
Mean	13.92	7.08	14.65	14.28
SD	0.69	1.32	2.31	2.39

Figure 7.2

Mean Scores of Groups on Societal Size and Social Conformity Dimensions

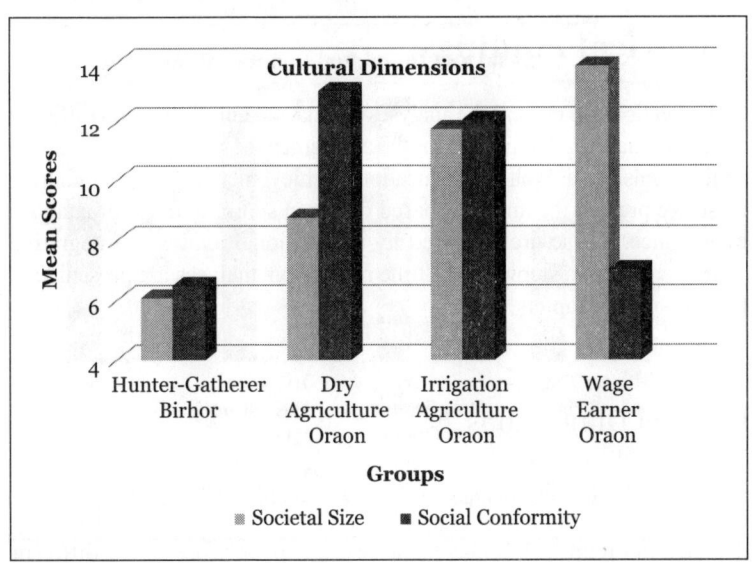

dimension of societal size, the scores indicate a progressive increase from hunting-gathering through the two agricultural groups to the wage-earning group, representing a linear relationship between subsistence strategies and societal size. The relationship of social conformity with subsistence strategies of groups appears to be curvilinear. Social conformity is low in hunting-gathering (HG) and wage-earning (WE) groups, but high in dry agriculture (DA) and irrigation agriculture (IA) groups. Social conformity dimension, thus, generally seems to be unrelated to societal size, at least for the DA and WE groups. These trends for both cultural measures are in line with our expectations.

Table 7.2 also presents the mean scores of the four groups on cultural dimensions of social connectedness and individual connectedness. These relationships are pictorially displayed in Figure 7.3, which presents the proportionate mean scores of the groups on the two dimensions.

The per cent mean scores were derived because the score range on 'social connectedness' (range: 8–40) and 'individual connectedness' (range: 6–30) measures were not equivalent. It is clear that the DA and IA groups are relatively highly placed in comparison to the HG and WE groups on both the dimensions. It is also to be noted that the level of individual connectedness in the HG and WE groups is slightly higher

Figure 7.3

Mean Per cent Score of Groups on Social and Individual Connectedness

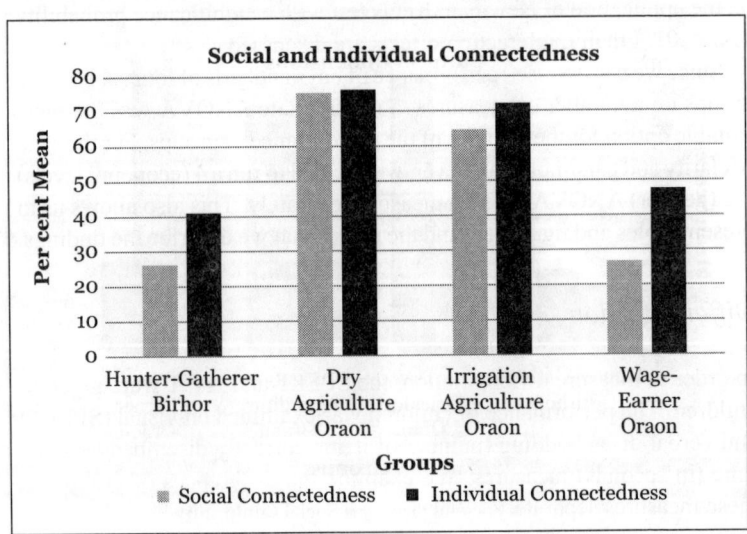

Cognitive Style and Educational Achievement of Adivasi Children 143

than the level of social connectedness. While this pattern of findings is less evident in the case of IA sample, both dimensions are represented to the same level in the DA group.

However, the trend of increase and decrease in the levels of individual and social connectedness is uniform, suggesting a covariation of individual and social connectedness in all the groups. Our expectation was that social connectedness would be low in hunter-gatherer and wage-earner groups than in rudimentary and irrigation agricultural groups. As for the measure of social conformity, the findings for social connectedness are clearly in line with the expectations.

Cognitive Style Dimensions

As discussed in Chapter 4, a number of tasks were used to measure the cognitive style dimensions of 'differentiation' (intra-unit distinctiveness) and 'contextualization' (extra-unit connectedness). In the following pages, the findings obtained on tasks measuring these cognitive style dimensions are presented separately. At the end, an attempt will be made towards their integration.

In presenting the findings, first the mean and SD are examined. Then the outcomes of analysis of variance (ANOVA) are discussed. Following that appear the mean comparisons of various subsistence groups based on the application of Newman–Keuls test with a significance probability of $p < .01$. Finally, interaction effects are discussed.

Since we had assessed performance of boys and girls of four subsistence groups on a number of measures, a multivariate ANOVA was the most suitable option for the analysis of the performance of groups. For the sake of clarity and parsimony, however, we decided to run a 4 (economy levels) × 2 (gender) ANOVA on each measure separately. This also allows us to present tables and figures around the places that we describe the findings.

Differentiation

In order to measure differentiation, the SPEFT and HWT were given to children. The performance of children was examined on visual (SPEFT) and verbal disembedding (number of items correctly disembedded) and time (in seconds) measures. We examine the differences of groups on these measures separately.

Story-Pictorial Embedded Figures Task (Visual Disembedding)

Mean scores obtained by groups on the visual disembedding measure of SPEFT are presented in Table 7.3 and pictorially depicted in Figure 7.4. The scores of HG and WE samples are higher than those of the DA and IA samples. Girls score higher than boys.

ANOVA (Table 7.4) revealed the main effects of economy and gender to be significant. Interaction effect of economy and gender was not

Table 7.3

Mean Score of Groups on the SPEFT

Groups	Disembedding		Time	
	Mean	SD	Mean	SD
Hunting-gathering	22.09	1.60	267.28	66.86
Dry agriculture	21.34	2.08	285.20	59.81
Irrigation agriculture	21.45	2.48	261.50	74.30
Wage-earning	22.66	1.53	225.91	71.79
Boys	21.69	2.13	266.84	74.48
Girls	22.08	1.80	253.10	67.84

Figure 7.4

Mean Scores of Groups on the SPEFT

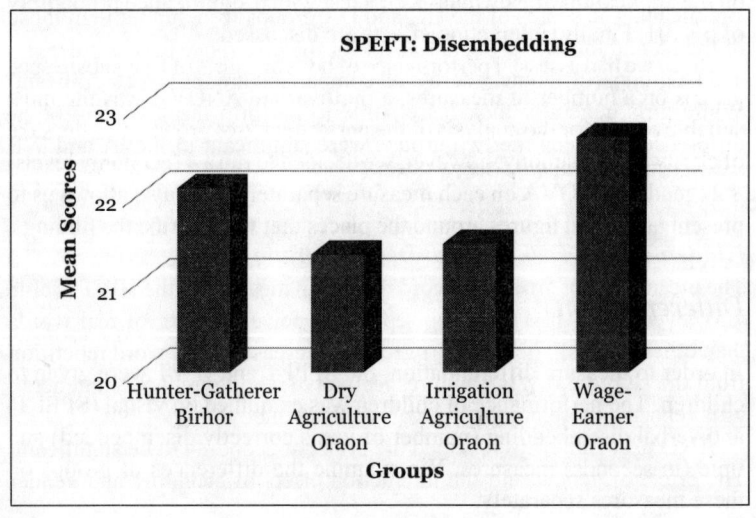

Table 7.4

ANOVA Outcomes on the SPEFT

		Disembedding		Time	
Source	df	Mean Square	F	Mean Square	F
Economy	3	37.63	9.92**	61747.12	13.48**
Gender	1	16.00	4.22*	18892.50	4.12*
Economy × Gender	3	4.89	1.29	13164.85	2.87*
Error: Within	392	3.79	–	4579.67	

Notes: *$p < 0.05$; **$p < 0.01$.

significant. Post-hoc comparison of means of various groups revealed that except for the difference between DA and IA samples, differences among other comparison groups were significant. Children of the WE group disembedded more number of objects in pictures than those of other groups, whereas children of the DA group disembedded the lowest. Gender differences in the performance of all groups were almost similar.

With regard to time taken to disembed objects, the mean scores (Table 7.3) revealed that children of the WE group took the least time. Successive increase in time was noted for the IA, HG and DA groups respectively. Boys generally took lesser time than girls in disembedding objects.

ANOVA (Table 7.4) revealed the main effects of economy and gender to be significant. The interaction effect of economy and gender was also significant. The scores of the HG and DA groups were higher than those of the IA and the WE groups. Except for the difference between the HG and IA groups, differences across all comparison groups were significant. While girls generally took lesser time to perform the task than boys, differences between the two groups were significant in the IA and WE groups, not in the HG and DA groups.

Hidden Words Task (Verbal Disembedding)

The mean score of groups on word repetition measure of the HWT (Table 7.5) reveals that the HG group repeated a fewer number of real words than other groups. There is a progressive increase in real word repetition from the HG to the WE group respectively (see Figure 7.5). In general, girls repeated more number of real words than boys.

ANOVA (Table 7.6) revealed the effect of economy to be significant. The effect of gender and the interaction effect of economy and gender

Table 7.5

Mean Score of Groups on the HWT

Groups	Real Words		Nonsense Words	
	Mean	SD	Mean	SD
Hunting-gathering	7.33	2.00	2.12	1.92
Dry agriculture	8.01	1.48	3.21	1.86
Irrigation agriculture	8.32	1.50	2.56	1.15
Wage-earning	9.94	1.32	2.06	1.98
Boys	8.30	1.84	2.28	1.08
Girls	8.49	1.87	2.69	1.37

Figure 7.5

Mean Scores of Groups on the HWT (word repetition)

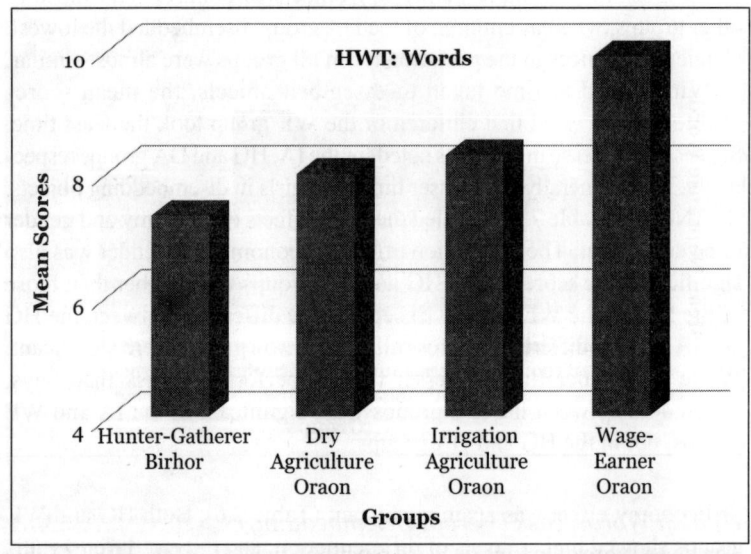

were not significant. Intergroup comparison of mean scores revealed that all groups differed significantly from each other.

Analysis of errors (repetition of nonsense words) revealed that the WE and HG groups made fewer nonsense word repetitions (errors) than the IA and DA groups respectively (Table 7.6), showing greater differentiation on the part of WE and HG groups. The mean scores of the groups are displayed in Figure 7.6.

Table 7.6

ANOVA Outcomes on the HWT

Source	df	Real Words		Nonsense Words	
		Mean Square	F	Mean Square	F
Economy	3	122.50	48.46**	28.46	9.92**
Gender	1	3.61	1.43	17.64	6.15**
Economy × Gender	3	3.99	1.58	2.18	0.76
Error: Within	392	2.53	–	2.87	

Notes: **$p < 0.01$.

Figure 7.6

Mean Scores of Groups on the HWT (nonsense word repetition)

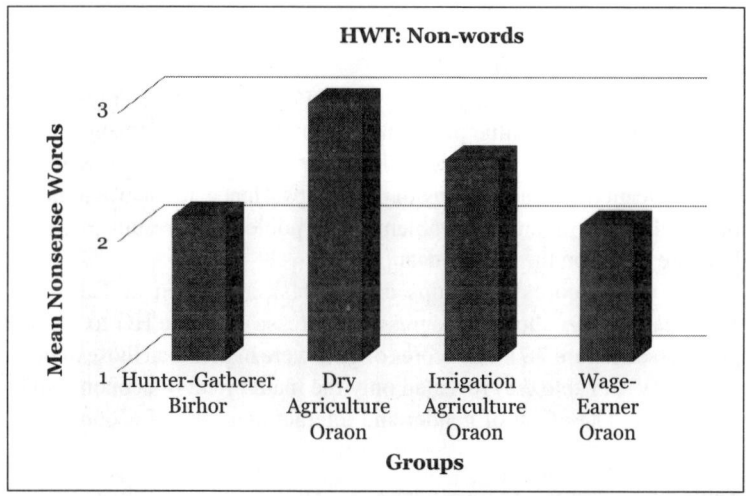

Economy effect was again significant (Table 7.6). Both HG and WE groups showed higher levels of differentiation, and did not differ significantly from each other, whereas other pairs of comparison were significant. Girls again scored higher than boys, and gender effect was statistically significant. The interaction of economy and gender was not significant, suggesting that in all groups boys and girls displayed almost a similar pattern of performance.

We also examined children's level of differentiation by analyzing the 'errors of intrusion' and 'errors of commission'. Intrusion errors are in evidence when a child speaks out a word, which is not included in the presented series of words. Commission error is evident when a child repeats any word of the presented series of words more than one time. In these analyses, we found no evidence for intrusion and commission errors in any of the groups, suggesting that all the groups were able to retain the words even though they were not able to repeat them. In a sense, this finding of similar ability on this verbal task across all groups suggests that the comprehension level of each group was much the same, and that no difference in their ability to understand verbal instructions for the tasks exists between them.

Contextualisation

For measuring this cognitive style dimension, we had used the RT, UWT and LOT. The findings obtained on various measures of these tasks are now presented.

Syllogistic Reasoning Task

Our initial plan was to analyse the pattern of performance of groups on the familiar and unfamiliar problems separately. The comparison of mean scores obtained on these problems, however, did not provide any evidence of significant difference for any of the groups. Hence, the scores obtained on familiar and unfamiliar problems were pooled. The results presented here are based on the pooled data.

The mean scores of groups on this task are given in Table 7.7. *Reasoning scores* showed progressive increase from the HG to the WE groups (see Figure 7.7). The scores of girls were higher than those of boys.

ANOVA (Table 7.8) revealed only the main effect of economy to be significant. The effect of gender and interaction effect of economy and

Table 7.7

Mean Score of Groups on the SRT

Groups	Reasoning		Request	
	Mean	SD	Mean	SD
Hunting-gathering	2.60	0.57	0.10	0.33
Dry agriculture	2.71	0.56	0.06	0.24
Irrigation agriculture	2.76	0.45	0.12	0.38
Wage-earning	2.84	0.37	0.13	0.36
Boys	2.69	0.54	0.10	0.32
Girls	2.77	0.46	0.10	0.46

Figure 7.7

Mean Scores of Groups on the SRT (reasoning measure)

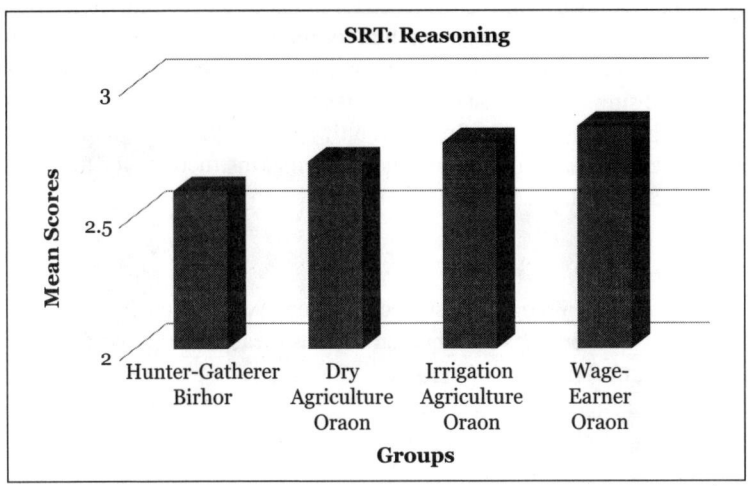

Table 7.8

ANOVA Outcomes on the SRT

Source	df	Reasoning		Request	
		Mean Square	F	Mean Square	F
Economy	3	1.01	4.20**	0.08	0.73
Gender	1	0.73	3.01	0.01	0.09
Economy × Gender	3	0.46	1.90	0.12	1.09
Error: Within	392	0.24	–	0.11	

Note: **$p < 0.01$.

gender were not significant. The comparison of mean scores across the four economy groups revealed all pairs of comparison to be significant.

On the *request measure* of this task (Table 7.7), the findings suggested high degree of variability in the score of groups. The DA group had the lowest score; The HG, WE and IA groups successively scored higher (see Figure 7.8). Boys and girls made the same amount of request. ANOVA (Table 7.8) revealed none of the main or interaction effects to be significant. Hence, the Newman–Keuls test was unwarranted. Due to high variability in score of participants, however, these results need to be taken with caution.

Figure 7.8

Mean Scores of Groups on the SRT (request measure)

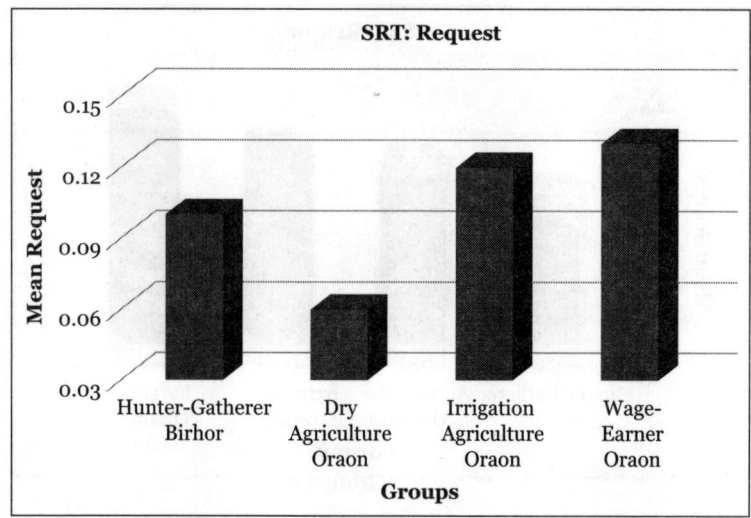

Unfamiliar Words Task

Mean scores of groups for 'meaning' as well 'request' measures of this task are given in Table 7.9. The *meaning scores* showed an increase from the HG to WE levels (Figure 7.9). The main effect of economy was significant (Table 7.10). All economy groups differed significantly from each other on the Newman–Keuls test. Gender effect was also significant. The scores of girls were higher than those of boys.

Table 7.9

Mean Score of Groups on the UWT

Groups	Meaning		Request	
	Mean	SD	Mean	SD
Hunting-gathering	1.27	1.04	9.27	3.67
Dry agriculture	1.63	0.96	8.43	2.54
Irrigation agriculture	2.02	1.13	7.01	2.15
Wage-earning	2.46	1.03	4.70	2.75
Boys	1.73	1.12	7.30	3.03
Girls	1.96	1.13	7.41	3.59

Figure 7.9

Mean Score of Groups on the UWT (meaning measure)

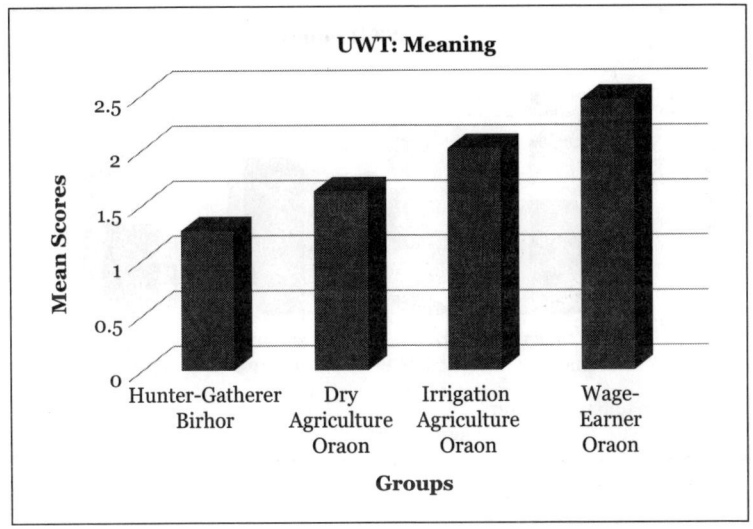

Table 7.10

ANOVA Outcomes on the UWT

Source	df	Meaning		Request	
		Mean Square	F	Mean Square	F
Economy	3	26.19	24.22**	399.70	49.31**
Gender	1	5.76	5.33*	1.10	0.14
Economy × Gender	3	0.09	0.08	1.87	0.23
Error: Within	392	1.08	–	8.11	

Notes: *p < 0.05; **p < 0.01.

On the *request measure* (Table 7.9), the lowest mean score was obtained by the WE sample. The scores of IA, DA and HG samples were successively higher than the score of the WE group (see Figure 7.10). Girls scored slightly higher than boys.

ANOVA (Table 7.10) yielded a significant F ratio for economy. The effect of gender and interaction effect of economy and gender were not significant. All pair-wise comparisons of mean scores of various economy groups revealed significant differences.

Figure 7.10

Mean Score of Groups on the UWT (request measure)

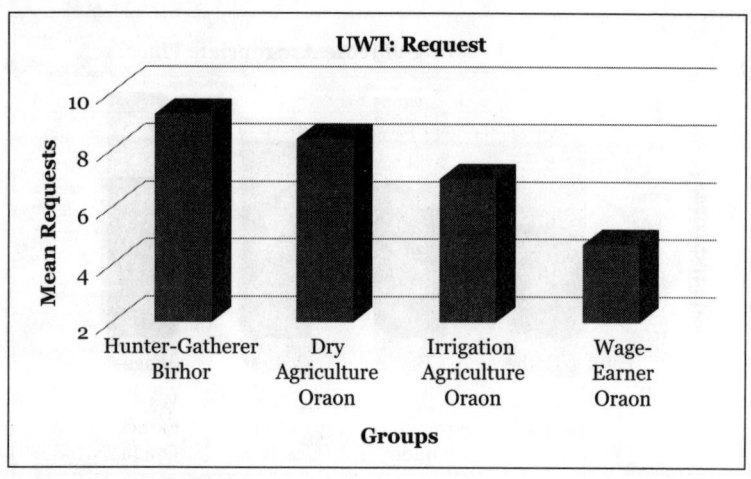

Locating Objects Task

Mean scores obtained by groups on this task are given in Table 7.11. In the appropriate place condition, the WE group was able to locate objects more quickly than the HG, IA and DA groups respectively (see Figure 7.11). Girls performed less quickly than boys.

ANOVA (Table 7.12) yielded significant F-ratio only for economy effect. Neither the main effect of gender nor the interaction effect of economy and gender was significant. Mean comparisons across the groups

Table 7.11

Mean Time Score of Groups on the LOT Under Appropriate (LOTA) and Inappropriate (LOTI) Object Place Conditions

Groups	Appropriate Place		Inappropriate Place	
	Mean	SD	Mean	SD
Hunting-gathering	14.62	5.06	15.67	4.94
Dry agriculture	16.89	5.52	19.91	6.67
Irrigation agriculture	15.47	6.62	19.40	9.44
Wage-earning	10.98	2.51	13.68	2.88
Boys	14.35	6.15	16.41	6.97
Girls	14.62	4.96	17.92	6.83

Figure 7.11

Mean Score of Groups on the LOT (appropriate place)

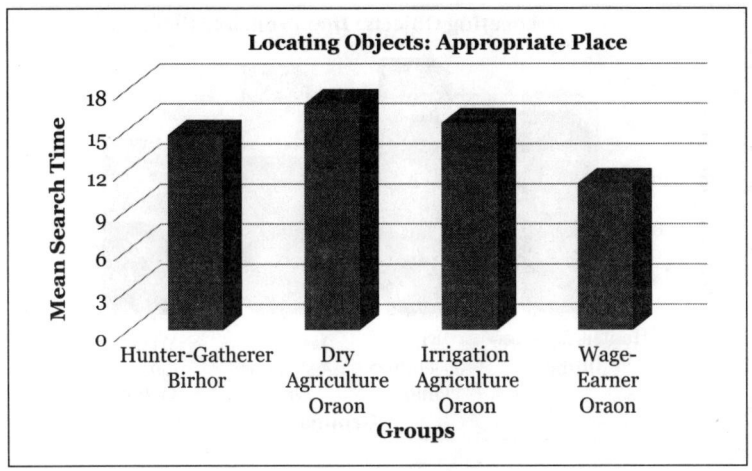

Table 7.12

ANOVA Outcomes on the LOT

Source	df	Appropriate Place		Inappropriate Place	
		Mean Square	F	Mean Square	F
Economy	3	635.25	24.11**	897.02	21.77**
Gender	1	7,29	0.28	231.04	5.61*
Economy × Gender	3	61.66	2.34	30.06	0.73
Error: Within	392	25.35	–	41.21	

Notes: *p < 0.05; **p < 0.01.

revealed all pairs of comparison to be significant, except for the difference between the HG and IA groups.

A similar pattern in results was noted on this task even in the inappropriate place condition (Table 7.11). The WE group performed the task more quickly than the HG group; the IA and DA groups were respectively next in the hierarchy (see Figure 7.12). Boys located objects more quickly (took lesser time) than girls.

ANOVA (Table 7.12) yielded significant F-ratios for both the economy and gender variables, suggesting significant effects of these variables on scores. Pair-wise comparison of mean scores of economy groups revealed

Figure 7.12

Mean Score of Groups on the LOT (inappropriate place)

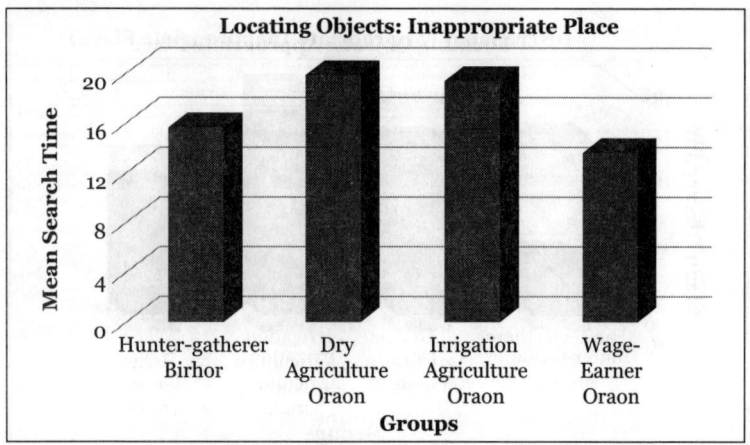

all comparisons to be significant, indicating that economic activities were associated significantly with differences in task performance.

In order to examine the level of contextualization among groups, we calculated a discrepancy score by subtracting the scores obtained by each group under the 'inappropriate place' condition from those obtained under the 'appropriate place' condition. Mean discrepancy scores of groups are given in Table 7.13. The lowest discrepancy in scores is evident in the HG group. Successively increasing discrepancy in scores between 'appropriate place' and 'inappropriate place' conditions can be noted in the WE, DA and IA groups (see Figure 7.13). Greater score discrepancy is evident in the case of girls than boys.

Table 7.13

Mean Discrepancy Score of Groups on the LOT

Groups	Discrepancy	
	Mean	SD
Hunting-gathering	1.05	0.65
Dry agriculture	3.02	0.96
Irrigation agriculture	3.93	1.26
Wage-earning	2.70	0.51
Boys	2.06	0.68
Girls	3.30	1.05

Figure 7.13

Mean Discrepancy Score of Groups on the LOT

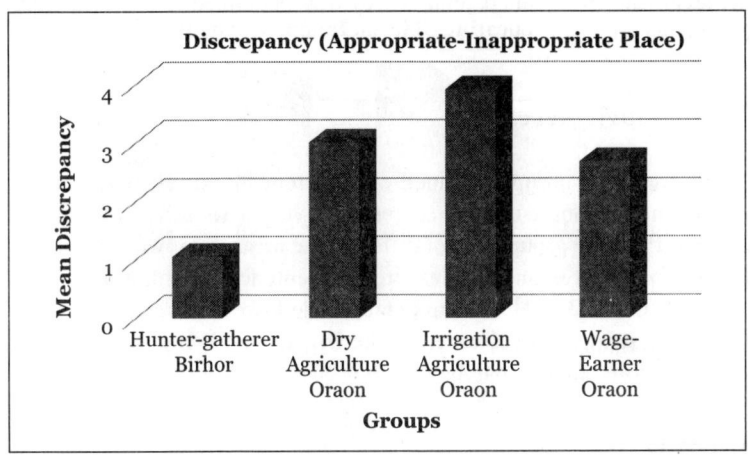

Table 7.14

ANOVA Outcomes for Discrepancy Scores on the LOT

Source	df	Mean Square	F
Economy	3	23.73	6.05*
Gender	1	13.07	3.33
Economy × Gender	3	2.33	0.59
Error: Within	392	3.92	

Note: *$p < 0.01$.

ANOVA (Table 7.14) revealed the effect of economy to be significant. The effect of gender and interaction effect of economy and gender were not significant. The comparison of different economy groups revealed all differences across their means to be significant. The evidence suggests greater contextualization in the DA and IA groups than in the HG and WE groups.

Educational Achievements

This section presents the findings for tasks related to the educational achievements of the four groups in language, mathematics and science subjects. The scores of groups on various measures within each area of achievement were highly inter-correlated. Hence, a composite score by pooling the scores obtained on different measures of a particular achievement area (called total score) was generated. ANOVAs were conducted on these total scores.

Language Achievement

Mean scores of groups obtained on different measures of Language Achievement along with total scores are given in Table 7.15. It may be observed that the groups do not differ on the measure of word meaning, but they do differ on the measures of sentence meaning and story comprehension. The HG group obtained the lowest score; successively increasing scores were obtained by the DA, IA and WE groups. Overall the girls scored higher than boys.

Table 7.15

Mean Score of Groups on the Language Achievement Measure (Lach)

Groups	Word Meaning	Sentence Meaning	Story Comprehension	Total
Hunting-gathering				
Mean	4.00	3.72	3.12	10.84
SD	0.00	0.47	0.74	0.43
Dry agriculture				
Mean	4.00	3.68	3.20	10.88
SD	0.00	0.53	0.78	0.47
Irrigation agriculture				
Mean	4.00	3.90	3.32	11.22
SD	0.00	0.30	0.66	0.36
Wage-earning				
Mean	4.00	4.00	3.47	11.47
SD	0.00	0.00	0.64	0.23
Boys				
Mean	4.00	3.88	3.42	10.90
SD	0.00	0.34	0.69	0.37
Girls				
Mean	4.00	3.77	3.14	11.30
SD	0.00	0.46	0.72	0.41

Table 7.16

ANOVA Outcomes on the Language Achievement Measure (Lach): Total Score

Source	df	Language Mean Square	F
Economy	3	8.91	11.86*
Gender	1	15.60	20.76*
Economy × Gender	3	5.31	7.07*
Error: Within	392	0.75	—

Note: $*p < .01$.

ANOVA (Table 7.16) revealed the main effects of economy and gender to be significant with evidence for a significant interaction effect of economy and gender. Mean differences across different subsistence groups were significant, but these differences were significantly linked with the gender variable. Mean comparisons revealed that gender difference was negligible in the HG and WE groups. In the DA and IA groups, on the other hand, the scores of boys were significantly higher than those of girls. This difference was especially noteworthy in the case of DA group.

Mathematical Achievement

Mean scores of groups on different measures of Mathematical Achievement are given in Table 7.17. It is noteworthy that the scores of all groups are close to the maximum possible score on this task. The DA group had the lowest score; the HG, IA and WE groups had successively higher scores. Boys scored slightly higher than girls.

Table 7.17

Mean Score of Groups on the Mathematical Achievement Measure (Mach)

Groups	Counting	Coin Arrangement	Coin Use	Total
Hunting-gathering				
Mean	4.00	5.93	2.94	12.87
SD	0.00	0.41	0.24	0.34
Dry agriculture				
Mean	3.94	5.87	2.86	12.67
SD	0.28	0.53	0.85	0.66

(Table 7.17 Continued)

(Table 7.17 Continued)

Groups	Counting	Coin Arrangement	Coin Use	Total
Irrigation agriculture				
Mean	3.98	5.97	2.98	12.93
SD	0.14	0.22	0.14	0.42
Wage-earning				
Mean	4.00	6.00	3.00	13.00
SD	0.00	0.00	0.00	0.00
Boys				
Mean	3.97	5.95	2.97	18.89
SD	0.21	0.29	0.17	0.21
Girls				
Mean	4.00	5.93	2.92	18.85
SD	0.00	0.41	0.27	0.17

Table 7.18

ANOVA Outcomes on the Mathematical Achievement Measure (Mach): Total Score

Source	df	Mathematics	
		Mean Square	F
Economy	3	0.37	2.18
Gender	1	0.01	0.01
Economy × Gender	3	0.17	0.97
Error: Within	392	0.17	

ANOVA (Table 7.18) revealed neither the main effect of economy or gender, and nor the interaction effect of economy and gender to be significant, indicating that mathematical achievement of children was unrelated to economy and gender variables. The application of Newman–Keuls test in this case was unwarranted.

Science Achievement

Mean scores of groups on the two measures of Science Achievement are given in Table 7.19. Reasoning scores revealed that the DA group had

Table 7.19

Mean Score of Groups on the Science Achievement Measure (Sach)

Groups	Reasoning	Scientific Reasoning
Hunting-gathering		
Mean	6.46	4.35
SD	0.90	1.00
Dry agriculture		
Mean	6.36	4.83
SD	1.11	0.94
Irrigation agriculture		
Mean	6.83	5.20
SD	0.99	0.93
Wage-earning		
Mean	6.88	4.99
SD	0.94	1.01
Boys		
Mean	6.88	5.10
SD	0.95	1.03
Girls		
Mean	6.39	4.59
SD	1.00	0.94

the lowest score with the HG, IA and WE groups scoring successively higher than each other respectively. The scores of boys were also higher than those of girls.

ANOVA (Table 7.20) revealed significant main effects of economy and gender. The interaction effect of economy and gender was also significant. The comparison of mean scores across the four economy groups revealed that all comparisons were significant except for the HG v. DA and the IA v. WE group comparisons. The interaction effect indicated no significant difference between boys and girls in the HG and IA samples, but a significant difference between them in the DA and WE groups.

Similar results were obtained on the *scientific reasoning* measure of this task. Mean scores (Table 7.19) revealed the highest level of scientific reasoning in the IA group. Other samples lower in hierarchy were the WE, DA and HG groups respectively. Boys scored higher than girls.

Table 7.20

ANOVA Outcomes on the Science Achievement Measure (Sach)

		Reasoning		Scientific Reasoning	
Source	df	Mean Square	F	Mean Square	F
Economy	3	6.81	8.08*	13.08	16.52*
Gender	1	24.50	29.08*	26.52	33.52*
Economy × Gender	3	9.93	11.78*	12.38	15.65*
Error: Within	392	0.84	–	0.79	

Note: $^*p < .01$.

ANOVA (Table 7.20) revealed the main effect of economy and gender to be significant; the interaction effect of economy and gender was also significant. Mean comparisons across all economy groups were found to be significant. More scientific reasoning among boys than girls was also statistically confirmed. However, the interaction effect revealed that boys and girls of the HG and IA groups did not differ in the level of scientific reasoning. In the DA and WE groups, on the other hand, the scores of girls were significantly lower than those of boys.

Overall Pattern of Relationships Between Ecocultural Context and Cognitive Style

On the whole, the findings suggest that the subsistence strategy of groups provides a basis for the differential patterning in performance on cognitive style tasks. The patterning is fairly consistent in the case of differentiation: the HG and WE groups show higher levels of differentiation than DA and IA groups respectively on visual (SPEFT) as well as verbal (HWT) differentiation tasks. This finding is highly consistent with our prediction. On the other hand, the patterning in performance is less consistent on contextualization tasks. In this case, the prediction is supported mainly for the agricultural group; contextualization in other subsistence groups appears to be 'task-specific'. In view of this pattern, it is not possible to draw any general conclusion regarding the relationship of contextualization with subsistence activities of groups. All we can say is that children from agricultural societies display the contextualization cognitive style more than the children of other subsistence societies.

Understanding Relationships

A significant feature of the present work is that a number of contextual variables (ecological, cultural and acculturation) and behavioural variables (cognitive style and educational achievement) were directly assessed, using culturally sensitive parameters, indices, scales, or tasks. All too frequently, previous work in this area has simply named the cultural group from which samples were drawn without attempting to characterize the specific features of the group that may be held to account for any similarities and differences in behaviour that are found (Berry et al., 2011; Irvine & Berry, 1984). The analysis of relationship of these contextual variables with each other, and with measures of cognitive styles and educational achievement are important for an understanding of psychological and educational processes of the Adivasi children. This section presents the outcomes of correlational analyses carried out in respect of ecocultural, socio-demographic, cultural and cognitive style variables that were employed in this work.

First, we look at the inter-correlations of cultural dimension variables. Table 7.21 presents for each of the four different subsistence groups the inter-correlation of the four variables related to cultural dimension.

Table 7.21

Inter-correlation among Cultural Dimension Variables for Different Subsistence Economy Groups

Samples and Variables	Societal Size	Social Conformity	Social Connectedness	Individual Connectedness
Hunting-gathering				
Societal size	*	0.93	0.86	0.84
Social conformity		*	0.79	0.80
Social connectedness			*	0.67
Individual connectedness				*
Dry agriculture				
Societal size	*	0.23	0.31	0.33
Social conformity		*	0.76	0.77
Social connectedness			*	0.97
Individual connectedness				*

(Table 7.21 Continued)

(Table 7.21 Continued)

Samples and Variables	Societal Size	Social Conformity	Social Connectedness	Individual Connectedness
Irrigation agriculture				
Societal size	*	0.94	0.78	0.81
Social conformity		*	0.82	0.86
Social connectedness			*	0.80
Individual connectedness				*
Wage-earning				
Societal size		−0.23	−0.16	−0.09
Social conformity		*	0.80	0.72
Social connectedness			*	0.86
Individual connectedness				*

It is to be noted that except for the correlation of societal size with other cultural variables in the WE group, all correlations are in the positive direction. While the correlation of societal size with other cultural variables (i.e., social conformity, social connectedness and individual connectedness) is of a relatively smaller magnitude in the DA and WE groups, the magnitude of all correlations in the other two groups is fairly high (correlation values ranging between 0.67 and 0.97).

This relationship of the four cultural variables in different subsistence groups carries a meaningful lesson for their treatment in cross-cultural research. In research with the HG and IA groups, the high correlation of 'societal size' and 'social conformity' may allow for their treatment as a single cluster representing a single cultural dimension. In research with the DA and WE groups, on the other hand, 'societal size' and 'social conformity' variables need to be treated as separate clusters, representing two independent cultural dimensions. In other words, the use of these two variables together as a single index of cultural variation for the whole range of subsistence populations may not be appropriate.

Inter-correlations among cognitive measures are equally interesting. Table 7.22 presents the inter-correlation of core measures of the cognitive style tasks employed in our work. These include the two tasks for differentiation (disembedding [on SPEFT] and real word repetition [on HWT]); and the four tasks for contextualization (syllogistic reasoning [on SRT]; word meaning [on UWT]; object location in the appropriate place condition [on LOTA] and object location in the inappropriate place condition [on LOTI]). The theoretical expectation was that the measures

Cognitive Style and Educational Achievement of Adivasi Children 163

Table 7.22
Inter-correlations among the Cognitive Style Measures

Measures	SPEFT	HWT	SRT	UWT	LOTA	LOTI
SPEFT	*	0.26	0.12	0.21	−0.24	−0.33
HWT		*	0.23	0.39	−0.37	−0.26
SRT			*	0.14	−0.13	−0.08
UWT				*	−0.15	−0.10
LOTA					*	0.69
LOTI						*

Note: $r = 0.10$ and above are significant.

of differentiation (SPEFT, HWT) will be positively correlated with each other, and that these differentiation tasks will be negatively correlated with the measures of contextualization (SRT, UWT, LOTA, LOTI).

The matrix of correlations reveals that the two measures of differentiation (SPEFT and HWT) are indeed positively correlated with each other as expected. The correlation between the LOTA and LOTI measures is also positive ($r = 0.69$, $p < 0.01$), but these measures are correlated negatively with SRT and UWT. On the other hand, SRT and UWT measures exhibit a positive correlation ($r = 0.14$, $p < .05$).

With respect to the relationship of the differentiation measures with those of contextualization, the findings reveal a positive correlation of SRT and UWT measures with SPEFT and HWT measures. On the other hand, there was a negative correlation of LOTA and LOTI measures with SPEFT and HWT. These correlations suggest that the measures of contextualization do not form a single cohesive cluster. Hence, a factor analysis of these measures was warranted.

We examined the pattern of coherence among the six measures used in the correlational analysis by running factor analysis. The principal components method with varimax rotation was used. The outcomes of this analysis are presented in Table 7.23.

The factor analysis revealed a three-factor interpretation to be the best outcome. Factor I was characterized by high positive loadings on the SPEFT and HWT measures. It accounted for approximately 45.7 per cent of variance in the scores; we refer to this as the 'differentiation' factor. Factor II was characterized by high positive loadings on LOTA and LOTI measures. It accounted for 13.4 per cent of the variance, and is referred to as the 'visual contextualization' factor. Factor III is characterized by high positive loadings on SRT and UWT measures, which accounted for

Table 7.23

Factor Analysis of the Cognitive Style Variables (pooled data)

	Factor Loadings		
Variables	I	II	III
SPEFT	0.74		
HWT	0.58		
LOTA		0.70	
LOTI		0.61	
SRT			0.50
UWT			0.63
% of variance explained	45.7	13.4	9.6

approximately 9.6 per cent of variance in the scores. This factor is referred to as the 'verbal contextualization' factor.

These findings provide clear and reliable evidence for the presence of three clusters of cognitive style variables, each being psychometrically distinct from others. The first factor indicating differentiation shows similar structure as noted in our previous studies (Berry et al., 1986; Mishra et al., 1996). In the present study, we proposed a new cognitive style, called contextualization. However, the contextualization variables are split into two independent factors: one is for contextualization in the visual domain; and another is for contextualization in the verbal domain. What is most important is that this factor structure is identical to the factor structure discovered in the international study with adults by using the same or similar tasks. We shall examine the implications of these cognitive style constructs later when we present a discussion of the findings.

While working with the Adivasi children, we had recorded and/ or measured a number of contextual variables. Besides the economy and gender used in our previous analyses, we have information about factors such as age, education, urban contact, parents' occupation, socialization pressure on children, societal size, social conformity, social connectedness and individual connectedness. Some of these were directly related to the child with whom we worked (e.g., their own age, education, socialization features), whereas others were related to the child's family (e.g., subsistence economy, occupation), or to the child's community (e.g., societal size, social conformity). The relationship of these contextual variables with cognitive style measures was examined. Table 7.24 presents the correlation of various contextual variables with cognitive style measures.

Table 7.24
Correlations of Contextual Variables with Cognitive Style Measures

Variables	Measures					
	SPEFT	HWT	SRT	UWT	LOTA	LOTI
Economy	0.10	0.49	0.17	0.39	−0.25	−0.10
Gender	−0.10	−0.05	−0.28	−0.11	−0.02	−0.11
Age	0.19	0.22	0.14	0.11	−0.12	−0.03
Education	0.16	0.51	0.16	0.40	−0.36	−0.19
Urban contact	0.26	0.48	0.10	0.31	−0.33	−0.27
Occupation	0.13	0.01	0.01	0.01	−0.13	−0.13
Socialization	0.14	0.43	0.13	0.31	−0.28	−0.14
Societal size	0.09	0.48	0.17	0.39	−0.22	−0.08
Social conformity	−0.21	−0.13	0.01	0.00	0.23	0.32
Social connectedness	−0.22	−0.04	0.01	0.01	0.26	0.32
Individual connectedness	−0.11	−0.01	0.04	0.03	0.27	0.30

Note: $r = 0.10$ and above are significant.

It may be noted that on the economy variable, wage-earning was scored higher than irrigation agriculture, dry agriculture, and hunting-gathering activities respectively. For gender, boys were scored higher than girls. Similarly, greater urban contact and non-traditional occupation were given higher weights than less urban contact and traditional occupation respectively.

The findings show that economy, gender, age, education, occupation, urban contact, socialization and societal size variables have a negative correlation with LOTA and LOTI measures, whereas they show a positive correlation with all other measures, except for the gender variable, which is negatively correlated with SRT, UWT, HWT and SPEFT measures. On the other hand, social conformity, social connectedness and individual connectedness are positively correlated with LOTA and LOTI measures. They also have a weak positive correlation with SRT and UWT measures, but a negative correlation with SPEFT and HWT measures.

It may also be noted that the SRT and UWT measures are positively correlated with all the variables in varying strengths except for the gender variable. Of the 66 values of correlation recorded in the table, 50 are found to be statistically significant.

The relationship of contextual variables with Educational Achievement measures was also analysed. Table 7.25 presents the values of correlation for the total score obtained in each domain of educational achievement.

Table 7.25

Correlations of Contextual Variables with Educational Achievement Measures

Variables	Language	Mathematics	Science
Economy	0.21	0.13	0.19
Gender	0.16	0.15	0.16
Age	0.22	0.07	0.10
Education	0.27	0.18	0.21
Urban contact	0.24	0.11	0.08
Occupation	0.10	0.07	0.05
Socialization	0.14	0.13	0.13
Societal size	0.19	0.14	0.15
Social conformity	−0.17	−0.07	−0.11
Social connectedness	−0.13	−0.07	−0.13
Individual connectedness	−0.11	−0.06	−0.11

Note: $r = 0.10$ and above are significant.

Generally speaking, the values of correlation are not very high. However, a positive correlation of economy, gender, age, education, urban contact, occupation, socialization and societal size variables with language, mathematics and science achievement measures is clearly in evidence. On the other hand, social conformity, social connectedness and individual connectedness show a negative correlation with all achievement measures.

The strength of correlations varies considerably across the three educational achievement measures. The values of correlation are relatively high on the Language Achievement measure (all values are significant) and moderate on the Science Achievement (9 values out of 11 are significant) as well as Mathematical Achievement (6 values out of 11 are significant) measures.

These findings suggest that all children acquire a functional level of competence not only in mathematical reasoning and language, but also in interpreting many familiar events in terms of principles, which involve scientific reasoning. Sociocultural factors tend to facilitate or arrest the development of these competencies to some extent.

The relationships of the six cognitive style measures with the three educational achievement variables were also analysed. Table 7.26 presents the value of correlations between cognitive style and educational achievement measures.

Table 7.26

Correlations between Cognitive Style and Educational Achievement Measures

Cognitive Style Measures	Achievement Measures		
	Language	Mathematics	Science
SPEFT	0.04	0.04	0.32
HWT	0.06	0.07	0.19
SRT	0.15	0.07	0.04
UWT	0.16	0.13	−0.12
LOTA	−0.17	−0.09	−0.10
LOTI	−0.14	−0.08	−0.06

Note: $r = 0.10$ and above are significant.

Although the values are not very high, all differentiation cognitive style measures show positive correlations with language, mathematics and science achievement, while two measures of contextualization (LOTA and LOTI) show a negative correlation. Language Achievement is positively and significantly correlated with SRT and HWT measures, and Mathematical Achievement with the UWT measure of contextualization.

On the other hand, Science Achievement is found to be positively correlated with SPEFT and HWT measures to a significant degree, but significantly in a negative manner with LOTA and UWT measures. It appears that contextualization in the visual domain tends to limit children's achievement in language and science, whereas differentiation facilitates achievement, particularly in science. Achievement in mathematics does not seem to be affected by any one of the cognitive style measures.

In order to have a comprehensive picture of the role of various factors examined in this work, the Multiple Regression Analysis (MRA) was carried out for all children. We had information on eleven variables of a contextual nature. These included economy, gender, age, education, urban contact, parental occupation, socialization pressure, societal size, social conformity, social connectedness and individual connectedness. These were used as predictor variables in the analysis of scores obtained by children on various tasks. A step-wise regression analysis was done, as it was difficult to specify the hierarchy of variables in terms of their potential influences for all measures.

Before presenting the MRA outcomes, it is necessary to explain the predictors, the direction of their relationship with criterion variables and some of the constraints of the analysis. Economy was scored: HG '1', DA

'2', IA '3' and WE '4'. Thus, a positive correlation would indicate that the WE group obtained a higher score. For gender, girls were scored '1' and boys '2'. Here, a positive correlation would suggest that boys obtained a higher score. Age and education were scored in terms of the number of years. Thus, a positive correlation would indicate that older and more educated children obtained a higher score. For urban contact, low contact was scored '1' and high contact '2'. Hence, a positive correlation would indicate that high contact children obtained a higher score. For occupation, traditional was scored '1' and non-traditional '2', suggesting that children of families engaged in non-traditional occupations obtained a higher score. Socialization was scored to give a positive correlation. Societal size, social conformity, social connectedness, and individual connectedness were scored as usual. For all of them, a positive relationship was indicative of the fact that those who scored high on the concerned variables obtained higher scores.

The outcomes of regression analysis for the overall sample are summarized in Table 7.27. Only the significant beta weights are presented in the table.

Table 7.27

Summary of MRA Outcomes

Variables	Significant Beta Weights								
	SPEFT	HWT	SRT	UWT	LOTA	LOTI	L ach	M ach	S ach
Economy	0.21	0.24	0.32	0.28					
Gender				0.11		−0.12	0.20		0.24
Age	0.16		0.11						
Education	0.19	0.38		0.25	−0.34	−0.21	0.43	0.19	0.32
Urban contact	0.18	0.33			−0.11	−0.22			
Occupation									
Socialization	0.17					0.15			
Societal size			0.15	0.23					
Social conformity									
Social connectedness	−0.16					0.28			
Individual connectedness					0.27			−0.13	
Per cent of variance explained	27.4	45.4	11.3	20.1	23.2	18.3	22.8	5.00	16.5

It may be noted that the prediction of scores on differentiation measures made by the economy variable has to be taken with caution. The correlation reported is of a linear relationship, but the relationship between these variables was predicted (and was found in our analyses) to be nonlinear. It was expected that for DA, IA and WE groups there would be a linear increase in scores. As noted earlier, the prediction of scores of the HG group would not fit this linear pattern. With this constraint, the MRA outcomes may be examined.

It is evident that except for occupation, all other variables have made some reliable prediction of scores on the various tasks. It is also evident that significant beta weights of different predictors vary considerably according to the specific features of the tasks. Yet, they present a fairly clear picture of the role of the contextual variables in the prediction of children's scores.

Economy contributed significantly to SPEFT, HWT, SRT and UWT. Gender contributed significantly to LOTI, UWT, Language Achievement and Science Achievement. Age made significant contributions to SPEFT and SRT. Education made significant contribution to all variables except for the SRT. Urban contact contributed significantly to SPEFT, HWT, LOTA and LOTI. Socialization contributed significantly to SPEFT and LOTI. Societal size contributed to SRT and UWT. Social connectedness contributed significantly to SPEFT and LOTI, whereas individual connectedness contributed significantly to LOTA and Mathematical Achievement.

The contribution of these variables varied from 5 per cent (Mathematical Achievement) to approximately 45 per cent (HWT). Beta weights for education were relatively stronger than those for other variables. In seven of the nine regression equations, education also appeared first in the equation. Economy appeared first in four of the nine regression equations. Urban contact was the third variable to appear frequently in regression equation; although it appeared in the first place only once in the equation, it was present as a significant variable in four regression equations.

It is possible to make some generalizations about the potential effects of these contextual variables based on these regression outcomes. In the ecocultural framework, two main input variables were proposed to influence cultural and behavioural outcomes: ecology and sociopolitical (acculturation). Viewed from all angles (appearance in MRA equations, strength of beta weights, direction of relationships, and the number of variables contributed), the acculturation variable of education turns out to be the most dominant and most pervasive influence on children's performance of both cognitive style and educational achievement tasks. The ecocultural variable of economy stands second in the hierarchy of influences. The third variable in importance is another acculturation variable, urban contact, which influences children's scores in important ways.

It should be pointed out that while the acculturation variables of education and urban contact seem to play dominant roles over the subsistence economy variable on some of the tasks, they have not been able to displace it as a source of influence. This observation corresponds with the findings from many previous studies of the relationship between subsistence economy strategy and measures of the differentiation cognitive style. Across variations in subsistence ranging from Arctic and Australian hunters to African and New Guinea farmers (Berry, 1976), and from Central African hunters and farmers (Berry et al., 1986) to Adivasi hunters and farmers (Mishra et al., 1996), the findings from the present study with the Adivasi children provide general confirmation of our predictions of children's cognitive style and educational achievements from the economic subsistence variable. In addition, this pattern of findings corresponds well with the finding presented in Chapter 6 on the development of cognitive style among adults that vary in their ecocultural and acculturation contexts.

As in these previous studies, in the present work the impact on cognitive style and educational achievements from contact with outside cultures (acculturation in the ecocultural framework, such as through formal schooling, wage employment and urban living) has also been shown to be important. In addition to these two exogenous variables of subsistence economy and contact with other cultures, the present study has shown that other exogenous variables also play a role in the patterning of cognitive style and educational achievement. What is of particular importance to note is that the prediction of all cognitive style and educational achievement variables has largely been in the direction that was generally anticipated from the ecocultural framework. This provides us with a strong evidence of predictive validity of children's scores on different tasks based on the knowledge of subsistence economy as well as of the acculturation experiences of the groups.

8
Revisiting the Culture–Cognition Relationship

Introduction

In the two preceding chapters, we presented and discussed the analyses carried out on several measures of cultural and cognitive dimensions. We also outlined the differences on these dimensions among groups, the direction of their differences, and the relationships between the ecological, cultural, acculturation and cognitive style dimension variables. In addition, we examined the probability of predicting cognitive performances from the knowledge of the ecological, cultural and acculturation features of the groups. In this chapter, we will examine the findings of our work from the theoretical perspective of the relationship between culture and cognition based on the ecocultural framework that was outlined in Chapter 2. Since we consider these findings useful for working towards an educational policy for the Adivasi children, this educational policy will be discussed in the next chapter in which we examine the implications of our findings for education of the Adivasi children in general, but especially for those who belong to the more traditional Adivasi communities.

It may be noted at the very outset that the analyses performed on various tasks used for the assessment of both cultural and psychological phenomena have produced a relatively complex set of results. However, in keeping with the ecocultural perspective it is fairly clear that subsistence economic activities, with which people engage in their day-to-day lives, play a crucial role in producing differences in cultural features of groups and psychological (cognitive) characteristics of children brought up in those contexts. These characteristics are clearly reflected even among the adult groups we have worked with. The patterning of gender difference in psychological makeup of children also seems to be linked with the cultural demands placed on boys and girls in different subsistence societies. On the other hand, the differences noted between boys and girls in different subsistence groups are mediated by the cognitive characteristics of the tasks so much so that gender differences do not always appear to be in one direction (i.e., in favour of a particular gender group) on all measures of the tasks.

It is also clear that, as expected from the ecocultural framework, contact with other cultures has brought about acculturation (particularly through schooling and urban experience), and that this in turn has influenced the cognitive style development and cognitive task performance of both the Adivasi children and adults in the international study. As in previous research using this framework (Berry, 1976a; Berry et al., 1986; Mishra & Berry, 2008; Mishra et al., 1996), the two exogenous variables (ecology and sociopolitical inputs) both play a role in the development of cognitive style.

There are seven broad questions that were raised at the beginning of this work. These questions emerge directly from the theoretical model that deals with the relationships among ecology, culture, acculturation and cognition (presented in Chapter 2). The first question concerns the evidence to support the existence of *societal size* and *social conformity* as two independent cultural dimensions that show variable relationship with subsistence strategies of the groups. The second question is about the existence of two cognitive dimensions of *differentiation* (intra-unit distinctiveness) and *contextualization* (extra-unit connectedness) as two independent and mutually exclusive cognitive processes. The third question concerns the relationship of cultural dimensions of societal size and social conformity with the cognitive style dimensions of differentiation and contextualization. The fourth question is about the relationship of subsistence strategies and acculturation features of the groups with the cognitive style variables of differentiation and contextualization. The fifth question is about the relationship of different cultural and cognitive style variables with the educational achievement of children reflected in the domains of language, mathematics and science. The sixth question concerns the patterning of gender difference in different subsistence groups on cognitive style tasks and educational achievement measures. The seventh issue is how the findings from the Adivasi work fit into the broader context of the international work. In addition to these questions of theoretical and academic interest, the last, but perhaps the most crucial, question concerns the utility of all this knowledge for educational purposes of the Adivasi children in India, and perhaps for children of the indigenous groups elsewhere in the world.

We will take up these theoretical and practical questions for discussion in this chapter. The last question concerning the implication of our findings for education of the Adivasi children will be addressed in the next chapter.

Cultural Dimensions

With regard to the first question of the existence of cultural dimensions of 'societal size' and 'social conformity', and their variable relationship with subsistence strategies, the results are generally in support of their existence as well as their linkage with ecology. In the Adivasi study, societal size has been found to show a systematic progressive increase from the HG to WE subsistence through DA and IA. The magnitude of increase from one subsistence strategy to another is also almost uniform (see Figure 7.2). On the other hand, the relationship of social conformity with subsistence strategies was curvilinear: social conformity was found to be low in the HG and WE samples, but high in the DA and IA groups. The amount of increase in social conformity from the HG to DA level groups, and the amount of decrease from the IA to WE level groups are particularly noteworthy (see Figure 7.2). These patterns are consistent with the analyses of Lomax and Berkowitz (1972), which provides some cross-validation for our measures of these two dimensions.

In addition to these two previously studied dimensions of cultural adaptation to ecology, we created and assessed two new dimensions: individual connectedness and social connectedness. Both these dimensions showed a curvilinear pattern that is similar to the dimension of social conformity (see Figure 7.3). Although the level of social connectedness is clearly higher than that of individual connectedness, the pattern of their relationship with subsistence strategies is identical. Both are found to be low in the HG and WE groups, and high in the IA and DA groups respectively.

The four cultural variables reveal an interesting pattern of similarities and differences. The HG and IA groups have low scores on all four cultural variables of societal size, social conformity, social connectedness and individual connectedness. In the DA and IA groups, all four scores increase, but much more so for social and individual connectedness. And while these three scores drop for the WE group, the societal size variable continues its linear increase. These findings show that all four cultural dimensions are similarly low in the HG group, but diverge in the other three groups.

The lesson from these findings is clear: the treatment of 'societal size' and 'social conformity' variables together as a single index of cultural variation is problematic for this whole range of subsistence adaptations. As noted in Chapter 3, this single dimension became questioned by new research, and so was replaced by the two dimensions used in the present study. Although this single dimension may be appropriate for research comparing hunting and gathering with agricultural societies (as for example in the earlier work of Berry, 1976a), the two dimensions are clearly more appropriate when extending this range of subsistence activities beyond them.

Cognitive Dimensions

Cognitive dimensions have received a more detailed treatment in our work by virtue of their association with a domain, which is relatively more easily amenable to psychological assessment. In psychological research, differentiation and contextualization have been identified as two different cognitive styles. Both differentiation and contextualization styles have been researched for many decades in general, and in cross-cultural research in particular. In differentiation, the individual starts with a well-organized cognitive unit (e.g., a complex figure in the EFT), which supplies the larger context, and is asked to differentiate out a part of it (e.g., a simple figure in the test). Taken in this sense, a differentiation cognitive style can be defined in terms of the fluency with which the internal aspects of a cognitive unit are separated from one another. Hence, it was referred to as 'intra-unit distinctiveness'. The differentiation style stands in sharp contrast to the contextualization style, which is evident when individuals try to link a cognitive unit (e.g., deductive reasoning problems such as the ones used by Luria) to other information outside that unit. Hence, it was referred to as 'extra-unit connectedness'.

Our focus in this book has been on the understanding of both the differentiation and contextualization cognitive styles. Viewed from the theoretical perspective presented in Chapter 3, one would expect a negative relationship of differentiation measures with contextualization measures—an expectation, which was not fully borne out by our findings in this work. Correlational analyses reveal that the two differentiation measures (SPEFT and HWT) are negatively correlated only with the LOT measures, which taps contextualization in the visual domain. With the other two measures of contextualization (SRT and UWT, which tap contextualization in the verbal domain), the relationship of both the differentiation measures has been found to be positive, which goes against our expectation.

Factor analytic treatment of the data provides some organization to the correlational picture obtained for cognitive style measures. In the work with the international groups, a three-factor solution of various measures turned out to be the best outcome. The first factor loaded the EFT and HWT, both of which were used as measures of 'differentiation'. A second factor loaded on LOT (one of the contextualization tasks), while a third factor loaded the SRT and UWT (the other contextualization tasks).

In the work with the Adivasi children also, we find a similar pattern of factor loadings. The analysis brought out three distinct factors. The first factor has high positive loadings on SPEFT and HWT measures. This factor clearly defines 'differentiation'. On the other hand, 'contextualization' does not turn out to be a unitary process; the tasks measuring contextualization dimension contribute to two independent factors. One has a significant positive loading on LOT measures, indicating visual contextualization; another, representing verbal contextualization, has a significant positive loading on SRT and UWT (i.e., the measures in which information have to be processed at the semantic level).

The degree of similarity noted in factor structure of measures between the international and the Adivasi children's studies is large. These outcomes bring out differentiation as a clear cognitive dimension. On the other hand, contextualization does not appear to be as neat a cognitive dimension as it has been generally conceptualized in studies carried out in the cognitive research tradition. While the status of differentiation remains unchanged, the scope of contextualization is narrowed by the organization of its measures into two separate independent factors, one contributing to visual measures (LOT) and another to verbal measures (SRT and UWT).

The findings of the work with both the international adult groups and the Adivasi children clearly indicate that contextualization is not a unitary process. The employment of this process presents evidence of considerable variation on tasks, which make use of visual (e.g., LOT) and verbal (SRT and UWT) stimuli. Contextualization is clearly in evidence on the visual measure. All discrepancy scores between LOTA and LOTI have been found to be in the expected direction. The level of discrepancy obtained for various samples also corresponds to the general prediction that was made in this respect.

In the case of verbal tasks, however, the evidence for contextualization is weak. For example, in the work with the Adivasi children, we find no difference in reasoning between familiar and unfamiliar problems of the SRT, although in the adult international groups the difference in reasoning between the two sets of problems is significant. The Adivasi children of all subsistence economy groups made very few requests for extra information on the SRT irrespective of the familiar or unfamiliar type of problems, a finding which is inconsistent with our expectation. On the other hand, a different pattern of performance is displayed by the Adivasi children on the UWT. On the 'request' measure of this task, the scores of the HG group are higher than those of the IA and WE groups, indicating greater contextualization in the case of children whose parents engage in hunting-gathering based economic activities.

How can we account for this unexpected differential pattern of responding to SRT and UWT? In the case of the Adivasi children, a probable reason can be traced back in their cultural life experiences. Verbal riddles are popularly used as a means of entertainment in almost all the Adivasi communities. They are considered as 'amplifiers' of children's intellectual processes (Mishra, 2005; Mishra & Sinha, 1998). It is possible that the familiarity of children with such riddles, which involve verbal reasoning type problems, helped them in processing syllogisms on the SRT in a decontextualized manner. They possibly treated the cognitive unit (conclusions on the SRT) in isolation from the background information. For example, they might have reasoned, 'Whatever soolems are, they won't grow well at Reetug, wherever it is'. It appears that on this task comprehension factor was seemingly more active in influencing children's responses than the context of the syllogism.

In the case of UWT, where the meaning of unknown words was to be guessed, a clear understanding of the context was essentially required. Requests for repetition of stories were made in order to comprehend their contexts. The tendency to process syllogisms in a decontextualized manner and stories in a contextualized manner presents us with findings, which go against the theoretical expectation. On the 'reasoning' and 'meaning' measures of the SRT and UWT, the HG group provides evidence for lesser contextualization as compared to other groups. In view of this, the manifestation of contextualization in task performance, at least in the case of the Adivasi children of different subsistence groups, needs to be considered with caution.

Evidence for selective engagement with cognitive processes, as described previously is not something new. It has been found to be in place in other studies in which cognitive development has been examined in an ecocultural perspective. For example, Dasen and Mishra (2010) in their studies of spatial frames of reference noted that in locations where the egocentric and geocentric spatial frames were potentially available (e.g., in Bali, Varanasi and Kathmandu), the participants clearly made choices between the two frames. Based on such observations they concluded: 'People have, as it were, the "choice", in so far as they have at their disposal, at the linguistic and the cognitive levels, both of the frames, and, depending on the situation, they activate one or the other. Sometimes they even activate one, but explain it by the other' (Dasen & Mishra, 2010, p. 297). Such a 'choice' indicates that individuals are equipped with all basic processes needed for dealing with problems encountered in their respective ecocultural contexts. This substantiates their status as psychological universals, a notion that claims that all psychological processes are present, but become active in culturally appropriate circumstances. However, which process is chosen and used more frequently, or even predominantly, in solving a cognitive problem may depend on several factors of which 'task demands' are most important.

Subsistence Economy and Cognitive Style Dimensions

The relationship between culture and cognition has been conceptualized in a number of ways (Berry & Dasen, 1974). The issue appears to be more complicated when this relationship is traced developmentally (see Dasen et al., 1979; Mishra, 1998a; Mishra, Sinha & Berry, 1999). A convenient and value-neutral way of comprehending the relationship of culture and cognition is to approach it through the analysis of day-to-day activities people carry out in their respective environments, using the perspective of 'indigenous cognition' (Berry, 1987). As we have indicated earlier, these environments not only place various cognitive demands on individuals for successful living, but also provide them with opportunities for the acquisition, development and mastery of various cognitive abilities to different degrees in order to carry out their daily activities (Mishra, 2001, 2011a, 2011b).

It was from this ecocultural perspective of human behaviour that the differing patterns of relationship of cognitive differentiation and contextualization with subsistence strategies of groups were predicted (see Chapter 3). The data analyses present us with results that are congruent with the theoretical expectation of a curvilinear relationship made with respect to differentiation. In the international study, it was expected that the hunting and gathering groups would be high on differentiation, the farming groups would be low and the urban group would be high. In the Adivasi children's study, it was expected that the HG and WE groups would be high on this dimension, whereas DA and IA groups would show low and moderate levels of differentiation respectively. The findings obtained on the visual disembedding measures (EFT and SPEFT) as well as the verbal disembedding measure (HWT) support these expectations.

In contrast, the findings obtained with respect to the contextualization cognitive style are relatively less consistent. In the work with the international adult groups, the findings of the syllogistic reasoning task (with both familiar and unfamiliar content) showed a pattern of low scores for the hunting and gathering groups, and increasingly high scores for the agricultural and urban groups. In contrast, the performance on the visual task requiring the search times for the identification of objects in the appropriate and inappropriate locations showed a curvilinear pattern. The hunting, gathering and urban groups had lower scores, while the farming groups had relatively high scores.

In the work with the Adivasi children, while the prediction about agricultural groups finds support on four out of five measures, the prediction about the WE group is confirmed only on two of the five measures. The prediction about HG group is supported by only one of the five measures (i.e., the 'request' measure of the UWT). These observations do not allow us to draw any general conclusion regarding the relationship of contextualization with subsistence economic activities of cultural groups. At best, we can say that children from agricultural societies engage in contextual processing of information more than the children of other subsistence societies.

The level of contextualization in other Adivasi groups appears to be 'task-specific'. For example, the WE group showed low contextualization on the LOT (discrepancy measure) and UWT (request measure), whereas the HG group showed more contextualization on the UWT (request measure). Theoretically, the predictive validity of UWT appears to be higher than that of the other two tasks of contextualization (i.e., LOT and SRT). In order to say anything conclusive about this cognitive style dimension, therefore, we need to evolve other alternative strategies for its assessment. The present analyses make the prediction tenable only for the agricultural groups.

Cultural and Cognitive Style Dimensions

The relationship of cultural variables with cognitive performance has attracted the attention of psychologists for several decades. The issue has remained active all through the past decades (Tomasello, 1999a, 1999b). In the discipline of cognitive science, this relationship is now being postulated and examined under the rubric of 'cognitive ecology' (Hutchins, 2010). Proposals have been made for the analysis of 'cultural cognitive ecosystems' for understanding human cognition (Hutchins, 2014). A relatively strong version of this proposition is the idea that cognition is fundamentally cultural (Bender & Beller, 2013).

Although these recent theoretical assertions are useful, in empirical analyses variables like societal size or social connectedness have neither been implicated directly and nor have they been assessed and quantified. Only the social conformity variable has received some serious attention, particularly in the context of the study of socialization in different ecocultural settings (see Berry, 1966, 1967, 1976; Berry et al., 1959, 1986; Mishra & Singh, 2008; Mishra et al., 1996). The social connectedness and individual connectedness variables are relatively new in research on cognition.

The relationship among the four cultural variables has already been examined. They are generally related positively with each other in all groups except for the WE group. However, to examine the relationship of these cultural variables with cognitive style variables in the case of the Adivasi children, an overall index for each one of them was prepared and the same was correlated with the scores obtained by overall groups on different cognitive style measures.

Broadly speaking, the variables of social conformity, social connectedness and individual connectedness yield correlations with cognitive style measures that are generally in the expected direction. All these variables are correlated negatively with differentiation measures, whereas they are correlated positively with contextualization measures. These relationships suggest that high social conformity, social connectedness and individual connectedness are likely to interfere with the development of differentiation as earlier concluded by Witkin (Witkin & Berry, 1975; Witkin et al., 1962), but promote the development of contextualization among children.

The relationship of societal size with cognitive style variables has turned out to be somewhat problematic. Societal size is correlated positively with measures of differentiation and the two (verbal) measures of contextualization, whereas its relationship with visual measures of contextualization is negative. These findings suggest that with an increase in societal size, a corresponding increase in the levels of differentiation and verbal contextualization also takes place. It is on the visual task alone that the societal size is negatively linked with contextualization. Hence, a distinction between visual and verbal tasks as measures of contextualization (as evidenced in the factor analyses) seems to be important, and this needs to be maintained in future studies. It will be rewarding to devise some other tasks for measuring visual and verbal aspects of contextualization, and examine their relationship with cultural and cognitive style variables.

Culture, Cognitive Style and Educational Achievement

From developmental as well as educational points of view, the search for relationships of cultural and cognitive style variables with children's educational achievement in language, mathematics and science has been an important pursuit of the present study; this is because it has direct policy implications for the education of the Adivasi children. The relationship of cultural variables with educational achievement measures examined in the work with the Adivasi children reveals that societal size is positively correlated with all achievement measures (i.e., language, mathematics and science), whereas the other three cultural variables (i.e., social conformity, social connectedness and individual connectedness) are correlated negatively. This pattern of correlation suggests that the probability of acquiring competence in and/or displaying them in different domains of educational achievement will be higher for children of the communities characterized by higher societal size. On the other hand, children of the communities characterized by greater social conformity, social connectedness and individual connectedness are likely to develop and/or display a lower level of competence in these domains of educational achievement.

The relationship of cognitive style variables with educational achievement measures reveals that differentiation as a factor is more important for educational achievement in science than in the domains of language and mathematics. Contextualization, as revealed on the visual measures of LOT, appears to be linked to lower levels of achievement in all educational domains. Reasoning (on SRT) is especially important for language achievement. Word meaning (on UWT) facilitates achievement in language and mathematics, but restricts the level of achievement in science.

Knowledge of these cognitive variables can be helpful in predicting the domains of achievement in which the Adivasi children can acquire and display greater competence, particularly when they attend school and pursue educational goals in life. This issue will be taken up for discussion in the next chapter when we bring out the educational implications of our work with the Adivasi children. For the present, it may be concluded that both the cultural and cognitive characteristics of children contain important clues for understanding their achievement in the domains of language, mathematics as well as science. Anyone concerned with developing educational policy for the Adivasi children has to be cognizant of and sensitive to the cultural characteristics of different Adivasi groups and of the cognitive characteristics of children belonging to those groups.

Gender, Cognitive Processing and Educational Achievement

Gender issues represent an important topic of public and academic discussion, and the education of girls belonging to 'underdeveloped' sections of the Indian population has posed serious challenges to education planners and policy makers in India for decades (Anandalakshmy, 1994). Gender differences in cognitive abilities have been analysed in several studies from early on (e.g., Berry, 1966, 1974, 1976; Sinha, 1980) and more recently (e.g., Caplan, Crawford, Hyde, & Richardson, 1997; Halpern, 2012; Mishra & Singh, 2008).

Decades ago, Maccoby and Jacklin (1974) addressed the issue of sex differences in great detail by summarizing the findings of large number of studies in a comprehensive volume. The magnitude of difference often was found to be too small to mark any significant difference between boys and girls. During the late childhood period (i.e., 6–11 years), the evidence of gender difference also appeared to be rather complicated. However, Maccoby and Jacklin (1974) concluded that a slight but consistent sex difference in verbal skills favouring women seemed to be demonstrated throughout the lifespan. The issue of sex differences in cognitive abilities still continues to be addressed and interpreted in terms of biological and sociocultural processes (see Halpern, 2012).

On the other hand, the review of studies dealing with sex difference in the performance of EFT and other tasks of differentiation (van Leeuwen, 1978) indicates that sex difference in performance cannot be accepted as a rule. Variables such as ecological pressures, social conformity and social pressures largely account for such differences in performance. For example, in nomadic hunting and gathering societies, sex differences are not at all evident (Berry, 1966; Mac Arthur, 1967), whereas they are noted quite often in studies carried out in agricultural societies (Berry, 1976; Shrestha & Mishra, 1996; Sinha, 1980). Sex role differentiation and greater pressure for social conformity on girls during socialization years seem to be largely responsible for sex differences in cognition in agricultural societies.

When we examine the findings of our work with the Adivasi children from this perspective, a moderate degree of evidence for gender difference in performance of children is found to be in place. In 8 of the 15 analyses of variance in which the gender variable was implicated, the main effect of gender was found to be significant; and in four of these instances, the interaction effect of gender and subsistence economy was also significant. The interaction effect of economy and gender suggests that gender difference seemingly has some cultural roots or routes. In our work, we notice that gender difference was generally non-existent in the HG group, less frequently evident in the WE sample, but more commonly in the DA and IA groups, indicating that gender difference is much more likely to take place in the agriculture-based societies than in other societies. This pattern suggests a link to the cultural dimensions of social conformity and individual and social connectedness. This largely reconfirms the findings of previous studies (Shrestha & Mishra, 1996; Sinha, 1980) carried out in India and Nepal regarding gender difference in psychological differentiation.

With respect to the direction of gender difference, the findings suggest the scores of girls generally to be higher than those of the boys on differentiation as well as contextualization measures. This finding for differentiation is inconsistent with those generally (but not always) reported in other studies. On the other hand, there is also some evidence to suggest that gender difference in psychological differentiation in rural Indian children, particularly in relation to socialization variables, is generally not present up to the age of adolescence (Mishra & Singh, 2008).

The direction of gender difference obtained on cognitive style measures (girls scoring higher than boys) in the case of the Adivasi children, however, becomes reversed on the measures of educational achievement.

Here, the scores of boys are generally higher than those of the girls. While early maturation of girls in the childhood years (see Halpern, 2012; Waber, 1977) can be partly held responsible for their higher scores on differentiation and contextualization measures, the higher score of boys than that of girls on educational achievement measures may be attributed to greater exposure to schooling and greater parental encouragement for school achievement for boys, particularly in the WE groups. It appears that differences in the level of acculturation of boys and girls are more responsible for differences in the level of their educational achievement than any other factor.

The socialization of boys and girls in the Adivasi communities constitutes an interesting area that has been very little studied. It is only on the basis of an in-depth empirical analysis that the mechanisms of gender difference reflected on various cognitive and educational achievement measures could be precisely known. As far as the independent gender effects are concerned, they are commonly evident on contextualization measures more often than on differentiation or educational achievement measures. From this pattern of results, it may be argued that in the Adivasi cultures, contextualized cognition is a more typical characteristic of the girls than of the boys, and that its roots and mechanisms can be discovered in the socialization process of children in the Adivasi communities.

Relationship between Adivasi and International Work

One of the goals of our work was to situate the findings with the Adivasi children within a broader international context. This was done by using similar concepts and measures in both studies, thus allowing some degree of comparability between them. We might have carried out work only with the Adivasi children, and then compared the findings with extant findings that are available in the general literature. Had we done this, we would have found a fair amount of consistency between previous findings and those with the Adivasi children. However, because not all cultural and cognitive measures were the same in previous work, it would have been difficult to say whether the patterns were really similar or different. But because we used the same concepts to assess the contexts, and many of the same measures to assess cognition, we are able to make a more direct comparison between the two studies. This allows us to conclude that the

Adivasi children fit rather well into the broader findings about systematic relationships between ecology, culture, acculturation and cognition. This conclusion is particularly clear with respect to the factorial structure of the cognitive styles, where similar factors were found in the performance of Adivasi children and international adults across range of subsistence strategies. It is also clear with respect to the broad pattern of relationships among all the major dimensions (ecology, culture, acculturation and cognition) in our work.

Concluding Comments

In this chapter, the major issues and findings emerging from our work with international adult groups and the Adivasi children have been reviewed and synthesized. In addition, there are a few other points that need to be addressed in order to bring out the implications of the work in more clear terms. It may be recalled that a major assumption underlying the organization of our work with the Adivasi and international adults was that subsistence strategies of societies and their individual members tend to generate certain unique cultural patterns to which individuals adapt by developing some appropriate psychological characteristics. Hence, subsistence economy was used as one of the two exogenous variables in this work, and groups were selected with a view to show considerable variation on this variable. In the case of the Adivasi children, in 13 of the 15 ANOVA outcomes was subsistence economy found to have significant effect on the performance of children. In the regression analysis also, subsistence economy made significant contributions to SPEFT, HWT, SRT and UWT scores. While the contributions on different tasks showed considerable variation, the contribution of subsistence economy to differentiation measures was relatively larger than its contribution to contextualization measures. These findings suggest that the long-lasting adaptations of individuals to their ecology play a vital role in the development and deployment of cognitive processes of differentiation and contextualization. In our previous research with the Adivasi children and adults in India (Mishra et al., 1996), we had noted a similar pattern of relationship in results. The long-standing effects of ecology on cognitive functioning of groups were found to be significant even after controlling all other factors. The recent acculturation experiences of groups were not able to displace the effects of ecology.

The second exogenous variable in the ecocultural framework is that of contact with outside cultures, resulting in acculturation taking place. In Chapter 4, we noted that education and urban contact variables covary with subsistence economy. In the case of the Adivasi children, the HG group was placed at the lowest end on both these acculturation variables, whereas the WE group was placed at the highest end. In regression analysis, however, both education and urban contact were found to make significant contributions to several cognitive measures. The role of education was particularly remarkable; it contributed significantly to all variables except for the SRT.

Despite having a pervasive influence on cognitive variables with relatively strong beta weights, however, education could not altogether displace the effect of subsistence economy on the cognitive performance and educational achievement of the Adivasi children. The urban contact variable also failed to displace the potential effect of subsistence economy. These results further strengthen our belief that long-term ecological adaptations of groups are as important in producing patterns of cognitive functioning among individuals as are the relatively more recent and clearly observable influences of education and urban contact. Thus, in any appraisal of the cognitive abilities, cognitive style and educational achievement of the Adivasi children, this particular dimension requires serious attention.

9
Adivasi Education in Cultural Context

Adivasi in the National Context

The relevance of psychological research to address the pressing problems of Indian society and the nation has been raised in a number of publications for the last several decades (Berry, Mishra, & Tripathi, 2003; Mishra, 2009; Sinha, 1973, 1975; Tripathi, 1988). Psychologists working in the western part of the world have also expressed similar concerns about the relevance of their research to the people of the Third World countries (Berry, 1995; Berry, Mishra, & Tripathi, 2003; Dasen, Berry, & Sartorius, 1988; Jahoda, 1973, 1975; Wagner, 1986, 1988, 2015). In developing nations, now called the 'majority world' (Dasen & Akkari, 2008), which confront a variety of social problems (such as poverty, and educational and social inequality), psychologists are expected to do research not merely for the satisfaction of academic curiosities, which by itself is a noble goal of the social as well as the physical sciences. The expectation is also that psychologists will engage in research activities with a sense of social responsibility and address research to the pressing problems of their society and nation, which can allow them a key player's role in social policy formulations (Tripathi & Sinha, 2014). Any research which does not address the application of its findings to practical problems, therefore, fails to fulfil its social and national obligations.

Our main focus in this book has been on the ecological, cultural and acculturation factors that underlie the cognitive functioning and educational achievements of the Adivasi children. For generations, the Adivasi peoples in India have been primarily concerned with the satisfaction of their basic needs. They were mainly dependent on forest resources for livelihood. They had their traditional family or community based institutions which imparted necessary knowledge and skills required for meeting the daily needs of life. These institutions played a vital role in the lives of the Adivasi children by providing them with economically viable and culturally meaningful life sustaining skills. The Adivasi groups managed to live their traditional life for centuries without having any major contact with the members of the larger groups of the Indian society.

After the country gained independence from the British rule in 1947, concerted plans (called Five Year Plans) were developed and executed at the national level for achieving different developmental goals (e.g., education, health, poverty, etc.). In every Five Year Plan since then, special provisions and budget allocations have been made for achieving the proposed objectives. Several new departments have been created in the central and state governments, as well as at the district level administration for the management of education, health and socio-economic development-related needs of 'weaker sections' of the society, including the people of the Adivasi groups.

As a result of these activities of the federal and state governments, the life of the Adivasi people in India has witnessed considerable change during the last decades (Mishra, 1996, 2008, 2015). Among many others, formal education through schooling is one of these activities, which can be claimed to have played a vital role in this process. As a social process, it has led to 'capacity building' and nurtured the Adivasi society by preparing children and adults to function in different spheres of life more effectively than before.

In spite of all good efforts made at the national level, social inequalities in the case of the Adivasi people still stand out clearly when we look at some basic indicators of human development. Most Adivasi people still represent groups that are 'weakest among the weak' (Singh & Jabbi, 1995). Government has recognized them as one of the most deprived and marginalized sections of the Indian society. Census data indicate an uneven level of educational achievement of the Adivasi groups in different states and across various Adivasi groups within the same states. For example, some states (e.g., Meghalaya, Mizoram, Nagaland) have done very well with respect to the literacy of the Adivasi populations, while many other states (e.g., Chhattisgarh, Jharkhand, Madhya Pradesh) are still struggling hard with the problem of literacy (Census of India, 2011). Since literacy has been equated with freedom, economic development, and even civilization (Wagner, 2010), the long standing priority and urgency of education of the Adivasi children have been reaffirmed in the policy document, 'Right of the Children to Free and Compulsory Education Act 2009'. Intervention through *Sarva Shiksha Abhiyan* (Education for All programme) in the last decade has resulted in positive trends in the Adivasi children's enrolment at schools.

While the national statistics presents us with some evidence for change in school enrolment, the 'quality of education' for a huge population of children in remote rural Adivasi settings still remains an issue of serious concern. Absence of the basic minimum facilities in schools is one of the major concerns commonly shared by researchers from the disciplines of education and psychology. Mishra (1999) indicates that many schools lack even such basic infrastructure as classrooms, black boards and safe drinking water. Teachers and their motivation to work with the Adivasi children are other important concerns. How can we think of effective learning outcome for children in the face of these limitations of basic resources? Hence, it is not surprising to find a high percentage of the Adivasi children dropping from school at some point of time during the early years of primary education (i.e., between Grades 1 and 5). Addressing these basic issues of school education, especially in remote rural Adivasi settings, is an essential step towards ensuring their development (Mishra, 2008; Sinha & Mishra, 1997).

Improvement in the education of the Adivasi children, thus, represents the goal, which still remains largely unfulfilled. Besides the government, several NGOs have also shown an interest and active involvement in this sphere. They have continued to work in the Adivasi regions for decades either by putting their own resources to work, or by using the resources made available by the government departments. In spite of all these good efforts, success achieved with respect to education of the Adivasi children remains much below the expected level even today (Mishra & Joshi, 2015).

A number of factors have been pointed out to account for the limited success of educational programmes in Adivasi society (Mishra, 2007, 2008; Mishra & Joshi, 2015; Mishra & Sinha, 1998; Singh, 1996). Many factors suggested in these studies are of a non-psychological nature (e.g., economic pressures, lack of resources, accessibility of schools). On the other hand, some researchers have also indicated that a general disregard of the socio-cultural context, within which the goals of education, health and sociocultural development have been pursued, is a crucial factor accounting for a low level of success of the programmes (Mishra, 2008; Sinha & Mishra, 1998).

Education and National Development

Much has been written about education and its role in the development of individuals and groups all over the world. The goals, forms, contents, modes of delivery and other aspects of education present considerable variation across as well as within many cultures (Dasen & Akkari, 2008). That schooling produces any new cognitive processes among individuals seems to be doubtful (Mishra & Dasen, 2004). However, that schooling increases the possibility of the existing cognitive processes and skills of children and adults to be applied to other situations is a generally accepted conclusion. There is also evidence to suggest that in unfamiliar encounters, schooling makes people feel more at ease because of which educated people can control and manage the affairs of their life more effectively than those who have not been to school (Mishra & Dasen, 2004). It is in this sense that school education is believed to lead to general 'empowerment' that gets manifested in individuals' functioning in several domains of life such as personal, social, economic and work. These positive influences of education are also perceived and acknowledged to a considerable extent by parents and other members of the community whose children participate in schools (Mishra, 1996b; Serpell, 1993).

The above-mentioned observations of researchers, who have worked with children of weaker, marginalized and remote rural communities in different parts of the world, generally find support from the findings of the studies carried out with Adivasi children in India. Parents of hunting-gathering as well as agricultural Adivasi societies perceive several benefits of school-based education, children's personal development being the most important among them. Parents generally indicate better economic possibilities (i.e., wage employment) and a better future for children; they also imagine a better life for children, including the greater chance of their movement away from home along with enhanced feelings of self-efficacy and empowerment (Mishra, 1996a; Mishra & Joshi, 2015). Thus, the idea that school education prepares future generations for change in any society gets resonated in the responses of the Adivasi parents in studies.

In psychological research, a distinction has been made between 'cognitive' and 'non-cognitive' effects of schooling (Mishra, 1996b). The cognitive effects are observed in the form of specific knowledge and general reasoning skills that children acquire while they negotiate life in schools. The non-cognitive effects are observed in the form of changes in beliefs, attitudes and values towards work, society and life in general. That school education can impart knowledge and skills to enhance chances for wage employment and improve economic conditions of individuals, and that it can prepare children to accept many responsibilities as adults in the society are the facts deeply realized by the Adivasi parents (Mishra & Joshi, 2015). Research indicates that Adivasi parents perceive children, village and their community as closely interlinked. They also believe that development of children can be instrumental in ameliorating the conditions of their own personal lives more than the lives of their family and community.

Mishra and Joshi (2015) indicate that such an optimism of parents is often not without preconditions. Children's engagement in economic activities and childcare responsibilities, possibly due to the lack of resources available with families, appear as important barriers in children's attendance at schools. Similarly, several factors have been suggested to be responsible for children's dropping out of schools. These factors include less attractiveness of schools, irregularity of teachers, children's difficulties in adapting to school environment (e.g., staying whole day in school surrounding) and inaccessibility of schools. It may indeed be difficult for psychologists to deal with economic conditions of people, but the latter set of factors are certainly manageable. What the findings of studies with the Adivasi people ask for is the ecologically appropriate and culturally sensitive processes of teaching and learning. In a review of studies carried out with primary school students, Mishra (1998) noted that a culturally sensitive and motivated teacher was a far more important factor in children's achievement in schools than physical conditions of schools, or economic conditions of children's families.

Education of children of the Adivasi groups is still a highly debated issue in India more or less similar to the issue of education of the Native, Indigenous or Aboriginal groups in other parts of the world. Research with the Adivasi children clearly suggests that their cognitive functioning has to be viewed and evaluated taking into consideration their ecological and cultural contexts, which place very different demands before them in daily life. Because of differences in the demands of ecology, the patterning of cognitive abilities of the Adivasi children shows considerable variation from those of other groups. A related and more important finding is that the Adivasi children are neither culturally inferior nor cognitively less competent than the children of other groups. Instead, many of their skills and abilities are highly developed and extremely sophisticated.

Whether education of the Adivasi children is effective or not, inroads from schools have been already made into the life of the Adivasi communities in India. The problems of children's enrolment in and drop out of school can be managed by paying careful attention to their ecological conditions, cultural contexts and cognitive strengths (Mishra, 2007). Sinha and Mishra (1997), based on a review of studies carried out with the Adivasi children and adults, have concluded that only an ecologically valid, culturally meaningful, economically viable and locally useful form of school education stands a chance of success in the Adivasi communities. Education that can build up culturally nurtured cognitive strengths of children of these communities can enhance their skills for negotiation of life in most effective ways in their respective cultural environments.

Culture-based Adivasi Education

The significance of the above-mentioned research findings for education and development of the Adivasi children are clear. A programme of school education which does not pay attention to the ecological, cultural and psychological characteristics of the Adivasi children is highly unlikely to make any significant impact. The educational pattern of the dominant non-Adivasi population is of very limited value in the Adivasi cultural milieu, because it does not match with the culturally nurtured cognitive skills and abilities of children, lifestyles of their families and needs of the Adivasi communities.

Researchers have described several qualities of the Adivasi children, which are highly desirable not only for participation in and success at school, but also outside the school. For example, the Adivasi students are more assertive, venturesome, imaginative, experimenting, emotionally stable and practical than non-Adivasi students (Srivastava, 1983). They also have an accepting, emotionally supportive and positively involved family (Singh, 1996), which has a positive association with higher academic achievement and creativity.

This evidence suggests that the Adivasi children do possess the basic cognitive processes and abilities, and the psychological dispositions for successful participation in schools. Less participation and low success of the Adivasi children in the programmes of school education point to our failure in evolving a sensitive model of education rooted in their psychological strengths. Our previous work with the Adivasi children indicates that, in comparison to other groups, children of hunters and gatherers possess a high level of visual and tactual differentiation, demonstrate capacity for fine judgement of shape and size of stimuli and spatial relations and produce fine categorization of an array of objects (Mishra et al., 1996). These abilities are greatly required for success in science, art, music, dance, athletic activities and vocations such as carpentry, tailoring, wood and stone crafts. These skills need to be utilized not only for education of children in schools, but also in the broader economic spheres of the Adivasi life. Attempts made in this direction will be helpful in generating and promoting the sense of competence, self-efficacy, self-respect and positive self-image among the Adivasi children.

Such attempts are also highly likely to provide the Adivasi children with a culturally meaningful, ecologically valid and economically viable alternative to life by reinforcing the dignity of their culture and identity. Contact of the Adivasi people with the outside world over the years has introduced several changes in their culture and life. These changes are reflected in their psychological characteristics also so much so that their ways of perceiving the world, categorizing objects, interpreting pictures and strategies of learning and memory become more similar to those with whom they interact and negotiate their life in these changed circumstances (e.g., Mishra et al., 1996). This suggests that the Adivasi children can acquire all those skills that the members of other groups of the society possess. What is important on our part is to develop a positive frame of mind about the Adivasi children. This is possible only through sensitivity to the Adivasi culture and life, recognition of cognitive strengths of the Adivasi children and appreciation of their psychological qualities.

Changes are essentially needed at the level of schools as well. While there is a general need for improvement in physical facilities in all schools located in remote tribal regions, change in the perception and outlook of teachers about the Adivasi children is equally important. They have to be sensitized about the cultural and behavioural strengths of the Adivasi children, and motivated for delivering their best to them in schools. Incentives have to be initiated to attract effective teachers to work in schools in the Adivasi areas. Only such motivated teachers are likely to generate interest among the Adivasi children towards school education by attempting to link the contents of the curriculum with the cultural context of the Adivasi communities through the use of innovative technologies.

The interest of the present book was in the analysis of selected cultural and cognitive style dimensions in relation to subsistence strategies of groups in general, but of the Adivasi groups of India in particular. Understanding the role of these factors in the Adivasi children's cognitive style and in their achievement in the domains of language, mathematics and science was pursued as a related goal. The findings of our work with the international groups of adults and the Adivasi children suggest that different cognitive styles are differently developed in different subsistence economic groups. These differences do not mean that some groups are cognitively more competent than others. They simply suggest that because of greater functional salience, different cognitive styles get relatively high premium in the life of individuals engaged in different subsistence economic activities. Opportunities available for learning and use of a certain cognitive style for successful negotiation of daily life in particular ecological contexts, along with their cultural support systems, have evolved in the respective societies. These ecological and cultural features of their lives promote the nurturing of those styles, and allow for their development in more refined manners than in those contexts in which the concerned styles have lesser premium in daily lives of people, and in which cultural support systems also do not encourage their development among children.

The differentiation cognitive style may be taken as an illustration. It seems to be at a high premium in the life of individuals or groups whose livelihood is based on hunting and gathering activities. Fruits, nuts, mushrooms and game animals must be perceived as standing out from the camouflaged forest surroundings for successful gathering and hunting activities. The forest ecology greatly encourages such differentiations by providing individuals with regular opportunities for disembedding of objects from the complex background during gathering and hunting. In this kind of ecology, socialization practices also emphasize independence, autonomy and achievement on the part of children, which (according to Witkin & Berry, 1975) support and further promote differentiation. In urban-industrial settings, differentiation is promoted by the demands of correct perception of symbols and many other things, which initiate variety of activities among individuals for successful living (Mishra, 2011b).

Research indicates that a high level of differentiation is required in many spheres of education. For example, it has been found to contribute significantly to the level of children's achievements in science, geometry, fine arts, music, dance and athletic activities (Witkin & Goodenough, 1981; see also Riding & Rayner, 2012). Since differentiation is found to be more strongly developed in the hunting-gathering and urban-industrial groups, the above mentioned areas may be brought into sharp focus in the education policy for hunting-gathering and wage-earning groups. This is true particularly in the Adivasi societies, but also for other similar societies internationally. Groups can be encouraged to choose some of these areas for education and helped along to develop fine competencies in them.

With respect to the contextualization cognitive style, the findings suggest that this cognitive style is more strongly rooted in agricultural and wage-earning groups. This process is greatly helpful in the acquisition of competence in literature and social studies, that is, the spheres which require an understanding of people, places and social contexts. These might be suggested as the fields of education for the development of children of agricultural societies. It may be noted that urbanized wage-earning samples display high levels of both differentiation and contextualization. For such groups, science, fine arts, music, geography as well as literature and social studies can constitute the potential areas on which the policy of education can focus.

These observations, however, do not necessarily ensure that the concerned groups would achieve highly in the respective fields of education we are suggesting here. They simply indicate the cognitive styles that are prevalent in groups, with their particular psychological predispositions and cognitive strengths (Mishra, 2005, 2008; Sinha & Mishra, 1997), and these may be utilized in sensitive ways for developing a policy for effective education of those groups. At best our findings indicate the probability that education in spheres in which the groups are already psychologically predisposed and cognitively strong can be expected to be a smoother sail if other conditions of education (which educationists call 'barriers' of the Adivasi education) are met successfully.

A second use of these findings is that they can be taken as starting points of education for children in different subsistence economy groups while operating within the existing framework of the policy of the Adivasi education. Informed by psychological predispositions and cognitive strengths of children of different subsistence economy groups, if the policy intends to strengthen those cognitive resources further, then a programme of a 'reinforcing education' will have to be developed, implemented and monitored.

On the other hand, if the policy intends to ignore the psychological strengths of groups, and decides to run a common programme of education for all groups of Adivasi children, then psychological weaknesses of children, particularly of those belonging to traditional groups, such as the Birhor, will have to be identified and carefully addressed. This step is seemingly essential for inculcating an optimal level of competence among the Adivasi children in all those areas in which they appear to be less competent than others. This would require area-specific programmes of education that seek to strengthen those areas that are less well-developed (Berry, 1976; Mishra et al., 1996), although looking at the outcomes of the compensatory educational programmes carried out in different parts of the world, the probability of effectiveness of this kind of education appears to be bleak.

The findings obtained with respect to cultural variables also carry some important implications for the education of the Adivasi children. They reveal a positive relationship between societal size and the differentiation cognitive style. This suggests that study areas in which the differentiation style can make potential contributions are likely to have a more successful transaction among children hailing from relatively high and low societal size cultures. On the other hand, social conformity, social connectedness and individual connectedness variables bear a positive correlation with contextualization. These cultural variables interfere with the development of the differentiation style, and they also correlate negatively with children's educational achievement in the domains of mathematics and science. Groups or individuals characterized by these cultural features may be encouraged to choose literature and social studies as areas of educational pursuits. Thus, knowledge of cultural features of the Adivasi groups is quite helpful in understanding cognitive competencies the groups are likely to develop. This knowledge is also helpful in identifying the areas of education in which children of different cultural characteristics might achieve excellence.

As far as the educational achievement measures in relation to cognitive style variables are concerned, our findings indicate that a high level of differentiation promotes achievement especially in the domain of science. For contextualization, while visual contextualization interferes with achievement in all domains, our findings indicate that verbal contextualization generally facilitates and promotes achievement in all domains. The implicit suggestion of these findings is that in order to promote achievement in different subjects of school education, children may be exposed to variety of riddles, stories and tasks that involve visual and/or verbal reasoning and inference. Plenty of these materials are available in the Adivasi cultural settings. In many Adivasi groups, the tradition of engaging children with riddles and stories is fairly strong and wide-spread in practice. What needs to be done is to reinforce these cultural traditions, which are 'at risk' of dying out with recent changes taking place in the Adivasi societies due to a number of developmental and acculturative influences. The salience of these age-old cultural practices needs to be explained to parents so that they could be preserved against extinction, and children are able to enjoy the benefits of this rich cultural knowledge.

Within the ecocultural framework, it is both the ecological and cultural adaptations that promote the development of particular cognitive styles, and the acculturation that results from the contact with other cultures, particularly the presence of urbanization and formal schooling variables. Both experiences produce differences in children's cognitive styles and their educational achievement measures. These relationships have been much in evidence in our findings with the Adivasi children. In fact, education has appeared to be such a pervasive factor that any cognitive task or educational achievement measure has hardly escaped its influence in these studies. Given this importance of formal school education, such programmes should be continued in the Adivasi society in whatever form they exist at the present time. On the other hand, there is also the need to broaden the scope, effectiveness and cultural appropriateness of the programmes so that they can easily make their way into the life of the Adivasi people and receive wider acceptance and recognition by the Adivasi community.

There is an ongoing debate at the international level with respect to 'appropriate schooling' for children. Smith and Sobel (2009) have indicated that an urbanized school life deprives children of many rich experiences, which are available in community environments. This happens due to the loss of children's connection with the life of natural environments characterized by the richness of landscapes, streams, rivers and a wide variety of flora and fauna. Such experiences are part of daily life of the Adivasi children in villages and forest dwellings. Schools situated in the Adivasi settlements can easily use these environmental resources to build up and strengthen the knowledge base of children through practical experiences and thereby make education a meaningful pursuit of life.

Tailoring educational programmes according to the ecological and cultural characteristics, daily life experiences and cognitive styles of different Adivasi groups will certainly be a positive step in the direction indicated above. The linking of the programmes of education with local strengths and needs of the Adivasi community stands in contrast to developing universal (a standard 'one size fits all') programmes of education. Whether the former can serve the needs of the Adivasi groups in general is a major issue of debate, and also a serious problem confronting the designers of the Adivasi education policy. More than five decades of experimentation with the Adivasi education seems to have given the lesson that the local needs of particular Adivasi groups should get priority over the needs of the Adivasi communities in general. This lesson appears to be sensible in view of the fact that the Adivasi represent a very heterogeneous group in terms of ecological, cultural, acculturational and cognitive features even today despite all efforts made towards their development and change over the decades (Mishra, 2007).

With respect to the effect of urban contact, our findings reveal that it plays a significant role in children's performance on almost all cognitive tasks. It promotes the processes of differentiation, but interferes with visual contextualization process. The differentiation cognitive style can be of use in education of the Adivasi children, which is promoted by urban contact.

With the fast growth of an urban-industrial economy in all parts of the country, the Adivasi peoples cannot be stopped or prevented from encountering such experiences. What needs to be guarded against is that urbanization is not 'forced' on them. Caution has also to be taken against the introduction of major inconsistencies between the traditional lifestyle of the Adivasi peoples and the one that is envisaged through educational and other developmental programmes currently underway. This caution is particularly important in the context of traditional Adivasi groups (such as the Birhor we have worked with) in order to prevent them from experiencing undesirable consequences of development and cultural change.

We believe that the work reported in this book has far-reaching implications for understanding culture–cognition relationship from an ecocultural perspective and for approaching the problem of education of the Adivasi children of different subsistence economic groups. For ensuring effective education in these groups, we need to understand their ecological engagements, their cultural features and the strengths of their cognitive life. We believe that the integration of ecological, cultural, acculturation and cognitive components of the Adivasi children in their educational programmes will constitute an important step in the direction of making the Adivasi education a fruitful, effective and successful enterprise.

References

Aberle, D., Cohen, A., Davis, A., Levy, M., & Sutton, F. (1950). The functional prerequisites of a society. *Ethics, 60(January)*, 100–111.
Allwood, C. M., & Berry, J. W. (2006). Origins and development of indigenous psychologies: An international analysis. *International Journal of Psychology, 41*(4), 153–72.
Anandalakshmy, S. (1994). *The girl child and the family: An action research study*. New Delhi: Ministry of HRD, Government of India.
Barker, R. G. (1968). *Ecological psychology: Concepts and methods for studying the environment of human behavior*. Stanford, CA: Stanford University Press.
Barry, H., Child, L, & Bacon, M. (1959). The relation of child training to subsistence economy. *American Anthropologist, 61*(1), 51–63.
Bender, A., & Beller, S. (2013). Cognition is ... fundamentally cultural. *Behavioral Sciences, 3*(1), 42–54.
Berland, J. C. (1982). *No five fingers are alike: Cognitive amplifiers in social context*. Cambridge, MA: Harvard University Press.
Berry, J. W. (1966). Temne and Eskimo perceptual skills. *International Journal of Psychology, 1*(3), 207–29.
———. (1967). Independence and conformity in subsistence-level societies. *Journal of Personality and Social Psychology, 7*(4), 415–18.
———. (1968). Ecology, perceptual development and the Muller-Lyre illusion. *British Journal of Psychology, 59*(3), 205–10.
———. (1969). On cross-cultural comparability. *International Journal of Psychology, 4*(2), 119–28.
———. (1970). Marginality, stress and identification in an acculturating Aboriginal community. *Journal of Cross-Cultural Psychology, 1*(3), 239–52.
———. (1971). Ecological and cultural factors in spatial perceptual development. *Canadian Journal of Behavioural Science, 3*(4), 324–36.
———. (1972). Radical cultural relativism and the concept of intelligence. In L. J. Cronbach & P. Drenth (Eds), *Mental tests and cultural adaptation* (pp. 77–88). Den Haag: Mouton.
———. (1973). Differentiation across cultures: Cognitive style and affective style. In J. Dawson & W. Lonner (Eds), *Readings in cross-cultural psychology* (pp. 167–75). Hong Kong: University of Hong Kong Press.
———. (1974). Sex differences in behaviour and cultural complexity. *Indian Journal of Psychology, 51*(2), 89–97.
———. (1975). An ecological approach to cross-cultural psychology. *Nederlands Tijdschriftvoor de Psychologie, 30*(1), 51–84.
———. (1976a). *Human ecology and cognitive style: Comparative studies in cultural and psychological adaptation*. New York: SAGE/Halsted.

Berry, J. W. (1976b). Sex differences in behaviour and cultural complexity. *Indian Journal of Psychology, 51*(1), 89–97.

———. (1979). A cultural ecology of social behaviour. In L. Berkowitz (Ed.), *Advances in experimental social psychology* (Vol. 12, pp. 177–206). New York: Academic Press.

———. (1980). Social and cultural change. In H. C. Triandis & R. Brislin (Eds), *Handbook of cross-cultural psychology* (Vol. 5, pp. 211–79). Boston: Allyn & Bacon.

———. (1987). The comparative study of cognitive abilities. In S. H. Irvine & S. Newstead (Eds), *Intelligence and cognition: Contemporary frames of reference* (pp. 393–420). Dordrecht: Nijhoff.

———. (1994a). An ecological approach to cultural and ethnic psychology. In E. Trickett (Ed.), *Human diversity* (pp. 115–41). San Francisco: Jossey-Bass.

———. (1994b). Ecology of individualism and collectivism. In U. Kim, H. C. Triandis, Ç. Kagitçibasi, S. C. Choi, & G. Yoon (Eds), *Individualism and collectivism: Theory, research and applications* (pp. 77–84). London: SAGE Publications.

———. (1995). Ecological approach to understanding cognition across cultures. In J. Altarriba (Ed.), *Cognition and culture: A cross-cultural approach to cognitive psychology* (pp. 361–75). Amsterdam: Elsevier.

———. (2000). Whatever happened to cognitive style? *Cross-Cultural Psychology Bulletin, 33*(2), 19–23.

———. (2003). Conceptual approaches to acculturation. In K. Chung, Balls-Organista & G. Marin (Eds), *Acculturation: Advances in theory, measurement, and applied research* (pp. 17–37). Washington: American Psychological Association Press.

———. (2006). Stress perspectives on acculturation. In D.L. Sam & J.W. Berry (Eds), *The Cambridge handbook of acculturation psychology* (pp. 129–41). Cambridge: Cambridge University Press.

———. (2011). The ecocultural framework: A stocktaking. In F. J. R. van de Vijver, A. Chasiotis, & S. M. Breugelmans (Eds), *Fundamental questions in cross-cultural psychology* (pp. 95–114). Cambridge: Cambridge University Press.

———. (2012). *Culture and societal development*. Patna: A. N. Sinha Institute of Social Studies.

———. (2015). *Intercultural adaptation to acculturation*. Paper presented at Annual Conference, Canadian Psychological Association, Ottawa, June.

———. (2017a). Ecocultural perspective on human behaviour. In A. Uskul & S. Oishi (Eds), *Socioeconomic environment and human psychology*. Oxford: Oxford University Press.

———. (2017b). Theories and models of acculturation. In S. Schwartz & J. Unger (Eds), *The Oxford handbook of acculturation and health* (pp. 15–28). New York: Oxford University Press.

———. (2017c). *Mutual intercultural relations*. Cambridge: Cambridge University Press.

Berry, J. W., & Bennett, J. A. (1991). *Cree syllabic literacy: Cultural context and psychological consequences*. Tilburg: Tilburg University Press.

———. (1992). Cree conceptions of cognitive competence. *International Journal of Psychology, 27*(1), 73–88.

Berry, J. W., Bennett, J. A., & Denny, P. J. (1995). *Ecological and cultural adaptation*. Unpublished manuscript.

Berry, J. W., Bennett, J. A., Denny, J. P., & Mishra, R. C. (2000). *Ecology, culture and cognitive processing*. Paper presented at IACCP congress, Pultusk, Poland.

Berry, J. W., & Dasen, P. R. (1974). *Culture and cognition: Readings in cross-cultural psychology*. London: Methuen.

Berry, J. W., & Irvine, S. H. (1986). Bricolage: Savages do it daily. In R. Sternberg & R. K. Wagner (Eds), *Practical intelligence: Origins of competence in the everyday world* (pp. 271–306). New York: Cambridge University Press.

Berry, J. W., Irvine, S. H., & Hunt, E. B. (1988). *Indigenous cognition: Functioning in cultural context* (pp. 9–20). Dordrecht: Nijhoff.

Berry, J. W., & Kalin, R. (2000). Multicultural policy and social psychology: The Canadian experience. In S. Renshon & J. Duckitt (Eds), *Political psychology in cross-cultural perspective* (pp. 263–84). New York: MacMillan.

Berry, J. W., Kalin, R., & Taylor, D. (1977). *Multiculturalism and ethnic attitudes in Canada*. Ottawa: Supply and Services Canada.

Berry, J. W., Mishra, R. C., & Tripathi, R.C. (2003). *Psychology in human and social development: Lessons from diverse cultures*. New Delhi: SAGE Publications.

Berry, J. W., Poortinga, Y. H., Breugelmans, S. M., Chasiotis A., & Sam D. L. (2011). *Cross-cultural psychology: Research and applications*. Cambridge: Cambridge University Press.

Berry, J. W., Poortinga, Y. H., Segall, M. H., & Dasen, P. R. (2002). *Cross-cultural psychology: Research and applications*. New York: Cambridge University Press.

Berry, J. W., Poortinga, Y. H., Pandey, J., Dasen, P. R., Saraswathi, T. S., Segall, M. H, & Kagitçibasi, C. (Eds). (1997). *Handbook of cross-cultural psychology* (Vols. 1–3). Boston, MA: Allyn & Bacon.

Berry, J. W., Poortinga, Y. H., Segall, M. H., & Dasen, P. R. (1992/2002). *Cross-cultural psychology: Research and applications*. New York: Cambridge University Press.

Berry, J. W., & Sabatier, C. (2011). Variations in the assessment of acculturation attitudes: Their relationships with psychological wellbeing. *International Journal of Intercultural Relations, 35*(5), 658–69.

Berry, J. W., Annis, R. C., Bahnchet, S., Cavalli-Sforza, L. L., Senechal, C., Van de Koppel, J. M. H., & Witkin, H. A. (1986). *On the edge of the forest: Cultural adaptation and cognitive development in Central Africa*. Lisse: Swets & Zeitlinger.

Berry, J. W., & Ward, C. (2016). Multiculturalism. In D. L. Sam & J. W. Berry (Eds), *The Cambridge handbook of acculturation psychology* (2nd ed., pp. 441–63). Cambridge: Cambridge University Press.

Bishop, A. J. (1978). Spatial abilities and mathematics in Papua New Guinea. *Papua New Guinea Journal of Education, 14*(Special Issue), 172–200.

Boldt, E. D. (1976). Acquiescence and conventionality in a communal society. *Journal of Cross-Cultural Psychology, 7*(1), 21–36.

———. (1978). Structural tightness and cross-cultural research. *Journal of Cross-Cultural Psychology, 9*(2), 151–65.

Boldt, E. D., & Roberts, L. W. (1979). Structural tightness and social conformity. *Journal of Cross-Cultural Psychology, 10*(2), 221–30.

Bond, M. H. (2013). A general model for explaining situational influence on individual social behavior: Refining Lewin's formula. *Asian Journal of Social Psychology, 16*(1), 1–15.

Bond, R., & Smith, P. (1996). Culture and conformity: A meta-analysis. *Psychological Bulletin, 119*(1), 111–37.

Boyd, R., & Richerson, P. J. (1983). Why is culture adaptive? *Quarterly Review of Biology, 58*(June), 209–14.

Boyd, R., & Richerson, P. J. (2005). *The origin and evolution of cultures*. Oxford: Oxford University Press.

Boyd, R., Richerson, P. J., & Henrich, J. (2011). The cultural niche: Why social learning is essential for human adaptation. *Proceedings of the National Academy of Sciences* (USA), *108*(2), 10918–925.
Bronfenbrenner, U. (1974). Development research, public policy and ecology of childhood. *Child Development, 45*(1), 1–5.
———. (1979). *The ecology of human development*. Cambridge, MA: Harvard University Press.
Brunswik, E. (1957). Scope and aspects of the cognitive problem. In H. Gruber, R. Jessor, & K. Hammond (Eds), *Cognition: The Colorado symposium* (pp. 5–31). Cambridge, MA: Harvard University Press.
Caplan, P. J., Crawford, M., Hyde, J. S., & Richardson, J. T. T. (1997). *Gender differences in human cognition. Counterpoints: Cognition, memory and language*. Oxford: Oxford University Press.
Census of India. (2011). *Census of India*. New Delhi: Government of India.
Chomsky, N. (2000). *New horizons in the study of language and mind*. New York: Cambridge University Press.
Ciborowski, T. (1980). The role of context, skill and transfer in cross-cultural experimentation. In H. C. Triandis & J. W. Berry (Eds), *Handbook of cross-cultural psychology* (Vol. 2, pp. 279–96). Boston: Allyn & Bacon.
Cole, M., Gay, J., Glick, J. A., & Sharp, D. W. (1971). *The cultural context of learning and thinking*. New York: Basic Books.
Darwin, C. (1859). *On the origin of species*. London, John Murray.
Dasen, P. R. (1975). Concrete operational development in three cultures. *Journal of Cross-Cultural Psychology, 6*(2), 156–72.
———. (1984). The cross-cultural study of intelligence: Piaget and the Baoulé. *International Journal of Psychology, 19*(1–4), pp. 407–34. Reprinted in P. S. Fry (Ed.), *Changing conceptions of intelligence and intellectual functioning: Current theory and research* (pp. 107–34). Amsterdam: North-Holland.
———. (2003). Theoretical frameworks in cross-cultural developmental psychology: An attempt at integration. In T. S. Saraswathi (Ed.), *Cross-cultural perspectives in human development* (pp. 128–65). New Delhi/Thousand Oaks, CA: SAGE Publications.
———. (2008). Informal education and learning processes. In P. R. Dasen & A. Akkari (Eds), *Educational theories and practices from the majority world* (pp. 25–48). New Delhi: SAGE
Dasen, P. R., & Akkari, A. (2008). *Educational theories and practices from the majority world*. New Delhi: SAGE Publications.
Dasen, P. R., Berry, J. W., & Witkin, H. A. (1979). The use of developmental theories cross-culturally. In L. Eckensberger, W. Lonner, & Y. H. Poortinga (Eds), *Cross-cultural contributions to psychology* (pp. 69–82). Lisse: Swets & Zeitlinger.
Dasen, P. R., Berry, J. W., & Sartorius, N. (1988). *Health and cross-cultural psychology: Toward applications*. Newbury Park: SAGE Publications.
Dasen, P. R., & Heron, A. (1981). Cross-cultural tests of Piaget's theory. In H. C. Triandis & A. Heron (Eds), *Handbook of cross-cultural psychology; Developmental psychology* (Vol. 4, pp. 295–342). Boston, MA: Allyn & Bacon.
Dasen, P. R., Lavallée, M., & Retschitzki, J. (1979). Training conservation of quantity (liquids) in West African (Baoulé) children. *International Journal of Psychology, 14*(1), 57–68.
Dasen, P. R., & Mishra, R. C. (2010). *The development of geocentric spatial language and cognition: An eco-cultural perspective*. Oxford: Oxford University Press.

Dasen, P. R., & Mishra, R. C. (2013). Cultural differences in cognitive styles. In B. R. Kar (Ed.), *Cognition and brain development: Converging evidences from various methodologies* (pp. 231–49). Washington D.C.: American Psychological Association.

Dasen, P. R., Lavallée, M., & Ngini, L. (1979). Cross-cultural training studies of concrete operations. In L. Eckensberger, Y. Poortinga, & W. Lonner (Eds), *Cross-cultural contributions to Psychology* (pp. 94–104). Amsterdam: Swets & Zeitlinger.

Dawson, J. L. M. (1967a). Cultural and *psychological* influences upon spatial-perceptual processes in West Africa (Part 1). *International Journal of Psychology*, 2(2), 115–28.

———. (1967b). Cultural and *psychological* influences upon spatial-perceptual processes in West Africa (Part II). *International Journal of Psychology*, 2(2), 171–85.

———. (1969). Theoretical and research bases of biosocial psychology. *University of Hong Kong Gazette*, 16(3), 1–10.

———. (1972). Effects of sex hormones on cognitive style in rats and men. *Behavior Genetics*, 2(1), 21–42.

Denny, J. P. (1986). Cultural ecology of mathematics: Ojibway and Inuit hunters. In M. Closs (Ed.), *Native American mathematics* (pp. 129–80). Austin: University of Texas Press.

———. (1991). Rational thought in oral culture and literature decontextualization. In D. R. Olson & N. Torrance (Eds), *Literacy and orality* (pp. 66–89). New York: Cambridge University Press.

Denny, J. P., & Davis, L. (1989). *Contextualization during reasoning: An experimental study of Amerindians.* Unpublished manuscript.

De Young, R. (2013). Environmental psychology overview. In A. H. Huffman & S. Klein (Eds), *Green organizations: Driving change with IO psychology* (pp. 17–33). New York: Routledge.

Dona, D., & Berry, J. W. (1994). Acculturation attitudes and acculturative stress of Central American refugees. *International Journal of Psychology*, 29(1), 57–70.

Dudgeon, P., Darlaston-Jones, D., Nikora, L. M., Pe-Pua, R., Rouhani, L., Tran, L. N., & Waitoki, W. (2016). Changing the acculturation conversation: Indigenous cultural reclamation in Australia and Aotearoa/New Zealand. In D. L. Sam & J. W. Berry (Eds), *The Cambridge handbook of acculturation psychology* (2nd ed., pp. 115–33). Cambridge: Cambridge University Press.

Ember, C. R., & Ember, M. (1999). *Anthropology* (9th ed.). Englewood Cliffs: Prentice Hall.

Eysenck, H. J. (1971). *The IQ argument: Race, intelligence and education.* New York: The Library Press.

———. (1988). The biological basis of intelligence. In S. H. Irvine & J. W. Berry (Eds), *Human abilities in cultural context* (pp. 87–104). Cambridge: Cambridge University Press.

Feldman, M. W. (1975).The heritability hang-up. *Science*, 190(4220), 1163–68.

Ferguson, G. (1956). On transfer and the abilities of man. *Canadian Journal of Psychology*, 10(3), 121–31.

Forde, D. (1934). *Habitat, economy and society.* New York: Dutton.

Gamble, J. J., & Ginsberg, P. E. (1981). Differentiation, cognition and social evolution. *Journal of Cross-Cultural Psychology*, 12(4), 445–49.

Gelfand, M. J., & Lun, J. (2013). Ecological priming: Convergent evidence for the link between ecology and psychological processes. *Behavioral and Brain Sciences*, 3(5), 489–90.

Gelfand, M., Raver, J., Nishii, L., Leslie, L., & Lun, J. et al. (2011). Differences between tight and loose societies: A 33-nation study. *Science*, 332(6033), 1100–04.

Georgas, J., & Berry, J. W. (1995). An eco-cultural taxonomy for cross-cultural psychology. *Cross-Cultural Research*, 29(2), 121–57.

Georgas, J., Berry, J. W., van de Vijver, F. J. R., Kagitçibasi, C., Poortinga, Y. H. (2006). *Families across cultures: A 30-nation psychological study*. Cambridge: Cambridge University Press.
Georgas, J., van de Vijver, F., & Berry, J. W. (2004). The ecocultural framework, ecosocial indices and psychological variables in cross-cultural research. *Journal of Cross-Cultural Psychology, 35*, 74–96.
Georgas, J., Weiss, L. G., van de Vijer, F. J. R., & Saklofske, D. H. (Eds). (2003). *Culture and children's intelligence. Cross-cultural analysis of the WISC-III*. San Diego, CA: Academic Press/Elsevier Science.
Gifford, R. (2007). *Environmental psychology: Principles and practice*. New York: Psychology Press.
Goody, J. (1977). *The domestication of the savage mind*. Cambridge: Cambridge University Press.
Goody, J., & Watt, I. (1963). The consequences of literacy. *Comparative Studies in Society and History, 5*(3), 304–45.
Graves, T. D. (1967). Psychological acculturation in a tri-ethnic community. *Southwestern Journal of Anthropology, 23*(4), 337–50.
Greenfield, P. M. (1972). Oral and written language: The consequences for cognitive development in Africa, the United States and England. *Language and Speech, 15*(2), 169–78.
Grusec, J., & Hastings, P. (2007). *Handbook of socialization*. New York: Guilford Press.
Halpern, D. F. (2012). *Sex differences in cognitive abilities*. New York: Psychology Press.
Heelas, P., & Lock, A. (1981). *Indigenous psychologies*. London: Academic Press.
Herrnstein, R. J., & Murray, C. (1994). *The bell curve: Intelligence and class structure in American life*. New York: Free Press.
Hofstede, G. (1991). *Cultures and organizations: Software of the mind*. London: McGraw Hill.
Honigmann, J. J. (1968). Interpersonal relations in an atomistic community. *Human Organization, 27*(2), 220–29.
Huntington, E., (1945). *Mainsprings of civilization*. Oxford, England: Wiley.
Hutchins, E. (1980). *Culture and inference*. Cambridge: Harvard University Press.
———. (2010). Cognitive ecology. *Topics in Cognitive Science, 2*(4), 705–15.
———. (2014). The cultural ecosystem of human cognition. *Philosophical Psychology, 27*(1), 34–49.
Irvine, S. H., & Berry, J. W. (1983). *Human assessment and cultural factors*. New York: Plenum.
———. (1988/2011). *Human abilities in cultural context*. New York: Cambridge University Press.
Iwawaki, S. (1986). Achievement motivation and socialization. In S.E. Newstead, S. H. Irvine, & P. L. Dann (Eds), *Human assessment: Cognition and motivation* (pp. 341–50). Dordrecht: Nijhoff.
Iwawaki, S., & Vernon, P. E. (1988). Japanese abilities and achievement. In S. H. Irvine & J. W. Berry (Eds), *Human abilities in cultural context* (pp. 358–84). New York: Cambridge University Press.
Jabbi, M. K., & Rajyalakshmi, C. (2001). Education of marginalised social groups in Bihar. In A. Vaidyanathan & P. R. G. Nair (Eds), *Elementary education in rural India: A grassroots view* (pp. 395–458). New Delhi: SAGE Publications.
———. (1997). Education of SC and ST groups in Bihar. *Social Change, 27*(1 & 2), 30–72.

Jahoda, G. (1973). Psychology and the developing countries: Do they need each other? *International Social Science Journal, 25*(4), 461–74.
———. (1975). Applying cross-cultural psychology to the Third World. In J. W. Berry & W. J. Lonner (Eds), *Applied cross-cultural psychology* (pp. 13–17). Amsterdam: Swets & Zeitlinger.
———. (1982). *Psychology and anthropology: A psychological perspective*. London: Academic Press.
———. (1995). The ancestry of a model. *Culture & Psychology, 1*(1), 11–24.
Jensen, A. R. (1969). How much can we boost IQ and scholastic achievement. *Harvard Educational Review, 39*(1), 1–123.
Joshi, S. (2009). The dynamics of education of Kharwar children of Chandauli. In A. Shukla (Ed.), *Culture, cognition and behavior* (pp. 98–109). New Delhi: Concept.
Kagitçibasi, C. (1997). Individualism and collectivism. In J. W. Berry, M. H. Segall, & C. Kagitçibasi (Eds), *Handbook of cross-cultural psychology: Social psychology* (Vol. 3, pp. 1–49). Boston: Allyn & Bacon.
Kagitçibasi, C. (2007). *Family, self, and human development across cultures: Theory and applications* (2nd ed.). Hillsdale, NJ: Lawrence Erlbaum.
Kardiner, A. (1939). *The individual and his society: The psychodynamics of primitive social organization*. Oxford, England: Columbia University Press.
———. (1945). *Psychological frontiers of society*: New York: Columbia University Press.
Keller, H., Poortinga, Y. H., & Scholmerich, A. (2002). *Between culture and biology: Perspectives on ontogenetic development* (pp. 215–40). Cambridge: Cambridge University Press.
Kim, U., & Berry, J. W. (Eds). (1993). *Indigenous psychologies. Research and experience in cultural context*. Newbury Park, CA: SAGE Publications.
Kim, U., Triandis, H. C., Kagitçibasi, Ç., Choi, S. C., & Yoon, G. (Eds). (1994). *Individualism and collectivism: Theory, method, and applications*. Thousand Oaks, CA: SAGE Publications.
Kim, U., Yang, K., & Hwang, K. (Eds). (2006). *Indigenous and cultural psychology: Understanding people in context*. New York: Kluwer Academic/Plenum.
Kottak, C. (1999). The new ecological anthropology. *American Anthropologist, 101*(1), 23–35.
Kroeber, A. (1939). *Cultural and natural areas of Native North America*. Berkeley: University of California Press.
Kvernmo, S. (2006). Indigenous Peoples. In D. L. Sam, & J. W. Berry (Eds), *The Cambridge handbook of acculturation psychology* (pp. 233–50). Cambridge: Cambridge University Press.
Lévy-Bruhl, L. (1910). *Les fonctions mentales dans les sociétés inférieures*. Paris: Alcan. English translation: *How natives think*. London: Allen & Unwin, 1928.
———. (1949). *Les carnets de Lucien Lévy-Bruhl*. Paris: Presses Universitaires de France.
Linton, R. (1939). The Marquesan culture. In A. Kardinar (Ed.), *The individual and his society* (pp. 138–96). New York: Columbia University Press.
Lomax, A., & Berkowitz, W. (1972). The evolutionary taxonomy of culture. *Science, 177*(4045), 228–39.
Luria, A. R. (1976). *Cognitive development: Its cultural and social foundations*. Cambridge: Harvard University Press.
Lynn, R. (2006). *Race differences in intelligence: An evolutionary analysis*. Augusta Ga: Washington Summit Publishers.

Mac Aurther, R. S. (1967). Sex differences in field dependence for the Eskimo: Replication of Berry's findings. *International Journal of Psychology, 2*(2), 139–40.
Maccoby, E. E., & Jacklin, C. N. (1974). *The psychology of sex differences*. Palo Alto: Stanford University Press.
McIntyre, L. A. (1976). An investigation of the effect of culture and urbanization on three cognitive styles and their relation to school performance. In G. E. Kearney & D. W. McElwain (Eds), *Aboriginal cognition* (pp. 231–56). Canberra: Australian Institute of Aboriginal Studies.
McNett, C. W. (1970). A settlement pattern scale of cultural complexity. In R. Naroll & R. Cohen (Eds), *Handbook of method in cultural anthropology* (pp. 872—88). New York: Natural History Press.
Mishra, K. (1996). *Cognitive style of Tharu children in relation to daily life activities and experience of schooling*. Unpublished doctoral thesis, Banaras Hindu University, Varanasi.
Mishra, R. C. (1996a). Perceptual differentiation in relation to children's daily life activities. *Social Science International, 12*(1–2), 1–11.
———. (1996b). *Cognitive processes, cultural adaptations, and education of children of some Adivasi groups*. New Delhi: National Council of Educational Research and Training (unpublished report).
———. (1997). Cognition and cognitive development. In J. W. Berry, P. R. Dasen, & T. S. Saraswathi (Eds), *Handbook of cross-cultural psychology: Basic processes and human development* (Vol. 2, pp. 147–79). Boston: Allyn & Bacon.
———. (1998a). A cross-cultural perspective on cognitive development theories used in Indian settings. *Psychology and Developing Societies, 10*(1), 21–33.
———. (1998b). Cognitive processes. In NCERT (Ed.), *Fifth survey of educational Research* (pp. 128–46). New Delhi: NCERT.
———. (1999). Research on education in India. *Prospects, 29*(3), 335–47.
———. (2001). Cognition across cultures. In D. Matsumoto (Ed.), *The handbook of culture and psychology* (pp. 119–35). New York: Oxford University Press.
———. (2005). Cognitive strengths of tribal children: Implication for their education. In A. Shukla (Ed.), *Indian tribes: Psychological and social perspectives* (pp. 53–64). New Delhi: Kanishka.
———. (2007). Psychological perspective on educational development of Adivasis. In M. B. Sharan & D. Suar (Eds), *Psychology matters: Development, health and organization* (pp. 1–17). New Delhi: Allied Publishers.
———. (2008). Education of Adivasi children in India. In P. R. Dasen & A. Akkari (Eds), *Educational theories and practices from the majority world* (pp. 145–67). New Delhi: SAGE Publications.
———. (2009). Psychology and the challenges of social problems and issues. In A. K. Tiwari (Ed.), *Psychological perspectives on social issues and human development* (pp. 17–33). New Delhi: Concept.
———. (2011a). Eco-cultural contexts and cognitive functioning. In P. N. Tandon, R. C. Tripathi, & N. Srinivasan (Eds), *Expanding horizons of mind science(s)* (pp. 287–305). New York: Nova Science Publishers.
Mishra, R. C. (2011b). Ecology, culture and cognitive functioning. In P. R. Sharma, R. S. Yadav, & V. N. Sharma (Eds), *Research methodology: Concepts and studies* (pp. 201–14). New Delhi: R. K. Books.
Mishra, R. C., & Berry, J. W. (2008). Cultural adaptation and cognitive processes of tribal children in Chotanagpur. In N. Srinivasan, A. K. Gupta, & J. Pandey (Eds), *Advances in cognitive science* (pp. 289–301). New Delhi: SAGE Publications.

Mishra, R. C., & Chaubey, A. C. (2002). Acculturation attitudes of Kharwar and Agaria Adivasi Peoples of Sonebhadra, *Psychology and Developing Societies, 14*(2), 201–20.
Mishra, R. C., & Dasen, P. R. (2004). The influence of schooling on cognitive development: A review of research in India. In B. N. Setiadi, A. Supratiknya, W. J. Lonner, & Y. H. Poortinga (Eds), *Ongoing themes in psychology and culture* (pp. 207–22). Yogyakarta: Kanisius.
———. (2007). The methodological interface of psychology and anthropology. In J. Wassmann & K. Stockhaus (Eds), *Experiencing new worlds* (pp. 21–35). Oxford: Berghahn.
Mishra, R. C., Dasen, P. R., & Niraula, S. (2003). Ecology, language and performance on spatial cognitive tasks. *International Journal of Psychology, 38*(6), 366–83.
Mishra, R. C., & Joshi, S. (2015). Acculturation and children's education in a rural Adivasi community. *Indian Educational Review, 53*(1), 7–24.
Mishra, R. C., & Kothiyal, D. (1995). Stress in relation to varying experiences of culture change. In O. P. Misra & S. K. Srivastava (Eds), *Ecological perspectives and behaviour* (pp. 89–102). Hardwar: Gurukul Kangri University.
Mishra, R. C., & Singh, D. V. (2008). Psychological differentiation in relation to some socialization variables: A study with rural children. *Psychology and Developing Societies, 20*(2), 241–56.
Mishra, R. C., & Sinha, D. (1998). Role models, socialization patterns and cognitive strength of tribals. In K. Sujatha (Ed.), *Modules of tribal education* (pp. 47–71). New Delhi: NIEPA.
Mishra, R. C., Sinha, D., & Berry, J. W. (1990). *Some aspects of cognitive functioning of Birhor and Oraon children in relation to acculturation.* Paper presented at the X Conference of the IACCP, Nara, Japan.
———. (1996). *Ecology, acculturation and psychological adaptation: A study of Adivasis in Bihar.* New Delhi: SAGE Publications.
———. (1999). Meeting the challenges of fieldwork in cross-cultural psychological research. *Psychology and Developing Societies, 11*(1), 91–104.
Moran, E. (1982). *Human adaptability: An introduction to ecological anthropology.* Boulder: Westview Press.
———. (1990). *The ecosystem approach in anthropology.* Ann Arbor: University of Michigan Press.
———. (2006). *People and nature: An introduction to human ecological relations* (3rd ed.). Malden, MA: Blackwell Publishing.
Murdock, G. P. (1969). Correlation of exploitative and settlement patterns. In D. Damas (Ed.), *Contributions to anthropology: Ecological essays* (Bulletin, No. 230, Anthropological Series, No. 86; pp. 129–46). Ottawa: National Museum of Canada.
———. (1975). *Outline of world cultures* (5th ed.). New Haven, CT: HRAF.
Nettle, D., Gibson, D., & Starr, R. (2013). Human behavioral ecology: Current research and future prospects. *Behavioral Ecology, 24*(5), 1031–40.
Nimkoff, M., & Middleton, R. (1960). Types of family and types of economy. *American Journal of Sociology, 66*(3), 215–25.
Nisbett, R. E. (2003). *The geography of thought: How Asians and Westerners think differently, and why.* New York: Free Press.
Norenzayan, A., Choi, I., & Peng, K. (2007). Perception and cognition. In S. Kitayama & D. J. Cohen (Eds), *Handbook of cultural psychology* (pp. 569–94). New York: Guilford Press.
Nsamenang, B. (1992). *Human development in cultural context.* Newbury Park: SAGE Publications.

Overton, W. (2013). A new paradigm for developmental science: Relationalism and relational-developmental systems. *Applied Developmental Science, 17*(2), 94–107.

Pelto, P. (1968). The difference between "tight" and "loose" societies. *Transaction, 5* (April), 37–40.

Poortinga, Y. H., van de Vijver, F. J. R., Joe, R. C., & van de Koppel, J. M. H. (1987). Peeling the onion called culture: A synopsis. In C. Kagitçibasi (Ed.), *Growth and progress in cross-cultural psychology* (pp. 22–34). Amsterdam: Swets & Zeitlinger.

Porteus, S. D. (1917). Mental tests with delinquents and Australian Aboriginal children. *Psychological Review, 24*(1), 32–41.

———. (1937). *Intelligence and environment.* New York: Macmillan.

Prasad, N. (1961). *Land and people of tribal Bihar.* Ranchi: Bihar Tribal Research Institute.

Redfield, R., Linton, R., & Herskovits, M. J. (1936). Memorandum on the study of acculturation. *American Anthropologist, 38*(1), 149–52.

Riding, R. J., & Rayner, S. (2012). *Cognitive styles and learning strategies: Understanding style differences in learning and behavior.* London: Routledge.

Reuning, H., & Wortley, W. L. (1973). Psychological studies of the Bushmen. *Psychologia Africana* (Monograph Supplement No. 7).

Richerson, P. J., & Boyd, R. (2005). *Not by gene alone: How culture transformed human evolution.* Chicago: University of Chicago Press.

Ridington, R. (1988). Knowledge, power and the individual in the sub-Arctic hunting societies. *American Anthropologist, 90*(1), 98–110.

Roberts, L. W., Boldt, E. D., & Guest, A. (1990). Structural tightness and social conformity: Varying the source of external influence. *Great Plains Sociologist, 3*(1), 67–83.

Rushton, J. P. (1995). *Race, evolution, and behavior: A life history perspective.* New Brunswick, NJ: Transaction.

———. (2000). *Race, evolution and behavior: A life history perspective.* Galapagos: Charles Darwin Research Institute.

Ryder, A., Alden, L., & Paulhus, D. (2000). Is acculturation unidimensional or bi-dimensional? *Journal of Personality and Social Psychology, 79*(1), 49–65.

Sam, D., & Berry, J.W.(Eds). (2016). *The Cambridge handbook of acculturation psychology* (2nd ed.). Cambridge: Cambridge University Press.

———. (Eds). (2017). *Cross-cultural psychology* (4 volumes). London: Routledge.

Sam, D. L., Hassan, G., Jasinskaya-Lahti, I., & Ryder, A. (2016). Health. In D. L. Sam & J. W. Berry (Eds), *The Cambridge handbook of acculturation psychology* (pp. 504–24). Cambridge: Cambridge University Press.

Sagayaraj, A. (2013). Christianity in India: A focus on inculturation. *Research Papers of the Anthropological Institute, 1,* 114–42.

Schliemann, A., & Acioly, N. M. (1989). Mathematical knowledge developed at work: The contribution of practice versus the contribution of schooling. *Cognition and Instruction, 6*(5), 185–221.

Schleimann, A., Carraher, D., & Ceci, S. J. (1997). Everyday cognition. In J. W. Berry, P. R. Dasen, & T. S. Saraswathi (Eds), *Handbook of cross-cultural psychology: Basic processes and human development* (Vol. 2, pp. 177–216). Boston: Allyn & Bacon.

Scribner, S. (1977). Mode of thinking and ways of speaking: Culture and logic reconsidered. In P. N. Johnson-Laird & P. C. Wason (Eds), *Thinking: Readings in cognitive science* (pp. 483–500). Cambridge: Cambridge University Press.

Scribner, S., & Cole, M. (1981). *The psychology of literacy.* Cambridge, MA: Harvard University Press.

Segall, M. H., Campbell, D. T., & Herskovits, M. J. (1966). *The influence of culture on visual perception.* Indianapolis: Bobbs-Merrill.
Segall, M. H., Berry, J. W., Dasen, P. R., & Poortinga, Y. H. (1999). *Human behavior in global perspective* (2nd ed.). Boston: Allyn & Bacon.
Serpell, R. (1993). *The significance of schooling: Life journeys in an African society.* Cambridge: Cambridge University Press.
Shrestha, A. B., & Mishra, R. C. (1996). Sex differences in cognitive style of Brahmin and Gurung children from the hills and plains of Nepal. In J. Pandey, D. Sinha, & D. P. S. Bhawuk (Eds), *Asian contributions to cross-cultural psychology* (pp. 165–174). New Delhi: SAGE Publications.
Shuey, A. M. (1958). *The testing of Negro intelligence.* New York: Social Science Press.
Singh, A. K. (1984). Health modernity: Concept and correlates in South Bihar. *Social Change, 14*(3), 3–16.
———. (1995). Development, deprivation and discontentment of tribals in India. In A. K. Singh & M. K. Jabbi (Eds), *Status of tribals in India* (pp. 13–26). New Delhi: Har Anand.
———. (1996). *Improving the educational status of the tribals in India.* Paper presented at the National Seminar on Research in Tribal Education, NIEPA, New Delhi.
Singh, A. K., & Jabbi, M. K. (1995). *Status of tribals in India.* New Delhi: Har Anand.
Sinha, D. (1973). Psychology and the problems of developing countries: A general overview. *International Review of Applied Psychology, 22*(1), 5–28.
———. (1975). Social psychologists' stance in a developing country. *Indian Journal of Psychology, 50*(2), 91–107.
———. (1977). Some social disadvantages and development of certain perceptual skills. *Indian Journal of Psychology, 52*(2), 115–32.
———. (1978). Story-pictorial E. F. T.: A culturally appropriate test of perceptual disembedding. *Indian Journal of Psychology, 53*(2), 160–71.
———. (1979). Perceptual style among nomadic and transitional agriculturalist Birhors. In L. Eckensberger, W. J. Lonner, & Y. H. Poortinga (Eds). *Cross-cultural contributions to psychology* (pp. 83–93). Lisse: Swets & Zeitlinger.
———. (1980). Sex differences in psychological differentiation among different cultural groups. *International Journal of Behavioral Development, 3*(4), 455–66.
———. (1982). Socio-cultural factors and the development of perceptual and cognitive skills. *Review of Child Development Research, 6,* 441–72.
———. (1984). *Manual for story-pictorial E. F. T. and Indo-African E. F. T.* Varanasi: Rupa Psychological Corporation.
Sinha, D., & Bharat, S. (1985). Three types of family structure and psychological differentiation: A study among the Jausar-Bawar society. *International Journal of Psychology, 20*(3–4), 693–708.
Sinha, D., & Mishra, R. C. (1997). Some personality, motivational and cognitive characteristics of tribals and their implications for educational development of children. *Indian Journal of Educational Planning and Administration, 17*(2), 283–95.
Sinha, D., & Shrestha, A. B. (1992). Eco-cultural factors in cognitive style among children from hills and plains of Nepal. *International Journal of Psychology, 27*(1), 49–59.
Sinha, G. (1988). Exposure to industrial and urban environments, and formal schooling as factors in psychological differentiation. *International Journal of Psychology, 23*(5), 707–19.

Smith, G. A., & Sobel, D. (2009). *Place- and community-based education in schools*. New York: Routledge.
Sommerlad, E., & Berry, J. W. (1970). The role of ethnic identification in distinguishing between attitudes towards assimilation and integration of a minority racial group. *Human Relations, 23*(1), 23–29.
Srivastava, R. K. (1983). Psychological characteristics of Tharus and non-Tharus: A cross-cultural study. Proceedings of the 70th Session of the Indian Science Congress, Tirupati.
Sternberg, R., & Grigorenko, E. L. (1997). Are cognitive styles still in style? *American Psychologist, 53*(7), 700–12.
Sternberg, R. J., & Grigorenko, E. L. (2004). Intelligence and culture: How culture shapes what intelligence means, and the implications for a science of well-being. *Philosophical Transactions: Biological Sciences, 359*(1449), 1427–34.
Steward, J. (1955). *The concept and method of cultural ecology: Theory of culture change*. Urbana: University of Illinois Press.
Stokols, D., & Altman, I. (1987). *Handbook of environmental psychology*. New York: John Wiley.
Super, C., & Harkness, S. (1986). The developmental niche: A conceptualization at the interface of child and culture. *International Journal of Behavioral Development, 9*(4), 545–69.
Super, C. M., & Harkness, S. (1997). The cultural structuring of child development. In J. W. Berry, P. R. Dasen, & T. S. Saraswathi (Eds), *Handbook of cross-cultural psychology: Basic processes and human development* (Vol. 2, pp. 1–39). Boston: Allyn & Bacon.
———. (2002). Culture structures the environment for development. *Human Development, 45*(4), 270–74.
Sutton, M. Q., & Anderson, E. N. (2010). *Introduction to cultural ecology*. Lanham, MD: Alta Mira.
Talhelm, T., & Oishi, S. (2017). How rice farming shaped culture in Southern China. In A. Uskul & S. Oishi (Eds), *Socioeconomic environment and human psychology*. New York: Oxford University Press.
Talhelm, T., Zhang, X., Oishi, S., Shimin, C., Duan, D., Lan, X., & Kitayama, S. (2014). Large-scale psychological differences within China explained by rice versus wheat agriculture. *Science, 344*(6184), 603–08.
Tomasello, M. (1999a). The human adaptation for culture. *Annual Review of Anthropology, 28*, 509–29.
———. (1999b). *The cultural origins of human cognition*. Cambridge, MA: Harvard University Press.
———. (2011). Human culture in evolutionary perspective. In J. M. Gelfand, C. Chiu, & Y. Hong (Eds), *Advances in culture and psychology* (Vol. 1, pp. 5–52). Oxford: Oxford University Press.
Townsend, P. K. (2009). *Environmental anthropology: From pigs to policies* (2nd ed.). Prospect Heights, Ill.: Waveland Press.
Triandis, H. C. (1995). *Individualism and collectivism*. Boulder, CO: Westview.
Tripathi, R. C. (1988). Applied social psychology. In J. Pandey (Ed.), *Psychology in India: The state-of-the art* (pp. 95–157). New Delhi: SAGE Publications.
Tripathi, R. C., & Mishra, R. C. (2016). Acculturation in South Asia. In D. L. Sam & J. W. Berry (Eds), *The Cambridge handbook of acculturation psychology* (2nd ed., pp. 337–54). Cambridge: Cambridge University Press.

Tripathi, R. C., & Sinha, Y. (2014). *Psychology, development and social policy in India*. New Delhi: Springer.
Troadec, B. (1999). *Le développement de la pensée chez l'enfant. Catégorisation et cultures*. Toulouse: Presses Universitaires du Mirail.
Uskul, A., & Oishi, S. (Eds) (2017). *Socioeconomic environment and human psychology*. Oxford: Oxford University Press.
Uskul, A. K, Kitayama, S., & Nisbett, R. E. (2008). Ecocultural basis of cognition: Farmers and fishermen are more holistic than herders. *Proceedings of the National Academy of Science* (USA), *105*, 8552.
Van Leeuwen, M. S. (1978). A cross-cultural examination of psychological differentiation in males and females. *International Journal of Psychology, 13*(2), 87–112.
van Oudenhoven, J. P., & Ward, C. (2012). Fading majority cultures. *Journal of Community and Applied Social psychology, 23*(1), 81–97.
Vayda, A. P., & Rappaport, R. (1968). Ecology: Cultural and non-cultural. In J. Clifton (Ed.), *Cultural anthropology* (pp. 477–97). Boston: Houghton Mifflin.
Vidyarthi, L. P., & Sahay, K. N. (1976). *The dynamics of tribal leadership in Bihar*. Allahabad: Kitab Mahal.
Waber, D. P. (1976). Sex differences in cognition: A function of maturation rate? *Science, 192*(4239), 572–74.
———. (1977). Sex differences in mental abilities, hemispheric lateralization and rate of physical growth at adolescence. *Developmental Psychology, 13*(1), 29–38.
Wagner, D. A. (1986). Child development research and the Third World: A future of mutual interest. *American Psychologist, 41*(3), 298–301.
———. (1988). "Appropriate education" and literacy in the Third World. In P. R. Dasen, J. W. Berry, & N. Sartorius (Eds), *Health and cross-cultural psychology: Toward applications* (pp. 99–111). Newbury Park: SAGE Publications.
———. (2010). Literacy. In M. Bornstein (Ed.), *Handbook of cultural development science* (pp. 161–73). New York: Taylor & Francis.
———. (2015). *Learning and education in developing countries: Research and policy for the post-2015 UN development goals*. New York: Palgrave Macmillan.
Ward, C. (1996). Acculturation. In D. Landis & R. Bhagat (Eds), *Textbook of cultural psychiatry* (pp. 124–47). Thousand Oaks, CA: SAGE.
Wassmann, J., & Dasen, P. R. (1994). Yupno number system and counting. *Journal of Cross-Cultural Psychology, 25*(1), 78–94.
Werner, C., Brown, B., & Altman, I. (1997). Environmental psychology. In J. W. Berry, M. H. Segall, & C. Kagitçibasi (Eds), *Handbook of cross-cultural psychology* (Vol. 3, pp. 255–90). Boston: Allyn & Bacon.
Weisner, T. S. (1984). A cross cultural perspective: Eco-cultural niches of middle childhood. In A. Collins (Ed.), *Elementary school years: Understanding development during middle childhood years* (pp. 335–69). Washington, D.C.: National Academy Press.
Whiting, B. B. (1980). Culture and social behavior: A model for the development of social behavior. *Ethos, 8*(2), 95–116.
Whiting, J. W. M., & Child, I. (1953). *Child training and personality*. New Haven: Yale University Press.
Whiting, B. B., & Whiting, J. W. M. (1975). *Children of six cultures*. Cambridge, Massachusetts: Harvard University Press.

Whiting, J. W. M. (1977). A model for psycho-cultural research. In P. H. Leiderman, S. R. Tulkin, & R. Rosenfeld (Eds), *Culture and infancy: Variations in the human experience* (pp. 29–48). New York: Academic Press.

Witkin, H. A. (1978). *Cognitive style in personal and cultural adaptation.* Worcester, MA: Clark University Press.

Witkin, H. A., & Berry, J. W. (1975). Psychological differentiation in cross-cultural perspective. *Journal of Cross-Cultural Psychology, 6*(1), 4–87.

Witkin, H. A., Dyk, R. B., Faterson, H. F., Goodenough, D. R., & Karp, S. A. (1962). *Psychological differentiation: Studies of development.* New York: John Wiley.

Witkin, H. A., & Goodenough, D. R. (1981). *Cognitive styles: Essence and origin.* New York: International University Press.

Witkin, H. A., Goodenough, D. R., & Oltman, P. (1979). Psychological differentiation: Current status. *Journal of Personality and Social Psychology, 37*(7), 1127–45.

Woodburn, J. (1982). Egalitarian societies. *Man, 17*(3), 431–51.

Wundt, W. (1910–1920). *Volkerpsychologie (10 vols.).* Leipzig: Engleman. [*Elements of folk psychology.* London: Allyn & Unwin, 1916].

Zimba, R. (2002). Indigenous conceptions of childhood development and social realities in southern Africa. In H. Keller, Y. H. Poortinga, & A. Schomerich (Eds), *Between culture and biology: Perspectives on ontogenetic development* (pp. 89–115). Cambridge: Cambridge University Press.

Zhang, L. F., & Sternberg, R. J. (2006). *The nature of intellectual styles.* Mahwah, NJ: Erlbaum.

Index

absolutism, 26
absolutist orientation, 5
acculturation, 38
acculturation influences on cognitive style, 56
acculturation influences on health and well-being, 44
  coexistence acculturation strategies, 45
  integration and/or coexistence acculturation strategies, 45
  inverted U-shaped relationship, 45
acculturation in India, 42
acculturation measures, 110
  influences, 110
acculturation psychology
  sister field of, 19
acculturation strategies, 38
adaptation to sociopolitical context acculturation, 34
adivasi children in India, 3
adivasi education
  culture-based, 191–197
  national context in, 185–188
adivasi groups
  acculturation strategies, 43
    attitudinal changes, 43
    Kharwar economy, 44
adivasi peoples of India, 12
  cognitive and other abilities of children, incongruence between, 13
  education, 12
  low achievers, 13
agricultural groups, 103

biological adaptation, 34

Canada hunters, 82
  adults, 84
  children, 85
  government efforts, 84
  hunting camps, 83
  notion of respect, 85
  urbanisation process, 84
Canada urban, 104
  British immigrants, flow, 104
  population, 105
  Protestants, groups, 104
child in context, 29
chit lifting technique, 138
claiming qualitative differences, 6
cognition and cognitive style
  recent work, 60
cognitive dimensions, 173–177
cognitive style
  educational achievement measures, correlations between, 167
cognitive style dimensions, 70, 111, 142-143
  LOT, 113
  SRT, 112
  UWT, 113
  cultural and, 178–180
  differentiation tasks
    HWT, 112
    SPEFT, 111
  educational achievements
    Birhor, 116
    coin counting task, 117
    coin recognition task, 117
    coin sequencing task, 117
    coin use task, 117
    comprehension task, 116
    dry agricultural Oraon groups, 116
    language tasks, 116
    mathematics task, 116
    science task, 117
    sentence meaning task, 116

interference rating scale, 115
international studies, 121
  EFT, 121
interview-cum-observation schedule, 114
Locating Objects Task, 120
parental strictness, 115
participants, 121
personal information sheet, 114
preliminary trials, 118
socialization questionnaire, 115
subsistence economy and, 176–178
tasking procedures, 119
tasks, 119
cognitive style measures
  correlations of contextual variables with, 165
  inter-correlations among, 163
cognitive styles, 20–21
cognitive style variables
  factor analysis of, 164
contextualization
  SRT
    mean per cent of persons, 129
contextualisation tasks
  LOT, 132–134
  SRT, 124–130
  UWT, 130–132
cross-cultural and acculturation psychology, 19
cross-cultural psychology, 18, 23
cultural adaptation, 33
cultural anthropology, 21
cultural dimensions, 140–143, 172–174
  mean per cent score of groups, 142
  mean score of groups, 141
  measures, 107
    individual connectedness, 110
    social conformity, 108
    social connectedness measure, 110
    societal size, 108
cultural dimension variables
  inter-correlation among subsistence groups, 161
cultural evolution, 23
culture and cognition
  issues
    Berry research, 2
    claiming qualitative differences, 6

classification, 8
cognitive processes, 2
collectivistic attitudes, 5
cross-cultural and indigenous psychologists, 7
cross-cultural research, 6
cultural differences, 3
educational factors, 6
empiric, 9
genetic interpretations, 4
illiterate adults, 9
indigenous psychologists, 7
individualistic attitudes, 5
intelligence, 5
lottery bookies, 10
Mishra reviewed, 3
racial/genetic factors, 4
studies of, 8
theoretic mode, 10
values and behaviours, 5
culture-behaviour relationship, 19
current issues in understanding cognitive styles, 63
current state of knowledge, 74

differentiation, 143
  EFT, 124
  Hidden Words Task (HWT), 148
  SRT, 150
  UWT, 151
differentiation and contextualization in relation
  social conformity, 71
    measures, 72
    multiple regression analyses, 72
  societal size, dimensions, 71
    measures, 72
    multiple regression analyses, 72
differentiation and contextualization in relation, studies of, 71
differentiation tasks, 124
  EFT, 125
  HWT, 127
  mean score of groups, 125

ecocultural dimension, 139
ecocultural framework, 27, 31
  cultural and biological adaptations, 31
ecocultural groups and participants, 137

Index

ecocultural influences on social Behaviour, 56
ecological and cultural adaptations, 24
ecological approach, 24
  absolutism, 26
  adaption, 24
  cultures and behaviours, 25
  ideas, 24
  interaction, 24
  psychological level, 25
  relativism, 26
  universalist perspective, 25
ecological influences on cognitive style, 48
  agricultural group, 51
  BDT, 51
  Brahmin cultural groups, 52
  ecocultural framework, 53
  evidence, 50
  FDI, 48
  gathering societies, members of, 49
  Gurung cultural groups, 52
  nomadic hunting, members of, 49
  polygynandrous families, 52
  SPEFT, 51
  TEFT, 51
ecological model, 27
ecology dimension, 107
education
  national development and, 191
educational achievement, 155
  culture, cognitive style and, 180–181
  gender, cognitive processing and, 180–183
  language, 155–157
  mathematical, 156–158
  science, 160
educational achievement measures
  cognitive style, correlations between, 167
  correlations of contextual variables with, 158–166
empiric, 9
empirical findings, 140
Euro-Canadians. *See* Canada Urban
Extra-unit connectedness, 71

factoral structure, 134
Field-Dependent/Independent (FDI), 48

genetic interpretations, 4
Ghana hunters
  Vagala, 80
    hunting skills and practices, 81
  Jang, 82
  living styles, 81

Hidden Words Task (HWT), 111–112, 125–127
  ANOVA outcomes, 147
  mean score of groups, 126, 146
hunting-gathering groups, 85
  Birhor group, 77

India hunters-gatherers
  adivasi Birhor, 76
  camps, 80
  life, continuous progression, 78
  settlements, 79
  shifting camps, 77
  Sun, believe, 77
individual psychological issues, 68
integrated model
  Dasen, 28
intelligence quotient (IQ), 4
international studies
  cognitive style dimensions, measures, 121

Jang, 82

Kohs Block Designs Test (Kohs BDT), 51

language achievement
  ANOVA outcomes, 157
  mean score of groups, 156
Locating Objects Task (LOT), 113, 134
  ANOVA outcomes, 153
    discrepancy scores on, 155
  mean discrepancy score of, 155
  mean score of groups, 153, 154
  mean search time, 133
  mean time score of groups on, 152

marginalization, 40
mathematical achievement measure (Mach)
  ANOVA outcomes, 158

Oji-Cree. *See* Canada Hunters

participants
  mean percentage of, 130
  patterns of ability, 20
  psycho-cultural, 28

relativism, 26

science achievement measure (Sach)
  mean score of groups, 159
  NOVA outcomes on, 160
simplistic assumptions, 21
Story-Pictorial Embedded Figures task
  (SPEFT), 50, 111–112

Syllogistic Reasoning Task (SRT), 112,
  126–130, 147–150
  ANOVA outcomes, 149
  mean per cent of correct responses,
    129
  mean score of groups, 148, 149

Tactile Embedded Figures Test (TEFT),
  51

Unfamiliar Words Task (UWT), 130–132
  ANOVA outcomes, 151
  mean score of groups, 131, 150–152
unitary process, 6
Unknown Words Task (UWT), 113

About the Authors

Ramesh C. Mishra (DPhil, University of Allahabad) is Professor Emeritus of psychology at Banaras Hindu University, India. He has been a post Doctoral research fellow and Shastri Research Fellow at Queen's University, Canada, and a visiting professor at the Universities of Konstanz (Germany) and Geneva (Switzerland). He has also been a Fellow-in-Residence of the Netherlands Institute of Advanced Study, Wassenaar (The Netherlands) and a Fulbright Scholar-in-Residence at Wittenberg University, Springfield (USA). He is the Past President and Fellow of the National Academy of Psychology (India). His research is focused on understanding ecological and cultural influences on human development. He is the co-author of *Ecology, Acculturation and Psychological Adaptation: A Study of Adivasis in Bihar* (SAGE) and *Development of Geocentric Spatial Language and Cognition: An Ecocultural Perspective* and co-editor of *Psychology in Human and Social Development: Lessons from Diverse Cultures* (SAGE).

John W. Berry (PhD, University of Edinburgh) is Professor Emeritus of psychology at Queen's University, Canada, and Research Professor, National Research University Higher School of Economics, Moscow, Russia. He received honorary doctorates from the University of Athens and Université de Geneve (in 2001). He has published over 30 books in the areas of cross-cultural, intercultural, social and cognitive psychology with various colleagues. He is a Fellow of the Canadian Psychological Association, the Netherlands Institute for Advanced Study, the International Association for Cross-Cultural Psychology and the International Academy for Intercultural Research. He received the Hebb Award for Contributions to Psychology as a Science in 1999, the award for Contributions to the Advancement of International Psychology in 2012 (from CPA), the Interamerican Psychology Award from the Sociedad Interamericana de Psicologia (in 2001) and the Lifetime Contribution Award from IAIR (in 2005). His main research interests are in the role of ecology and culture in human development and in acculturation and intercultural relations, with an emphasis on applications to immigration, multiculturalism, educational and health policy.